GEOPOLITICS AND CONFLICT
IN SOUTH AMERICA

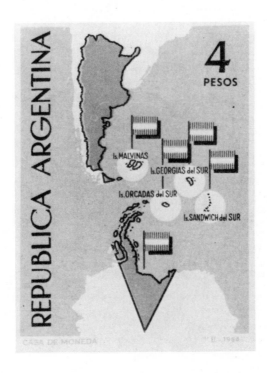

POLITICS IN LATIN AMERICA
A HOOVER INSTITUTION SERIES

General Editor, **Robert Wesson**

Copublished with Hoover Institution Press,
Stanford University, Stanford, California

GEOPOLITICS AND CONFLICT IN SOUTH AMERICA

Quarrels Among Neighbors

Jack Child

PRAEGER SPECIAL STUDIES • PRAEGER SCIENTIFIC

New York • Philadelphia • Eastbourne, UK
Toronto • Hong Kong • Tokyo • Sydney

Library of Congress Cataloging in Publication Data

Child, Jack.
  Geopolitics and conflict in South America.

  Bibliography: p.
  Includes index.
    1. Geopolitics—South America.   2. South America—
National security.   3. Latin America—Foreign
relations—1948–   I. Title.
F2237.C48   1985   327.1'01'1098   84-18326
ISBN 0-03-001453-0 (alk. paper)

Published in 1985 by Praeger Publishers
CBS Educational and Professional Publishing
a Division of CBS Inc.
521 Fifth Avenue, New York, NY 10175 USA

56789 052 987654321

Printed in the United States of America
on acid-free paper

CONTENTS

LIST OF FIGURES

EDITOR'S FOREWORD

The Argentine thrust against the Falklands/Malvinas Islands in 1982 drew much attention to territorial disputes in Latin America. Since then, the world's gaze has turned away, and it is to be hoped that the geopolitics of South America does not again become the focus of news — that is, that quarrels among neighbors do not turn into wars. The republics of South America have enough problems in trying to check impoverishment without spending their energies and resources on nationalistic claims, mostly for jungles of little benefit to the titleholder.

That there has been no major war between South American states since the Chaco conflict (1932–35) is encouraging but is no guarantee of peace. As Dr. Child makes clear, antagonisms are numerous and grave. They have been nourished in a framework of militaristic, power-oriented thinking, which the armed forces take very seriously. So far as states are democratic, they are less likely to resort to arms, but the military remains the residual power in all South American countries, and civilian governments are not free to abandon claims the generals hold sacred. Indeed, the civilian administration may cultivate a foreign quarrel to divert military attention from domestic politics.

The likelihood of conflict between states of this hemisphere rises as the ability of the United States to impose peace declines. Whatever this probability, however, it is essential to understand geopolitical thinking and issues in order to gain a better appreciation of the environment of politics in that troubled continent. Dr. Child has made a signal contribution.

Robert Wesson

PREFACE

Until the outbreak of the Anglo-Argentine war over the Malvinas/Falkland Islands in 1982, relatively little attention was paid to the possibilities or causes of interstate conflict in South America. The shock of that brief but damaging war attracted interest in other possible conflict situations in the area, and in exploring their likely causes.

Among the causes that might contribute to the heightening of tensions between states in South America is a mental framework subsumed under the heading of geopolitics. The very term had been something of a taboo word in the United States and Western Europe for many years after World War II because of its association with Adolf Hitler. However, in this same period, certain geopolitical theories and concepts survived and prospered in some of the larger military establishments of South America. When these military establishments took power in several South American nations in the 1960s and 1970s, they began to apply some of these geopolitical concepts to the internal development of their nations as well as to the international relations of the Southern Cone. During this same period the ability of the United States to influence the South American military establishments diminished markedly, and this increased the impact of these geopolitical ideas as they were applied to problems of development, governance, and international relations in the area. Even in those South American nations where the military had a more limited political role, there are indications that geopolitical modes of thought have influenced national policies and viewpoints, especially with regard to tensions with neighboring states.

This book examines the nature and impact of geopolitical thinking in South America and explores the possible relationship between these forms of thought and a series of conflict situations in the region. Some attention is given to the legacies of classical geopolitical thinking, especially in terms of how they influenced the development of subsequent currents of geopolitical thinking in the principal countries of the area. These subsequent currents are then explored for each of the major nations, and an assessment is made of the relationship they have had with the national security states in South America. The major portion of the book analyzes some 12 potential conflict situations in South America; it includes information on the historical background, recent developments, and the relationship to other conflicts and modes of geopolitical thinking in the countries involved.

Many colleagues, friends, and students contributed to the development of this book in a variety of ways. I would like to note the special contributions of: Eric Simmons, Steve Parkinson, Evelyn Weil, and their associates; my long-suffering students in the Fall 1983 Colloquium on Latin American Conflicts; Howard Pittman, Robert Wesson, Harriett Blood, Zack Nakos, Maria Manzana; and Leslie Morginson-Eitzen, "colega, compañera, y amiga."

POLITICS IN LATIN AMERICA
A HOOVER INSTITUTION SERIES

Robert Wesson, Series Editor

PART ONE
INTRODUCTION

THE SETTING: GEOGRAPHY, INTERNATIONAL RELATIONS, GEOPOLITICAL THINKING, AND CONFLICT IN SOUTH AMERICA

INTRODUCTION

South America: Peaceful or Conflictive?

For many years it was possible to consider South America as a region of peace in comparison to so many other areas of the world. For a number of reasons, this state of affairs began to change markedly in the middle and late 1970s and reached a dramatic and bloody climax in the Anglo/Argentine Falklands/Malvinas conflict of 1982. There are few informed optimists today who would predict that the South Atlantic war was an isolated event that could not be repeated in some other battlefield of the Western Hemisphere.

One consequence of the Falklands/Malvinas war, and of the changes that are being seen in the security environment of the Western Hemisphere, is a reexamination of the international relations of Latin America with a view toward explaining the causes of interstate conflict and its possible resolution.

This book suggests that one of these possible causes, at least in South America, may lie in the arcane, little studied, and less understood field of geopolitical thinking. It is not possible to establish strict causal relationships between geopolitical thinking and conflict in South America. However, a careful study of these links may provide a useful tool for understanding an important facet of the international relations of the subcontinent.

The argument can be illustrated using the Falklands/Malvinas conflict. The decision of the Galtieri regime to invade (or "recover") the islands was undoubtedly motivated by a number of considerations, including personal ambition, military politics, and the rising pressure of internal economic and social problems. However, it is also true that there is a rich lode of Argentine

geopolitical writings that for many years has stressed the geostrategic significance of the Malvinas/Falklands Islands and their relationship to Argentina's
Antarctic claims and the dispute with Chile over the Beagle Channel Islands.
Not much of this geopolitical thinking has found its way into English translation, and there is very little understanding outside of South America regarding the influence this mental framework of geopolitical thinking has had on
military decision makers. Thus, a careful study of these writings in London
and Washington might have eliminated much of the surprise that occurred
when the Argentines finally moved.

The disturbing implication of links between conflict and geopolitical
thinking is heightened by the fact that this mode of analysis is most prevalent
and advanced in the military establishments of three South American countries with a recent history of military rule: Brazil, Argentina, and Chile. As
has been noted elsewhere,[1] a small group of military and civilian analysts in
these three countries has developed a sophisticated and prolific current of geopolitical thinking that has been applied to national and international politics,
development, economics, and military strategy. As Pittman has observed, in
Brazil, Argentina, and Chile these currents of geopolitical thinking are beginning to have a significant impact on national policies and the international
relations of the region.[2] Further, it is these three states that have most fully
developed the concept of the national security state based on the doctrine of
national security, to the point that one author has taken note of "the diplomacy of national security" in the Southern Cone of South America.[3]

The Number and Scope of Potential Conflicts

The possibilities for conflict situations in South America have generally
received little attention in the past. Analysts have listed anywhere between
a half-dozen and over 30 possible conflict situations in the area, depending
on criteria and judgments on the level of seriousness. In a study commissioned
by the Stockholm International Peace Research Institute, this author assessed
20 such situations in the Western Hemisphere in terms of the type of conflict,
the military potential, the tension level, and the impact on arms purchases.[4]
In an analysis limited to mainland Central and South America, Dominguez[5]
addresses 12 conflicts, while Nolde[6] lists a total of some 26 in South America
alone. This present work will focus on the following conflicts.

The Southern Cone conflicts:
  The Southern Andean conflict: Argentina-Chile (the Beagle Channel)
  The Central Andean conflict: Chile-Bolivia-Peru
  The Northern Andean conflict: Peru-Ecuador (Amazonian territories)
  The Argentine-Brazilian rivalry (to include a consideration of the nuclear
  issue and the question of influence on other states in the subregion)
  Tensions in the buffer states (Bolivia, Paraguay, Uruguay)

The South Atlantic-Antarctic conflicts:
    The Malvinas/Falkland Islands crisis
    Influence in the South Atlantic
    The control of Antarctica
South American/Caribbean conflicts:
    Nicaragua-Colombia: San Andrés and Providencia Islands
    Colombia-Venezuela: the Gulf of Venezuela dispute
    Venezuela-Guyana: the Essequibo dispute
    Guyana-Suriname: the New River Triangle dispute

The Changing Nature of Latin American Conflicts

The conflict typology developed further on in this chapter will examine the way these conflicts can be classified and analyzed; however, it would be useful to note here that in the past most Latin American conflicts have been over border and territorial issues and have tended to involve those states with lower levels of war-making capacity. The conflicts now dominant in Latin America are increasingly motivated by ideology and competition for influence and resources. Over the years the Inter-American System has proven to be much more successful at resolving border and territorial disputes between small states than disputes involving influence, ideology, or resources, especially those between larger states. These considerations suggest that the conflict panorama of the next few years in Latin America may be increasingly dangerous and may include tensions that are much harder to ameliorate by the traditional means.

The Importance of Geopolitical Thinking

As this author indicated in a 1979 bibliographic survey of geopolitical writings in Latin America,[7] an analysis of these writings provides insight into the mentality of a politically significant group of Latin American military leaders and their civilian associates. Geopolitics is taken quite seriously by these individuals, especially in the Southern Cone of South America, and a study of this discipline can provide valuable insights into how these leaders view the roles played by their nation, by other international actors, and by the international system in general. When geopolitically influenced individuals assume positions of national leadership and begin to govern using geopolitical strategies and designs, then geopolitics can provide a rather consistent explanation for schemes of national development, territorial integration, and relations with neighboring states. Southern Cone geopolitical writings frequently present an almost Darwinian vision of a cruel and competitive international environment in which the most aggressive nations not only survive, but also increase their power, influence, and territory. This, in turn, may help explain certain expansionary and aggressive attitudes held by military leaders in the Southern Cone and ultimately may offer an explanation for some of the enduring conflicts. Barros[8] has suggested yet another reason why geopolitical thinking is important in the Southern Cone: geopolitics has been the dominant approach to conflict studies even in publications and among individuals whose approach is not explicitly geopolitical. In other words, geopolitical frameworks for analysis have begun to penetrate academic journals and mass media of the Southern Cone nations. As we shall see in the chapter dealing with South Atlantic conflicts, this phenomenon was especially prevalent in analyses of the Falklands/Malvinas conflict.

Geopolitics, Power Politics, and the Balance of Power

As the last chapter of this book brings out, one of the characteristics of international relations of southern South America in the future may well be a return to a balance of power system involving the principal nations of the subcontinent (Brazil, Argentina, Chile, and Peru), with the buffer states (Uruguay, Paraguay, and Bolivia) playing a subordinate role, and with some involvement by the peripheral states (Ecuador, Venezuela, Colombia, and the Guyanas). Such a balance of power system would involve crosscurrents of conflict and cooperation and a network of alliances, understandings and antagonisms. The geopolitical thinking prevalent in the Southern Cone would provide the ideological underpinnings for this balance of power system. It would also be closely linked to the national security state and a diplomatic style that would have a strong element of national security.

The redemocratization process evident in several South American nations in the mid-1980s would seem to signal the demise of the national security state and mitigate against the emergence of this balance of power system. However, as will be argued below, geopolitical thinking is so ingrained in these countries that it will survive the departure of the military regimes that encouraged and nurtured it.

THE GEOGRAPHY OF CONFLICT IN THE WESTERN HEMISPHERE

Major Geographic Areas

The simplistic division of the Western Hemisphere into North, Middle, and South America is not an adequate frame of reference for analyzing the relationship between geopolitics and conflict. Spykman suggested a more helpful division into six zones: the North American Buffer Zone, the North American Continental Zone, the American Mediterranean, the West Coast of South America, the South American Buffer Zone, and the South American Equidistant Zone.[9]

For our purposes we will use the following classification:

The North American Buffer Zone: the essentially empty northern portions of Canada and Alaska.
The North American Heartland: the industrial, cultural, political, and military core area made up of southern Canada and the United States.
The Caribbean Basin: Mexico, Central America, the Caribbean Islands, and the northern portions of Colombia, Venezuela, and the Guyanas.
The Southern Cone of South America: the remaining portion of the subcontinent.
The Southern Islands: Falklands/Malvinas, South Georgia, South Sandwich, South Orkney, South Shetland, the Tierra del Fuego Islands, and the major Pacific Ocean islands (Galapagos, Easter, and Juan Fernandez).
Antarctica.

The significance of this division is that it recognizes the geopolitical and strategic unity of the Caribbean and of the Southern Cone and begins to set the stage for the very different conflict situations in these two areas. The Orinoco River is a boundary between these two areas, and the vast interior areas of the Orinoco and Amazon Basins serve as a buffer between the Caribbean Basin and the Southern Cone. From the geopolitical perspective Colombia and Venezuela (and the Guyanas: Guyana, Suriname, and French Guiana) are more Caribbean than South American and lie in the transition area between these two major geopolitical zones.

At a somewhat greater level of detail, we can also classify the states and areas of interest to us in the following manner.

The major actors: Brazil, Argentina, Chile, Peru
The buffers: Uruguay, Paraguay, Bolivia
The peripherals: Ecuador, Colombia, Venezuela, Guyana, Suriname, French Guiana
Antarctica
The Southern Islands
The Southern Pacific and Atlantic Oceans

The concept of a *Southern Cone*, is an important one in the geopolitical thinking of Latin America. It is closely tied to the notion of a system of power politics involving the major actors listed above (Brazil, Argentina, Chile, and Peru) and the smaller actors (Uruguay, Bolivia, Paraguay), which play roles as buffer states. The remaining South American states are somewhat on the periphery of this power relationship. As Selcher has pointed out,[10] the Southern Cone of South America includes approximately half of Latin America's population, economic output, and military expenditures. The Southern Cone is also the bastion of geopolitical thinking in Latin America and is the area where the concepts of the national security doctrine and the national security state have been developed and put into practice. It should be noted in passing that some Latin American military analysts speak of the "two Southern Cones" (the other one is South Africa) as being the last remaining strongholds of Western, Christian civilization in the face of the moral decay of the West and the advances of Marxism-Leninism.

There are other ways of classifying the major areas of Latin America, and we will be referring to them on occasion. One of these emphasizes the maritime aspects and would divide the region into the Caribbean Basin, the South Atlantic States (Brazil, Argentina, Uruguay, and Paraguay), and the South Pacific States (Chile, Bolivia, Peru, and Ecuador). A second alternate classification would be more topographic: Amazon Basin, Patagonia-River Plate Basin, and the Andean states. A third approach would use the concept of "core areas" or poles of cultural, economic, and political development that would be contrasted with the essentially empty areas in between; the principal core areas in the Southern Cone would be Rio-São Paulo-Santos, Buenos Aires Province and Uruguay, the Central Valley of Chile, and the Lima-Callao area of Peru.

The Military Geography of South America

The importance of geographic factors in military operations cannot be overemphasized, and this is particularly true in the South American case where the problems posed by distance, mountains, rivers, and climatic extremes can severely limit military capabilities. This situation is compounded by the fact that the South American military establishments have only limited logistical means with which to overcome these formidable obstacles, and have not focused their attention on efforts to solve their basic logistical problems of transportation, communications, and supply.

In general the military geography of South America is dominated by the "core area" features described above, with considerable distances between the core areas. Difficult terrain of various types (mountains, swamps, jungles, rivers, and so on) separates these core areas and in turn separates military bases from their logical targets. The logistical problems of supporting military operations in South America can be put into perspective when compared with an area like the Middle East, where distances between cities and nations are relatively short and the geography far less hostile. A similar comparison can also be made with Central America, where the geography, while still difficult, is not as extreme as in South America, and the distances between cities are much shorter. South America is also characterized by the absence of foreign military bases (except, of course, for the British installations on the Falklands) and the relatively low level of foreign military influence. Again, comparisons with the Caribbean Basin area, the Middle East, and Europe are relevant. Because of the distances and the hostile terrain, it would seem logical that the Latin American military establishments should emphasize their air forces and navies over their ground armies. However, for a number of historical, political, and cultural reasons, this is not the case, and this situation further contributes to the hampering of the South American military's ability to effectively project and employ forces.

Analyses of the most suitable geography for military operations[11] suggest that there are relatively few such areas. The most prominent ones are: the coastal zone from Buenos Aires Province to the northeastern Brazilian salient; the River Plate estuary system and the lower portions of the Paraná River; northern Chile; and the Guajira Peninsula-Maracaibo Basin area of Colombia-Venezuela. Military operations are especially difficult in the far South Atlantic and the vicinity of Antarctica.

The Politico-Geographic Legacy of the Past

As can be quickly grasped from a glance at a map of South America, most of the major cities in the subcontinent are on the coast or within a hundred miles of the sea. Historically, the European settlement patterns were such that South America was settled on the rim, leaving the less attractive center empty. The coastal core areas that did develop tended to become the central nuclei of the emerging nations of South America. Thus, few borders cut through core areas, and there was no particular sense of concern over the need to determine borders accurately during the colonial period or in the first years of independent national existence. As one geopolitician has put it, "lack of space mastery was one of the unfortunate legacies the South American states received from their mother country."[12] In the late nineteenth and twentieth centuries, this lack of space mastery and well-defined borders became the source of a number of interstate disputes and even conflicts.

A further unfortunate legacy was a sense of rivalry and competition between the Spanish-speaking nations of South America and the lone Portuguese-speaking nation, Brazil. This rivalry is a particularly important factor in the geopolitics of the Argentine-Brazilian relationship, but to a lesser or greater degree is a significant element in the relationship of each South American country with Brazil. Brazil's conscious (and even subconscious) path to its "destiny" as the emerging super-power of South America has given rise to unease and concern in the neighboring states and has created in the Spanish-speaking nations a perception of Brazil as an expansionary power, albeit through peaceful means. As Pittman has pointed out,[13] the history of conflict in South America begins with rivalries between the kings of Portugal and Spain, and many of the territorial disputes of today can be traced back to the colonial era.

One last category of conflicts concerns Great Britain. Two of the most serious conflict situations in South America involve legacies of British colonialism: the Falklands/Malvinas conflict and the Venezuela-Guyana dispute. The issue of colonialism gave Argentina a very significant weapon in lining up Latin American support against Great Britain and mystified many U.S. and European analysts who could not understand how the banner of anticolonialism could carry much weight in 1982. The matter, however, does not end here, since a much more dangerous conflict situation involving Great Britain (and the United States, the Soviet Union, and a number of other nations) has the potential to erupt in Antarctica and the far South Atlantic.

THE CHANGE IN HEMISPHERE SECURITY RELATIONS

The Nature of the Change

Any consideration of the relationship between geopolitical thinking and conflict in South America must be set in the broader context of the evident changes in Western Hemisphere security relations over the last 15 to 20 years. The old hemisphere security relationship was built on the institutional basis of what came to be called the Inter-American Military System. This system had been painstakingly built up by the United States since World War II and reached its peak during the counterinsurgency years of the early and mid-1960s. With the increasing U.S. involvement in Vietnam in those years, and with the perception that the guerrilla warfare threat had declined after the death of Che Guevara in 1967, the Inter-American Military System began a slow and steady decline that accelerated dramatically during the Carter presidency and then suffered an almost mortal blow during the Falklands/Malvinas conflict of 1982. The system had, in effect, become dysfunctional, and there was little agreement on threats, policies, or military cooperation with the United States. During the Falklands/Malvinas conflict, some Latin American governments (and many of their military officers) began to speak of a "Latin-only" security relationship that would exclude the United States. At times it almost seemed as though the one thing that was holding the Latin American elements of the security system together was the feeling of opposition to the United States, a situation that prompted one senior Latin American military officer to comment that the United States was going to achieve what the Liberator Simón Bolívar had not been able to: the unification of Latin America.[14]

Causes of the Change

One fundamental cause for the changing security relationship is the general decline in the ability of the United States to influence events in the Western Hemisphere. This decline is in part relative and reflects the growing national capabilities and ambitions of the Latin American nations themselves, which have shown an increasing and understandable inclination to break away from what they perceive as an excessive dependency on the United States. This period has seen a growth in multipolar power centers in the Western Hemisphere and a resulting diffusion in the power that was once held overwhelmingly by the United States as the dominant and even hegemonic player in the hemisphere.[15]

Specific U.S. policies that, although well intentioned, did considerable damage to the hemispheric security structure, include a series of congressional restrictions on arms sales to Latin America and the linking of military assistance to human rights performance. Forcefully implemented under the Carter administration, these policies had a very negative impact on hemispheric security arrangements, although they contributed to the spread of civilian rule and undoubtedly saved the lives of numerous political dissidents.

The conservative military and civilian regimes in Latin America viewed with alarm the collapse of U.S.-supported governments in Vietnam, Iran, and Nicaragua, and came to the conclusion that the United States was either unable or unwilling to fulfill its international security obligation and had become, in effect, an unreliable ally. As one Brazilian geopolitician put it after the cutoff of U.S. military assistance to Chile, Argentina, and Uruguay, "the Southern Cone was abandoned, just as Angola was abandoned, and just as South Africa is being abandoned now."[16]

During this period there has been a parallel loss of confidence in the Organization of American States (OAS), and in particular its peace-keeping and peace-making machinery. The traditional, and reasonably effective, methods for settling territorial and nonideological disputes of the past between the smaller states of Central America and the Caribbean proved to be increasingly impotent in the face of contemporary conflict situations. These have tended to be more ideological, to involve the larger states as well as the smaller, and to involve important resources (real or perceived). The OAS has not shown itself to be particularly effective in dealing with potential conflicts arising from geopolitical doctrines, from national security diplomacy, or from the increasing military capabilities of several of the South American nations. Demographic pressures, a greater demand for land and resources, and the stimulus of geopolitical doctrines have combined to create a greater interest in filling the previously "empty spaces" in the heartland of South America.

One last major cause that must be considered in assessing the changing security relationship in the Western Hemisphere is the Falklands/Malvinas conflict. Of particular importance is the manner in which the majority of the Spanish-speaking nations in the hemisphere perceived the roles of the United States, Brazil, Chile, and the Organization of American States. We will examine these perceptions in greater detail below, but it should be pointed out that the conflict had a strong negative impact on the OAS, greatly reduced the credibility of the Rio Treaty (and its effectiveness in future employment), and further confirmed the suspicions of those who doubted the reliability of the United States as an ally. The careful neutrality of Chile and the less-than-enthusiastic support for Argentina by Brazil have also contributed to the increasing sense of mutual distrust in the Southern Cone.

Impact and Implications

One of the implications of this changing security situation is that geopolitics in the Southern Cone may begin to fill the strategic gap left by the declining power of the United States and the other factors outlined above.[17] It would also be reasonable to assume that associated with this use of geopolitics will be an increased reliance on power politics as a diplomatic instrument. The decline of U.S. domination of the Inter-American Military System thus leaves the Latin American military establishments freer to establish more links among themselves or to insist on a greater Latin American role in the remaining institutions of the system. One example of this tendency occurred during the Falklands/Malvinas battles when the Venezuelan military raised the possibility of moving the Inter-American Defense Board from Washington to Caracas in order to get it out from under excessive U.S. influence.

New types of disputes are beginning to emerge within the hemisphere, and especially the Southern Cone. Previously, most of the territories in dispute were not perceived as containing resources of any great value. This perception is now changing, and in fact several of the areas in contention (for example, the area of the Peruvian-Ecuadorean dispute, the Malvinas/Falkland Islands basin, and the Gulf of Venezuela) are believed to contain significant hydrocarbon reserves.

These increasing concerns over the implications of power politics and geopolitics as a driving force in Southern Cone international relations are not simply theoretical in nature. The principal nations of the Southern Cone have considerably increased their military capabilities in the last decade. One of the "lessons learned" by the Latin American military from the Falklands/Malvinas conflict appears to be the utility of high-technology weapons such as the Exocet missile. Reports from the area after the Malvinas/Falkland conflict indicate that several countries displayed interest in purchasing this type of weapon. At the same time local arms industries in countries such as Brazil and Argentina continue to produce and export weapons.

An Alternate View

As will be seen below, geopolitical thinking in South America is not entirely hostile in nature, and there are two currents that permit an alternate view that is considerably more optimistic than the one sketched out above.

The first current concerns the purely internal aspects of geopolitical thinking, which stresses that a nation must fully and effectively occupy its own national territory in order to maximize the opportunities that its geographic position and resources permit. This attitude is not aggressive or hostile toward neighbors; if carried out intelligently, it can make a contribution toward national development and general progress in each of the countries in the area.

The second current stresses the need for international integration among the Southern Cone nations through geopolitical concepts that deal with the pooling of resources and the joint development of frontier areas. This current is especially notable in the geopolitical writings of the Argentine "integrationalist" group, and in the proposals of the Uruguayan Bernardo Quagliotti de Bellis. Taken as a body of ideas, these writings suggest that geopolitical thinking in the Southern Cone nations may be an important element in helping them overcome years of suspicion and distrust, and as a result reduce the possibilities of conflict.

A TYPOLOGY OF CONFLICT IN LATIN AMERICA

In connection with the study commissioned for the Stockholm International Peace Research Institute mentioned above, a typology of conflict[18] in Latin America was developed that offers a useful starting point for this book. The typology, subsequently modified, establishes the following classification for conflicts in the Western Hemisphere:

1. Territorial conflicts. These conflicts stem from disputes over the possession and sovereign rights of portions of the earth's surface, be they land or water. Although this type of conflict initially focused almost exclusively on possession of land, in recent years there has been an increased emphasis on extending sovereignty for considerable distances into the ocean, thus creating additional areas for potential conflict.

2. Border conflicts. Such conflicts flow from the strains and tensions that seem to emerge almost inevitably when two sovereignties meet at a frontier. In the past the intensity of this type of conflict in Latin America was ameliorated by the fact that most Latin American international borders went through empty areas far removed from national core areas. However, with the slow but steady filling up of these empty areas, and the discovery of valuable resources near some of them, we can anticipate greater strains over border conflicts in the future.

3. Resource conflicts. Usually this type of conflict also involves territory (land or ocean), but the driving force behind the conflict is not so much territorial as it is the perception that important resources are at stake. Competition for energy resources, such as petroleum or hydroelectricity, is now becoming increasingly important. There is also competition and even conflict over other types of resources, such as strategic territory (key terrain, islands, and sea lanes) or biological assets (fish and krill).

4. Ideological conflicts. These deal with the struggle to impose (or resist the imposition of) sets of political, economic, and social values. This type of conflict tends to be particularly bitter, complex, and uncompromising. In the Southern Cone of South America, ideological conflicts have not been prevalent because of the relatively homogeneous nature of the ideologies of the regimes in power.

5. Influence conflicts. These involve competition to increase and project national power and prestige. In the Southern Cone the fundamental influence conflict is between Brazil and Argentina (or between the Portuguese-speaking state and the Spanish-speaking states led by Argentina), and this influence conflict is an important element in the balance of power system to be described in the analysis that follows.

6. Migratory conflicts. These deal with the strains caused by the movement of people across frontiers. In general (with the exception of Colombia-Venezuela) these are not prominent in South America. This is because population densities in South America are still relatively low and because the national core areas in the region are generally at considerable distances from each other.

These categories can now be used to classify 20 different conflicts in the hemisphere. These are presented in summary form in Table 1 and Figure 1. Table 1 also summarizes the linkages to other conflicts and makes a preliminary assessment of the significance of geopolitical thinking in the conflicts. As can be seen from Table 1, most of the conflicts involve more than one of the categories described above; any analysis is further complicated by the fact that adversaries may have different perceptions of the type of conflict, and that the type of conflict may vary over time. For example, what might have begun as a historical territorial squabble over land that was empty and useless in colonial times now becomes much more serious if there is a strong belief that important resources (such as oil) are to be found in the area.

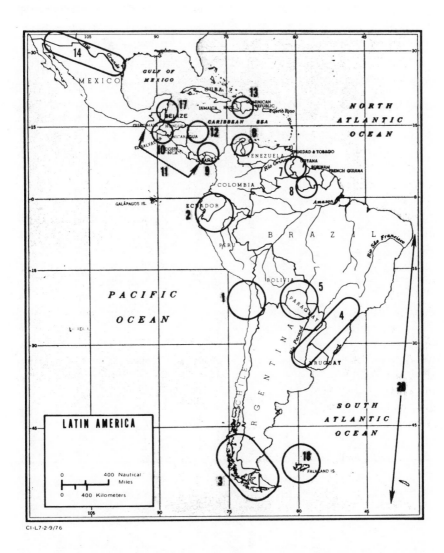

Figure 1. Map of potential conflict situations. (See Table 1 for identification. Not shown: 15. Law of the Sea 16. Caribbean 17. Antarctica)

Table 1: Potential Conflict Situations in Latin America

No.	Conflict	Parties	Type of Conflict	Linkages to Other Conflicts	Relationship to Geopolitical Thinking
1	Central Andean	Chile, Peru, Bolivia	Territorial; also resource (Bolivia)	Nos. 2, 3	Strong, especially in Chile
2	Northern Andean	Peru, Ecuador	Territorial; also resource	No. 1	Slight
3	Southern Andean (Beagle Channel)	Argentina, Chile	Resource, territorial, border, migratory	Nos. 1, 4, 18, 19, 20	Very strong
4	Argentine-Brazilian rivalry	All Southern Cone countries	Influence, resource	Nos. 3, 5, 19	Very strong
5	Bolivia-Paraguay	Bolivia, Paraguay	Territorial, resource	Nos. 1, 4	Slight
6	Gulf of Venezuela and border	Colombia, Venezuela	Territorial, resource, migratory	Nos. 7, 12	Slight in Colombia; strong in Venezuela
7	Essequibo (Western Guyana)	Venezuela, Guyana	Territorial	Nos. 7, 16	Slight in Guyana; strong in Venezuela
8	New River Triangle	Guyana, Suriname	Territorial; also resource	None identified	None identified
9	Panama Canal	Panama, United States	Territorial, resource	Potentially to no. 16	U.S. geopolitical interest in the canal
10	Honduras-El Salvador	Honduras, El Salvador	Territorial, resource, migratory	No. 11	None identified

16

11	Central American	All Central America, U.S., Cuba, USSR	Ideological, migratory, influence	No. 16 and various border conflicts	U.S. strategic thinking; Central American unity
12	San Andrés and other islands	Colombia, Nicaragua	Territorial	Nos. 6, 15, 16	None identified
13	Island of Hispaniola	Dominican Republic, Haiti	Border, migratory	None identified	None identified
14	United States-Mexico	United States, Mexico	Resource, migratory	None identified	None identified
15	Law of the sea, maritime zones	Whole region	Territorial, resource	Nos. 3, 6, 12, 14, 18	Strong in Brazil, Argentina, Chile, Ecuador
16	Caribbean	U.S., Cuba, USSR, Caribbean states	Ideological, resource, migratory	Potentially to all in area	U.S. and Soviet strategic thinking
17	Belize	Belize, Guatemala, Great Britain, U.S.	Territorial	Possibly no. 11	None identified
18	Malvinas/Falkland Islands	Great Britain, Argentina	Territorial, resource	Nos. 3, 7, 19, 20	Very strong in Argentina
19	Antarctica	Members of the "club," others	Territorial, resource	Nos. 3, 4, 18, 20, and U.S.-USSR	Strong in Argentina, Brazil, Chile; also in others
20	South Atlantic, Atlantic Narrows	U.S., USSR, Great Britain, Brazil, Argentina	Resource, influence	Nos. 3, 4, 8, and U.S.-USSR	Strong in Argentina, Brazil; also in others

Source: Compiled by the author.

NOTES

1. Jack Child, "Geopolitical Thinking in Latin America," *Latin American Research Review* (Summer 1979), pp. 89–111.

2. Howard T. Pittman, "Geopolitics and Foreign Policy in Argentina, Brazil and Chile," in *Latin American Foreign Policies*, ed. Elizabeth G. Ferris and Jennie K. Lincoln (Boulder, Colo.: Westview Press, 1981).

3. Alexandre S. C. Barros, "The Diplomacy of National Security: South American International Relations in a Defrosting World," in *Latin America: The Search for a New International Role*, ed. Ronald G. Hellman (New York: John Wiley, 1975).

4. Jack Child, *Conflicts in Latin America: Present and Potential*, unpublished manuscript prepared for the Stockholm International Peace Research Institute (SIPRI), 1980.

5. Jorge I. Dominguez, *Ghosts from the Past: Territorial and Boundary Disputes in Mainland South and Central America since 1960*, unpublished manuscript, Harvard University, 1980.

6. Kenneth Nolde, "Arms and Security in South America: Towards an Alternate View, Ph.D. dissertation, University of Miami, 1980, pp. 285–87.

7. Child, "Geopolitical Thinking."

8. Alexandre S. C. Barros, "Conflict Studies in Higher Education: The Case of South America with Emphasis on Argentina and Brazil," unpublished paper, 1980.

9. Nicholas J. Spykman, *America's Strategy in World Politics: The United States and the Balance of Power* (New York: Harcourt, Brace, 1942), p. 399.

10. Wayne Selcher, "Recent Strategic Developments in South America's Southern Cone," in *Latin American Nations in World Politics*, ed. Geraldo Munoz and Joseph Tulchin (Boulder, Colo.: Westview Press, 1984).

11. Geoffrey Kemp, "The Prospects for Arms Control in Latin America: The Strategic Dimensions," in Philippe C. Schmitter, *Military Rule in Latin America*, ed. Philippe C. Schmitter (Beverly Hills: Sage, 1973), pp. 216–217.

12. Andreas Dorpalen, *The World of General Haushofer* (New York: Farrar and Rinehart, 1942), p. 92.

13. Howard T. Pittman, "Geopolitics in the ABC Countries: A Comparison, Ph.D. dissertation, American University, 1981, pp. 2–5.

14. General Gustavo Leigh, quoted in the *Times of the Americas*, April 13, 1977.

15. Jack Child, *Unequal Alliance: The Inter-American Military System, 1938–1978* (Boulder, Colo.: Westview Press, 1980).

16. Terezinha de Castro, "El Atlántico," in *Geopolítica y Relaciones Internacionales*, ed. Luis Dallanegra Pedraza (Buenos Aires: Pleamar, 1981), p. 61.

17. Augusto Varas, *Geopolítica y Seguridad Nacional: Continuidad y Cambio en las Relaciones Militares Latino-americanas*, paper presented at the tenth annual conference of the Latin American Studies Association, Washington, D.C., 1982, p. 15.

18. This basic typology was developed by the author for the SIPRI study cited in footnote 4 above; it was also presented at the October 1981 annual meeting of the Conference of Latinamericanist Geographers (Buffalo, N.Y.) and was published in the proceedings for that meeting.

2

CLASSICAL GEOPOLITICAL THINKING

GEOPOLITICS: DEFINITIONS AND NOTIONS

The Semantic Problem

Part of the difficulty in coming to grips with the essence of geopolitical thinking is that there are at least five different notions of what geopolitics means:

First there was the "classic" nineteenth (and early twentieth) century concept of geopolitics, which grew out of various European approaches and was on its way toward becoming a respected branch of knowledge that bridged the gap between geography, political science, and international relations.

A current of this classical approach was captured by German nazism and was used to give the Third Reich a pseudoscientific rationale for its expansionist aims and racist doctrines. This experience was a severe blow to the discipline of geopolitics, and it has never really recovered from this setback.

In the contemporary context a third, and almost simplistic, notion of geopolitics is that it is little more than political geography (that is, the relationship between politics and geography).

A more realistic contemporary view holds that geopolitics is the relationship between power politics and geography. This notion thus begins to get closer to the concept of geodiplomacy and geostrategy, reflecting the concerns that the diplomat and the military planner keep in mind as they analyze how geographic factors can hinder or enhance their actions in the world arena.

Lastly, there is the concept of geopolitics that predominates in the Southern Cone of South America. It is a mix of classical and power politics approaches (with a strong Germanic influence) and is linked to the national security doctrine and to the Latin American military's sometimes strongly felt need to justify its existence by making a contribution to national development plans and strategies.

Areas of Interest to the Geopolitician

The basic conern of geopoliticians is the nation-state. Geopolitics is thus interested in the dynamic evolution of the state and the impact of geographic, racial, historical, and economic factors that have influenced that evolution; from this analysis geopoliticians draw certain political conclusions that will permit them to make projections into the future. The relationship of national space and geopolitics can be expressed as the study of how to best organize and plan for the effective utilization of national resources. However, nation-states do not exist in isolation, and geopoliticians must constantly be concerned with how the development of one nation-state relates to the development of its neighbors.

As these considerations suggest, one of the basic tasks of the geopolitician is to act as an advisor to diplomats as they give the nation-state political direction. This point is strongly made by South American geopoliticians; perhaps the best example of this is given by General Augusto Pinochet of Chile, who assumed the presidency in 1973 after overthrowing Salvador Allende and who is the author of Chile's best-known work on geopolitics. The book, *Geopolítica*, was written as his war college thesis when he was a colonel but was quickly re-edited and published by a prestigious Santiago editorial house after he assumed the presidency.[1] One of General Pinochet's close associates and geopolitical advisors has defined geopolitics as "the science and the art of the statesman."[2]

Major areas of interest to the geopolitician are national security (both internal and external) and geostrategy, which is usually defined as the application of geopolitics to the art of high-level military planning so as to make best use of national defense and war-making resources. As one Latin American geopolitical writer has put it, "for each geopolitic there is a corresponding geostrategy."[3]

Basic Geopolitical Concepts

The starting point of classical geopolitical writers is the "organic theory of the state," a concept maintaining that the nation-state is a living organism that requires living space, resources, and a purpose; the state also has a life cycle in which it is created, matures, declines, and finally disappears. Unfortunately, there are other organic nation-states competing for these same resources and for this same living space — thus, the sense of competition and rivalry that tends to run through most geopolitical writings.[4]

In the view of some classical geopolitical writers, this sense of competition becomes almost Darwinian, with the stronger states devouring the weaker ones and incorporating them into their spheres of influence. The geopolitical writer would refer to these spheres of influence as *pan-regions* where one nation-state is the dominant power.

Geopolitical writers, perhaps out of a concern that their "science" is not being accepted as such, frequently strive to find and prove certain underlying geopolitical "laws" that would govern the actions of states regardless of time or physical setting. Likewise, there has been a long debate between the deterministic and possibilistic schools of classical geopolitical thinking over whether the choices available to people and nations are severely limited or whether people can overcome these limitations.

THE HISTORICAL EVOLUTION OF GEOPOLITICAL THINKING

The Beginnings: Ratzel and Kjellen

The fundamental geopolitical concept of the nation-state as an organic entity began with Friedrich Ratzel (1844–1904), who coined the German word *anthropogeographie* to suggest a combination of the disciplines of anthropology, geography, and politics. The state, according to Ratzel, had many characteristics of living organisms and could be usefully studied from this perspective. Ratzel also introduced some of the basic ideas that governed how states dealt with other states in geopolitical frameworks. These included the concept that a state had to expand (that is, grow at the expense of others) or die, and the related concept of the "living frontiers," which argued that international borders were dynamic and subject to change if the stronger nations required expansion for their own existence.

Rudolf Kjellen (1864–1922), a Swede, first used the term *geopolitics* in the context of the relationship between a nation's power and the geographic factors that enhanced or limited that power. His approach was much more Darwinian than Ratzel's, and he portrayed the international environment as one in which states had to struggle for survival in the competition for limited space and resources.[5]

Mahan and Mackinder

Alfred Thayer Mahan (U.S., 1840–1914) and Sir Halford Mackinder (British, 1861–1947) were the chief proponents of two geopolitical world views described in the next section. Mahan, who reached the rank of admiral in the U.S. Navy, stressed the significance of sea power and the control of the sea lines of communications as the most effective way of exerting national power. In contrast, Mackinder, who was a professional geographer, stressed the significance of land transport as the key to control and power. Thus, both of these men were arguing that humanity, through technology, and specifically the technology of transportation, could overcome the obstacles posed by geography.

Haushofer and the Nazis

The German geopolitical school built on the work of Ratzel and Kjellen rose to prominence in the years after World War I under Karl Haushofer (1869–1946). Haushofer, who was a retired army officer, had considerable influence in military circles and is believed to have given Adolf Hitler many of his geopolitical ideas. Haushofer's academy and the *Journal of Geopolitics* (Zeitschrift für Geopolitik) were used by the Nazis to develop a number of concepts they later applied to policies. Geopolitics, in effect, served to provide some pseudoacademic and pseudoscientific legitimacy to Nazi programs of expansion, conquest, and genocide. General Pinochet of Chile has summed up the principal ideas of the German Haushofer school of geopolitics as follows:

Lebensraum or the vital space that a state must have to breathe, grow, and expand.
The notion that a state's frontiers must be natural and should expand out to the full extent of its *Lebensraum.*
The concept of *autarky*, whereby the strong states develop their own complete economic base, including the defense economy, so that they will not be dependent on any other state.
The idea that strong nation-states expand their spheres of influence out to an optimum maximum, which then becomes the pan-region associated with that state.

General Pinochet concludes: "The German school was repudiated by the Allies at the end of World War II; nevertheless, after more than 20 years we can observe that many of the studies it carried out are being fulfilled."[6]

The Rejection of the German Geopolitical School

General Pinochet's comment accurately summarizes the sharp rejection of not only the German school of geopolitics, but also the whole discipline, which had become tainted by association. Indeed, some authors have argued that the slow decline of geographical studies in Western Europe and the United States is linked to this unfortunate association. The very term *geopolitics* had a sharp pejorative connotation after World War II (it became known as "the geography of fascism"), and very little use was made of the term except as it was linked to the Third Reich or to neofascist ideas. Ladis Kristoff notes the irony of this, especially in the United States, where many chapters in our national history (for example, Manifest Destiny, the Monroe Doctrine, the Big Stick Policy) were based on frankly geopolitical notions of power, geographical advantage, and power politics.[7] Kristoff ascribes this ambivalent attitude to the U.S. tendency to shy away from the terms *imperialism* and *power politics* despite the fact that much U.S. growth was obtained precisely through these means.

The rejection of the German geopolitical school was at times propagandistic, especially during the war. A 1942 text on world politics printed in the United States described Haushofer's geopolitical doctrine, and the Nazis' use of it, in phrases such as these: "All life is a brutal, lawless struggle for existence, and internationally every nation must cede to the stronger, otherwise it delays the 'wave of the future', the rule of a racially pure nation, Germany."[8]

The Survival of Geopolitics, New Ideas, and a Renaissance

Despite the strong condemnation after World War II, geopolitical concepts did survive, and were added to, in two different ways. The first was that explicitly geopolitical thinking and writings continued after the war in the Southern Cone of South America, especially in Brazil, Argentina, and Chile. Some South American authors made it a point of arguing that the victorious Allies were unjustly using geopolitics as an anti-Nazi propaganda device and that it was up to the nations of the Southern Cone to keep the discipline of geopolitics from disappearing.[9] As a result, geopolitics remained alive and well in South America for the quarter-century when it was a taboo word in Western Europe and the United States. The second way in which geopolitical ideas survived was by acquiring new and sometimes euphemistic names. In effect, military strategists and diplomats in the North Atlantic basin continued to use the ideas, but now they came under the rubrics of *national defense planning, strategic studies,* and *elements of national power,* among others.

In the last ten years or so, the term *geopolitics* has begun to creep back into the vocabulary of academics, strategists, and diplomats in the United States and Western Europe. If one man deserves the credit for this process, it is probably Henry Kissinger, who as national security advisor, and later secretary of state, used the term and made it more respectable and indeed even fashionable. However, the Kissingerian concept of *geopolitics* owed more to raw power politics linked to geography than to classical geopolitical thinking. This renaissance of geopolitical thinking, and the increasing respectability of the term, was especially noteworthy in South America, where it emerged when the previously overwhelming U.S. strategic influence began to decline after 1967.

GEOPOLITICAL WORLD VIEWS

Ever since the nineteenth century debates between proponents of Mahan's ideas and those of Mackinder, geopolitical thinkers have presented a series of global visions of international power relationships and how geography affects them.[10] Prior to the advent of the strategic bomber and the nuclear-tipped missile, these global visions basically repeated the two contesting world views (maritime and continental) presented by Mahan and Mackinder. Several geopolitical writers wrote elaborate theories of history around the idea that human development went through cycles in which either the maritime or the continental thrust predominated. After World War II a third world view, that of the aerospace school, was added. Competition for increasingly scarce resources in the postwar period suggested that the geopolitics of resources (especially energy and strategic minerals) would be another relevant world view. Lastly, the significant role of guerrilla warfare in the contemporary period seemed to indicate that there should be some kind of a "revolutionary" geopolitical perspective associated with this type of conflict, although many geopolitical analysts do not accept this perspective precisely because the guerrilla makes no claim to territory or space.

The brief analysis that follows will bring out the relationship between the predominant geopolitical world view and technology, especially the technology of transportation and of the dominant strategic weapon. There are also strong links between geopolitical world views and certain map projections; indeed, cartography has always been a basic instrument of the geopolitical writer. The sections that follow will also make brief mention of the relevance of each geopolitical world vision to Latin America and to the Southern Cone in particular.

The Maritime Geopolitical Perspective

The maritime perspective stresses that the control of the oceans is the best way to project power. Technologically it is linked to water-borne commercial transport and to the naval ship as the principal strategic weapon. The concept of *sea lanes* (or *lines*) *of communications* is fundamental here, since control of the sea lanes implies control of trade, transport, and movement of military assets. The relationship of water to land is also seen in terms of the idea of the *choke point*: a site where land tends to compress the sea lane and make it easier to control it since it is so restricted. Classical choke points are canals, straits, and capes. Professor Lewis Tambs, one of the premier U.S. geopoliticians today and President Reagan's ambassador to Colombia, has defined the world's 12 major choke points as follows:[11]

- Four inland seas: the South China Sea, Mediterranean, North Sea, and Caribbean.
- Two interoceanic canals: Suez and Panama.

- Six critical passage points: Singapore, the Horn of Africa, Gibraltar, Ceylon (Sri Lanka), Cape of Good Hope, and the Strait of Magellan.

The relevance of the maritime geopolitical view to Latin America focuses on three of the choke points identified by Tambs: the Caribbean, the Panama Canal, and the Strait of Magellan. It should be noted in passing that the Tambs citation came from his congressional testimony in which he strongly opposed the 1977 Panama Canal Treaty on the grounds that turning the canal over to the Panamanians would severely weaken the ability of the United States to move its trade and naval power through the canal. As the present author has pointed out,[12] the first strategic approach the United States ever took toward Latin America (and one that remains very much alive today) was the idea that the Caribbean was an "American Lake" that should be under firm U.S. control for both commercial and military reasons. The Panama Canal was a key element in this approach since, as Mahan pointed out, it would permit the United States to concentrate its naval power as needed and would thus gain a two-ocean navy at the cost of one. In a sense the third Latin American choke point (the Strait of Magellan) is also linked to the Panama Canal, since it is an alternate transoceanic passage to the canal and would acquire much greater significance if the Panama Canal were to be closed or become obsolete. Southern Cone geopolitical writers (especially, and understandably, naval officers in Argentina and Chile) have consistently stressed the significance of the Strait of Magellan. As illustrated below, one element in the tension between Argentina and Chile concerns their relative roles in controlling the strait. Further, one explanation for the Argentine invasion (or "recovery") of the Falkland/Malvinas Islands was the interest of its geopoliticians in strengthening Argentina's position in the South Atlantic so as to better control the access to the strait and Antarctica.

The Continental Geopolitical Perspective

In contrast, those who hold the continental geopolitical perspective tend to view armies and control of land as the key strategic factors. Navies and air forces serve mainly to transport and support the soldier in the field, and it is the soldier who is seen as the ultimate instrument for projecting military power and national will. The continental geopolitical perspective bases its ideas on the theories of Mackinder, and especially the concept that the central portion of Europe was the political and strategic key to controlling what he called the "World-Island" (the European-Asian-African land mass). As he put it in his famous maxim:

Who rules East Europe commands the Heartland.
Who rules the Heartland commands the World-Island.
Who rules the World-Island commands the world.[13]

The continental geopolitical perspective has relevance in South America in terms of the dreams of Brazilian geopoliticians that their path to greatness rests on filling the Amazon Basin and exploiting its resources. This dream becomes reality through actions such as moving the capital of Brazil inland and embarking on a massive road-building project to penetrate the Amazonian "heartland" of South America. To a greater or lesser degree, all of the Amazon Basin countries (Brazil, Bolivia, Peru, Ecuador, Colombia, Venezuela) share this interest in penetrating the Amazon heartland, and there is a definite sense of geopolitical competition involved in this interest. The heartland theory shows up in yet another country: Bolivia. As we shall see below when assessing Bolivian geopolitical thinking, there is a school of thought in that country which holds that Bolivia is in a key position because it is the South American heartland. This theme has also been picked up by Argentine, Brazilian, and U.S. geopolitical analysts, and to some extent the Brazilian-Argentine rivalry is based on influence or control of Bolivia. Lewis Tambs has argued this point and has paraphrased Mackinder to illustrate:

Who rules Santa Cruz [Bolivia] commands Charcas.
Who rules Charcas commands the heartland.
Who rules the heartland commands South America.[14]

The Aerospace Geopolitical Perspective

The aerospace vision was the logical offshoot of the strategic bomber and then later the nuclear intercontinental missile. Not surprisingly, its strongest proponents have been air force officers and their supporters. In essence, this view holds that these powerful strategic weapons have rendered the old ideas about the role of the battleship and the land army obsolete, and that real national power in the nuclear age stems from the nuclear weapon and its aerospace delivery means. Its principal proponent, Alexander de Seversky, argued that both the United States and the Soviet Union have areas of air dominance based on the ranges of their strategic aerospace weapons. These areas, which look startlingly like spheres of influence, overlap in an "area of decision" consisting roughly of North America and the northern portions of the Eurasian-African land mass. The rest of the world was either in one of the superpower's exclusive "areas of dominance" or, if outside of these spheres, was simply too far away to have much strategic significance. The aerospace geopolitical vision was also the product of the cold war and tended to see nations as strategic objects within the spheres of influence of the two superpowers.

For Latin American geopoliticians the aerospace view has both positive and negative elements. On the one hand, there is a certain resentment that they are for the most part in the circle of U.S. air dominance (which they tend to interpret as "U.S. hegemony"). On the other hand, there is a sense that if the world does experience a nuclear war they will be outside of the area of decision and therefore would presumably escape much of the destruction that the area of decision would suffer. In the contemporary context the aerospace geopolitical vision has some interesting facets in the Southern Cone. There is, for example, an appreciation for the key role that Argentine air power played in the battles against the British fleet in the summer of 1982, and especially the role of high-technology weapons such as the air-to-air and air-to-surface missile of the Exocet type. There is also a school of thought that is presenting an Antarctic polar projection (analogous to the Arctic one used by de Seversky) to show how a Southern Cone nation could project power across the Antarctic toward Africa, the Indian Ocean, and the South Pacific.

The Resource Geopolitical Perspective

The resource geopolitical perspective is a relatively recent world vision, which received its greatest impetus with the oil crisis of 1973. Although centered principally on the competition for scarce oil and other energy resources, it has also included a sense of competition for strategic minerals, for water, and for food.

The theme is not yet well developed in Latin American geopolitical writings, although Venezuelan and Ecuadorean authors have noted the implications of their oil assets. There also has been a major geopolitical debate between Brazilian, Argentine (and to a lesser extent Uruguayan and Paraguayan) writers over the geopolitics of the development of hydroelectric energy in the Paraná-Plata River Basin. Further, Argentine geopolitical writers have also stressed the theme of "the geopolitics of food" in terms of the advantages that they have as one of the world's leading exporters of grain and meat.

The Revolutionary Geopolitical Perspective

As Collins has noted, some authors argue that more attention should be paid to the geopolitical perspectives of proponents of guerrilla warfare, such as Marx, Lenin, Giap, Ho Chi Minh, and Che Guevara.[15] Classical geopolitical writers would probably reject this suggestion, arguing that geopolitics is based on control of space and that guerrillas do not try to take or hold land until the final stages of their struggle for power. Guerrilla warfare is also not so much a purely military or strategic phenomenon as it is a political, social, and psychological one. Thus, the "space" involved is not a portion of the surface of the earth but rather the "inner space" of people's hearts and minds.

In Latin America such a revolutionary geopolitical perspective would rest on the writings of theoreticians and practitioners such as Che Guevara and Carlos Marighella (the Brazilian proponent of urban guerrilla warfare)

Although he is not a Latin American, the Frenchman Regis Debray also belongs in this group, along with a number of lesser figures. It should be noted, however, that most of the professional military officers in Latin America who write on geopolitical matters do not consider guerrilla warfare to be a geopolitical process and would probably reject the notion of a "revolutionary" geopolitical vision. There is a sense among regular military personnel that only many years of training in military and strategic matters can properly equip one to analyze these areas adequately; the guerrilla is looked upon with some contempt as one who has little, if any, professional military training.

NOTES

1. Augusto Pinochet, *Geopolítica* (Santiago: Editorial Andrés Bello, 1974), p. 142.

2. Julio von Chrismar, "Geopolítica y Seguridad Nacional," *Seguridad Nacional* (Chile) no. 21 (1981):21.

3. Bernardo Quagliotti de Bellis, *Constantes Geopolíticas en Iberoamérica* (Montevideo: Tarino Libros, 1979), p. 5.

4. See Harm de Blij, *Systematic Political Geography* (New York: John Wiley, 1967), p. 165; Pinochet, *Geopolítica*, p. 21; and Ulises Walter Perez, "Geopolítica del Uruguay," *Geopolítica* (Uruguay), reedición de 1981, pp. 19–20.

5. For a more complete treatment, see James E. Dougherty and Robert L. Pfaltzgraff, Jr., *Contending Theories of International Relations* (Philadelphia: J. B. Lippincott, 1971), pp. 50–61: Howard T. Pittman, "Geopolitics in the ABC Countries: A Comparison," Ph.D. dissertation, American Univeristy, 1981.

6. Pinochet, *Geopolítica*, pp. 60–61.

7. Ladis Kristof, "The Study of Geopolitics: Diversity of Traditions and Approaches," paper presented at the Congress of the International Political Science Association, Rio de Janeiro, August 1982.

8. Thorsten V. Kalijarvi, *Modern World Politics* (New York: Cromwell, 1942), pp. 619–20; Jeannette E. Muther, *Geopolitics and World War II* (Seattle: University of Washington, Bureau of International Relations, 1947), p. 16.

9. See, for example, Jorge E. Atencio, *¿Qué es la Geopolítica?* (Buenos Aires: Pleamar, 1965), p. 360 and passim.

10. For more detailed treatment, see John M. Collins, *Grand Strategy: Principles and Practices* (Annapolis, Md.: Naval Institute Press, 1973), pp. 17–18, 168–70.

11. Lewis A. Tambs, "Panama Canal Treaties," testimony before the Senate Foreign Relations Committee, pt. III, 1977, p. 154.

12. Jack Child, "Strategic Concepts of Latin America: An Update." *Inter-American Economic Affairs* 34 (Summer 1980): 61–82.

13. Sir Halford Mackinder, "The Geographic Pivot of History," *Geographic Journal* 23 (1904): 421–44.

14. Lewis A. Tambs, "Geopolitical Factors in Latin America," in *Latin America: Politics, Economics and Hemisphere Security*, ed. Norman A. Bailey (New York: Praeger, 1965), p. 36.

15. Collins, *Grand Strategy*, p. 18.

PART TWO
THE NATURE
AND IMPACT OF
GEOPOLITICAL THINKING
IN SOUTH AMERICA

3

THE NATURE OF GEOPOLITICAL THINKING IN THE INDIVIDUAL COUNTRIES

INTRODUCTION

Geopolitical Writings and Processes

This chapter can only summarize the considerable volume of geopolitical writings that has emerged in South America since the first significant publication in the 1930s. The reader who wishes to delve deeper into these writings should consult the bibliographic survey that appeared in the *Latin American Research Review*,[1] as well the works of Tambs, Pittman, and others mentioned in the last section of the previous chapter. Pittman's contribution merits special attention, inasmuch as it concerns the geopolitical literature of Brazil, Argentina, and Chile and provides an invaluable reference in English to geopolitical thinking in the ABC countries. He includes extensive quotes from a number of authors in these countries, and in many cases this is the first time these extracts have been published in English translation. His doctoral dissertation runs a total of 1,725 pages. (It is widely reported that only five people have read it in its entirety—and there is doubt about some of these five: Pittman himself, his typist, and the three members of his doctoral committee, which included this author.)

Pittman also introduces the notion of *applied geopolitics* (that is, the application of geopolitical theory to government policy and action) and takes note of the several stages through which this process takes place. In the first stage scholars, in their search for explanations or solutions to national problems, adapt existing geopolitical theories to local conditions in the Southern Cone. In the second stage this concept is transmitted to governing elites (and later the masses) through an educational process involving the national war colleges and the specialized geopolitical institutions. The third stage involves employing these geopolitically trained elites in important government positions so they can translate these geopolitical theories into policies, plans, and action. The final stage involves the reaction to these geopolitical theories and policies by scholars, military personnel, and officials from other countries. These individuals are then encouraged to come up with their own geopolitical theories and apply them in a similar manner.[2]

The Geopolitical Institutes

In most of the South American nations, there are one or more institutes devoted to the study of geopolitics and its dissemination. These geopolitical institutes are usually linked to national war colleges, national diplomatic academies, or other institutes for high-level education of government officials. An interesting phenomenon is that even in the military colleges the percentage of civilian students is quite high, reaching as much as 50 percent of the student body. This suggests a confirmation of Pittman's point that the educational role of elites is a key to the successful propagation and implementation of geopolitical ideas.

In the period from 1978 to 1980, there was an attempt made to bring these various national geopolitical institutes together in the Asociación de Estudios Geopolíticos e Internacionales at the initiative of Bernardo Quagliotti de Bellis of Uruguay. The roster of those who signed the "Declaration of Montevideo" of June 1979 establishing the association includes many of the major figures active in the field: General Carlos de Meira Mattos (Brazil); General Edgardo Mercado Jarrín (Peru); Professor Lewis Tambs (U.S.); Professor Therezinha de Castro (Brazil); Gustavo Cirigliano (Argentina); General Alvaro Valencia Tovar (Colombia); Professor Juan Carlos Moneta (Argentina); Licenciado Luis Dallanegra (Argentina); Dr. José Felix Fernández Estigarribia (Paraguay); General Roberto Iriarte (Bolivia). Although the association has had little success in bridging the gap between national geopolitical perspectives, Quagliotti de Bellis's journal, *Geosur*, continues to advocate a closer relationship between the national institutes; it acts as a sort of clearinghouse for articles on this theme, as well as a source of news regarding various conferences and activities dealing with geopolitics.[3]

The Integration Theme

The name of Quagliotti de Bellis has also been closely associated with the overall theme of Latin American integration in various fields: economic, cultural, strategic, and political. The journal *Geosur* has been a vehicle for this theme, as have been a number of monographs and books written by Quagliotti de Bellis. The integration theme among Southern Cone geopolitical writers has acquired a more intense thrust since the 1982 Falkands/Malvinas conflict and carries with it an implicit (and sometimes explicit) message of strong criticism of U.S. actions during that crisis. The theme of Latin American military and strategic integration is also closely linked to the notion that the United States is abandoning the Southern Cone, a theme that was especially prevalent during the Carter administration.[4]

The concept of some sort of Southern Cone "bloc" is a delicate one for a number of reasons, including the problem of leadership of the bloc (Argentine or Brazilian), and the belief that such a block might be a coalition of harsh authoritarian regimes in Latin America. A commentary in a Buenos Aires newspaper in 1980 speculated on the possible Southern Cone bloc, noting that such an arrangement would run counter to traditional Latin American diplomacy. It concluded that the principal commonality of the Southern Cone nations was "the unanimous rejection of subversion and the assertion of the right to fight it with all the means at the disposal of the state."[5]

Those South American geopoliticians who have felt that the United States has abandoned them have, on occasion, looked across the South Atlantic to another nation with similar feelings: South Africa. As previously mentioned, there is a "doctrine of the two Southern Cones" (South American and South African), which holds that these two regions are becoming the last bastions of Western, Christian values against the onslaught of godless Marxism-Leninism and the corruption and decay of the United States and Western Europe. As a Uruguayan geopolitician put it, "Argentina, Brazil, South Africa and Uruguay, states which border this most important oceanic space, have the responsibility of creating a geopolitical doctrine which will sustain the values and the interests of the Western world. . . . "[6]

Discord and Fragmentation between National Geopolitical Schools

Unfortunately, these currents of geopolitical thinking that stress integration and harmony, and that would presumably tend to make South American conflict less likely, are not the prevailing ones. Much more common are highly nationalistic themes that view neighbors with suspicion and even hostility, particularly when dealing with issues involving competing territorial or resource claims. Despite the best efforts of the integrationists, these chauvinistic currents in the geopolitical thinking of Southern Cone analysts tend to fragment the subcontinent and contribute to the discord and tension that is a common feature of the international relations of this region. This negative contribution of geopolitical thinking is the major topic of this book, and we turn now to a country-by-country summary of the principal elements of this outlook.

The country analysis in the next sections can be summarized as follows. There are two well-developed "schools" of South American geopolitical thinking: the Brazilian and the Argentine (although the Argentine school is one that devotes much of its efforts reacting to the Brazilian school). Strong currents of geopolitical thinking also exist in Chile, where the long-lasting President Pinochet is a classical example of the geopolitician as ruler. Individual geopolitical writers exist in all the remaining Spanish-speaking countries, and in some cases they have associated themselves into groups with important links to the government and the military.

BRAZIL

Significance

The Brazilian geopolitical school is without a doubt the most significant in Latin America. This is true not only because of its impact on contemporary Brazil, but also because it has served as a model for others and has produced strongly reactive geopolitical thinking, especially in Argentina. The significance of the Brazilian school is also a function of the creative and prolific nature of the Brazilian geopolitical writers and national advisers. The Brazilian school is the most deeply rooted such current in the continent. Many authors argue that the Portuguese (and later the Brazilians) were instinctive geopoliticians during the period when Brazil was a colony and an empire and that the twentieth century geopolitical analysts and writers merely put into words what their predecessors had done subconsciously. When these writers began to publish in the 1920s and 1930s, they were strongly influenced by Kjellen and the contemporary German geopolitical school, and there was communication between figures such as Haushofer and the Brazilian geopolitical writers of the prewar period. This is not to say, however, that the Brazilian school closely imitated the German school, especially when it became coopted by the Nazis. In fact, when Brazil came down on the Allied side in World War II, Brazilian geopolitical thinkers deliberately distanced themselves from the German school. At the same time, the pro-Axis neutrality of Argentina, and to a certain extent Chile, permitted their own links to the German school to remain. Perhaps because of these circumstances, the stronger legacies of the German school can be found today in Argentina and Chile, and not in Brazil. The single dominant characteristic of Brazilian geopolitical thinking (a characteristic that has greatly influenced Spanish Latin American reactions to Brazil) has been the emphasis on the seemingly inevitable Brazilian path to *grandeza*, the code word for the moment when (and never if) Brazil will become the first superpower to emerge from the Southern Hemisphere. Ever since the early 1920s, and in a sense ever since the first Portuguese arrived, Brazil has been embarked on a Latin American version of Manifest Destiny. Brazil's geopolitical writers have carefully analyzed this process and have charted out a path that flows from the full and effective filling of Brazil's national territory to a continental projection of power (to the Pacific, to the

Amazon Basin and the Caribbean, to the River Plate Basin, to the South Atlantic and Antarctica) and finally to achieving great-power status and international respect outside of the boundaries of Latin America.

Major Themes

This search for Brazil's greatness, and its perceived rightful role in the world, is the most important theme in Brazilian geopolitical writing. Interestingly, thoughts along these lines are not usually expressed aggressively or shrilly by Brazilian geopolitical writers (as is the case in Argentina); rather, it is almost taken for granted that it will happen and that all objective observers should be in agreement that this is a natural and inevitable occurrence. These same Brazilian geopolitical thinkers are sometimes puzzled when Spanish-speaking neighbors take them to task for their expansionistic nature, and they are frequently on the defensive when discussing these concepts with outsiders.[7]

An important subissue in this search for greatness and Manifest Destiny is Brazil's relationship with the United States. Brazilian geopolitical writers from the 1940s through the 1960s were quite frank in acknowledging that part of this path was to be traversed as a junior partner of the United States. The so-called *barganha leal* was to be the deal in good faith by which the United States would help Brazil at a time when Brazil was its principal ally in Latin America. The Argentine response to this "deal" was to accuse the Brazilians of being the lackeys of the United States and to declare that Argentina would never accept such a subordination. This subservient position of Brazil disappeared quickly during the Carter presidency, when a combination of factors (greater Brazilian maturity and self-reliance, Carter's ineptness in dealing with Brazil, and Argentine sniping) came together to force a quick change in what had once been an unusually close relationship and one that greatly enhanced Brazil's development for a period of some 35 years. Brazil, in effect, broke out of its geopolitical dependence on the United States during these years.[8]

Although it is not, strictly speaking, a geopolitical concept, the idea of integral security and development is fundamental to an understanding of how Brazilian geopoliticians believe they can move down this path to greatness. One should recall the words in the center of the Brazilian flag (*ordem e progresso*), placed there by nineteenth century Brazilian military positivists. The descendants of these men have, in a sense, transformed the original words into their contemporary slogan of *seguranca e desenvolvimento* (security and development). The two concepts are interlinked and can be summed up as follows: there can be no meaningful progress toward Brazil's destiny of greatness unless there is order and discipline (as defined by the Brazilian civilian-military elites who have ruled since 1964). At the same time order and peace are enhanced by movement down this path of national development. Part of the concept of order is an internal one having to do with control of subversive movements and keeping a watchful eye on individuals or groups who might be tempted to come forth with their own definitions of Brazilian greatness.

A second part of the idea of *ordem* has to do with international order, and it is this idea that has affected some of Brazil's international relations as it takes steps to enhance the stability of some of its neighbors. As President Joao Figueiredo put it in April of 1983:

> Where Brazil has common borders with countries whose politico-social development can represent a danger to national security, the Brazilian Government will do everything possible to prevent the region from falling under the influence of foreign powers, especially the Soviet Union. Regarding countries with which Brazil has no common borders, Brazil is not involved with the problem, although the problem may be of great interest to other nations of the continent.[9]

Evidence of this type of Brazilian concern includes maneuvers near the Uruguayan border during unrest there and recent Brazilian overtures toward the Bouterse regime in Suriname.[10]

An important theme in Brazilian geopolitical writings that has both national and international implications is the problem of filling the "empty spaces" of Brazil and the South American continent. This translates neatly into the question of the Amazon Basin and represents in a very concrete sense an application of Mackinder's heartland theory. Brazilian emphasis on the Amazon and on such international instruments as the Amazon Pact reflect a concern that Brazil must make sure that it fully and effectively occupies all its territory and that it is the dominant power in the vast empty spaces of the South American heartland. Here the technology of transportation, and specifically of road building, is fundamental to the plans of Brazilian geopoliticians. As we shall see below when analyzing geopolitical thinking in both Peru and Venezuela, there is some concern in those countries over this predominant Brazilian role in the heartland.[11]

The concept of filling the "empty spaces" of the South American heartland has been extended by some Brazilian geopolitical writers to encompass a "Manifest Destiny" for Brazil not unlike that of the United States of the early and mid-nineteenth century. In its extreme form it would include expansion of Brazilian influence to the Pacific as Brazil strove to become a two-ocean power like the United States. Peruvian geopolitical analysts are quite sensitive to this implicit threat, and in a sense the Peruvian plan to establish a vast road network on their eastern slope of the Andes is an attempt to ensure that they fill their empty spaces before the Brazilians do it for them. Or, as a senior Peruvian military officer told this author, "Brazil is like the United States a hundred years ago as it expands to the Pacific, and Peru is California." Other analysts have used this Brazilian interest in the Pacific to explain the attention Brazil has paid Bolivia and Chile, although in the Bolivian case its energy and natural resources alone would account for Brazilian interests, while in the Chilean case the value of Chile as an ally in the sometimes strained Argentine-Brazilian rivalry would also justify Brazilian attention.

Brazil's energy deficiency accounts for another major theme in its geopolitical writings: the search for energy self-sufficiency to guarantee Brazil's industrial development without placing it in economic bondage. Although important efforts have been made to search for oil, few expect any major finds. Instead, the effort focuses on the hydroelectric energy resources of the upper Paraná River and in the development of nuclear energy. Both of these areas have been the focus of considerable diplomatic attention. The Itaipú and other hydroelectric projects have become a major factor in the international relations between Brazil, Paraguay, and Argentina, while the nuclear issue was an important element in the strained relations with the United States during the Carter years.[12]

As Brazilian geopoliticians moved conceptually from the occupation of their national territory to continental projection, they developed an increasing interest in the South Atlantic and the Atlantic Narrows (that rather wide choke point between the northeastern Brazilian salient and West Africa). Not surprisingly, this particular theme was vigorously promoted by Brazilian naval officers, who saw in this area the possibility for an expanded naval role. The interest had been aroused during World War II, when the United States placed great emphasis on the strategic contributions made by the northeastern salient as a departure point for air traffic to West Africa and the Mediterranean.[13] This interest was further heightened when oil supertankers began to use the South Atlantic as their principal route from the Persian Gulf and the Middle East. The moves to push national ocean boundaries out beyond the traditional three-mile limit also contributed, as did the Falklands/Malvinas conflict. These concerns have on occasion found an outlet in the proposals for a South Atlantic Treaty Organization (SATO), which would form a mirror image to NATO, and in which Brazil and its navy could be expected to play a key role.[14]

Much to the alarm of their Argentine colleagues, the interest of Brazilian geopoliticians does not stop with the South Atlantic: it in fact extends to Antarctica. The relative strength of Brazilian and other Antarctic claims will be assessed in Chapter 6, but it would be useful to note here that the interest is a relatively recent one and relies on the novel concept of the "frontage" theory developed by Professor Therezinha de Castro. This theory argues that each South American nation should have a sector of Antarctica that corresponds to the easternmost and westernmost meridians of its territory that are not blocked by another nation to the south (see Figure 2). Regardless of how seriously the Brazilians (or anyone else) intend to take this theory, the fact is that the Brazilians have already mounted their first Antarctic expedition and are determined to establish a presence in the area.[15]

Figure 2. The Brazilian "frontage" theory of Antarctic sectors. The "frontage" theory is based on the idea that each South American country facing the Antarctic would have a sector corresponding to the territory between its unobstructed meridians to the South Pole.

The Historical Development of Brazilian Geopolitical Thinking

Although many Brazilians would call their Portuguese settler ancestors the first Brazilian geopoliticians, and others would argue that that honor should fall to the Baron Rio Branco, the individual who clearly stands out as the first explicitly geopolitical thinker and writer in Brazil was Mario Travassos.[16] He was an army officer who fought in World War II with the Brazilian Expeditionary Force and played a key role in influencing the next generation of Brazilian military leaders from his position on the faculty of the

Staff College. Travassos began his analysis with a study of population distribution in Brazil, which revealed the obvious: that Brazil's population was concentrated along the coast (or, as it is sometimes more poetically put, "Brazilians cling to the warm sensuous beaches like crabs clinging to a rock"). Travassos argued that if Brazil were ever to achieve its true national and international destiny, it must also develop along East-West axes to become what he called *longitudinal Brazil*. He identified two such axes: one along the Amazon River and a second across the Matto Grosso and into the "magic triangle" heartland area, defined by the Bolivian cities of Cochabamba, Sucre, and Santa Cruz. Travassos argued that time was of the essence, because Brazil had to establish itself in this magic triangle before Argentina did. Brazilian control of this triangle would offset Argentina's domination of the River Plate Basin and the buffer states of Uruguay, Paraguay, and Bolivia. Brazil's "continental destiny" would be enhanced by becoming longitudinal along these two East-West axes, which would give Brazil a much stronger base from which to project its power.[17]

A contemporary of Travassos, Everardo Backheuser, focused his attention on the theory of borders and borrowed many ideas from the German geopolitical school, with which he was in close contact (some of his articles were published in General Haushofer's journal). Backheuser is generally credited with developing the concept of the *living frontier*, which has caused some alarm among Brazil's neighbors. This theory, derived from the German geopolitical school's ideas on *Lebensraum* and the need for natural frontiers, holds that frontiers are not static but are more like flexible diaphragms that move in response to the relative pressure exerted by the nations on each side of the border. Thus, the theory suggests that a strong nation would inevitably move its border into the territory of the weaker neighbor. Backheuser also argued that Brazil must effectively populate and control the vast empty territories obtained from its neighbors through the skillful diplomacy of the Baron Rio Branco.

The principal contemporary figure (now in semiretirement) is the legendary General Golbery do Couto e Silva, who has been an influential advisor to the presidents of Brazil since the 1964 revolution. He has also been the director of the National Intelligence Service and has exercised great influence on the military and civilian leadership of contemporary Brazil through his geopolitical writings and teaching at the Escola Superior de Guerra (ESG). To a considerable degree, Golbery follows the same analytic path taken by Travassos, starting with the problem of Brazil's skewed population distribution. He viewed Brazil as an archipelago consisting of a series of isolated islands and peninsulas. In order for Brazil to develop, it must somehow link these various isolated regions together through a network of transportation links (primarily roads). Golbery's geopolitical ideas go considerably beyond internal Brazilian development and include a coherent path toward *grandeza*, which progresses from control of Brazil's national territories to continental projection and growing international influence. His geopolitical prescriptions include national integration and the effective use of the national territory; interior expansion and pacific external projection; containment along the frontier; participation in the defense of Western civilization; continental collaboration; collaboration with the developing world; and national geostrategy in response to the two great external superpowers. His vision of South America can be seen in Figure 3, which illustrates his concept of a continental heartland "welding area" (Brazilian Matto Grosso plus Paraguay and Bolivia) that

CI-L7-2-9/76

Figure 3. Golbery's geopolitical division of South America.   1.   Reserve area 2.   Amazon area   3.   Plata-Patagonia   4.   Continental welding area   5. Brazilian Northeast

must come under Brazilian control in order for Brazil to play its rightful international role. Golbery also explored the nature of Brazil's special relationship with the United States: Brazil can offer its strategic geography (especially the "aircraft carrier of the Northeast") and assistance in securing the South Atlantic in exchange for concessions.[18]

As can be readily seen, the major emphasis of the ideas of Travassos, Backheuser, and Golbery is a continental one. Other Brazilian geopolitical writers have emphasized the need for a maritime focus to project Brazilian power into the South Atlantic, and ultimately Antarctica. The ideas of Terezinha de Castro and numerous naval geopoliticians have been significant in this regard.

In recent years the name of General Carlos de Meira Mattos has begun to eclipse that of Golbery. Meira Mattos has synthesized and popularized much of the work of his predecessors and has succeeded in articulating these ideas in a number of Brazilian and international forums. His contribution has focused on the need for a rational and steady development of Brazil toward its destiny. This includes the need for Brazil to integrate its own heartland, play its rightful role in defending the American continent, take advantage of the strategic importance of the northeastern salient, cooperate with (but not be dominated by) the United States, and be a factor in the security of the South Atlantic and West Africa. Meira Mattos has also paid special attention to the economic possibilities inherent in the development of the Amazon Basin and in the beneficial effect of cooperative relationships between the Amazon and River Plate Basins.[19]

ARGENTINA

Significance

Geopolitical thinking in Argentina is as important as in Brazil but shows differences that in a sense are a reflection of the ways in which Argentina is different from Brazil. As in Brazil, there is a "school" of geopolitical thinking in Argentina in the sense that there are long historical roots, a considerable volume of publications, and individuals and institutes devoted to the subject. It is also true that geopolitical thinking in Argentina reveals deep chasms and a fundamental lack of agreement on what the solutions to Argentina's problems should be. In fact, there is even much disagreement about what Argentina's basic problems are, and Argentine geopoliticians often seem to be involved in harsh polemics among themselves as much as with their geopolitical adversaries in Brazil and Chile. As Pittman has pointed out,[20] current geopolitical thinking in Argentina is concerned with two broad and interrelated topics: the restoration of Argentina's rightful place in the world, and the drafting and implementing of a "National Project" that will unify Argentina and allow the nation to progress to its destiny as a great nation.

On the surface, the Argentine geopolitical school is far more prolific and creative than the Brazilian, if one judges by the sheer volume of geopolitical books, journals, and commentaries in the specialized press and the mass media, as well as the introduction of geopolitical ideas into the official primary and secondary school curricula. However, this volume is somewhat deceptive since it is a reflection of the infighting between Argentine geopoliticians, and the reactive nature of Argentine geopolitical thought. The label of *reactive* is valid in at least two directions: Brazil and Chile. Argentine geopolitical writers follow the output of their Brazilian and Chilean colleagues quite closely; whenever an article or book appears in Rio, Brasilia, or Santiago that seems to touch on delicate issues (such as the Beagle Channel, the Malvinas, international hydroelectric projects, or Brazilian-Argentine relations), a chorus of Argentine geopoliticians seems compelled to comment on it or contradict it. There is also reason to believe that the Argentine school of geopolitical writings (like the Chilean, but unlike the Brazilian) accepted many of the German school's ideas rather uncritically and never fully repudiated the link to nazism as most of Brazil's geopolitical writers did.

A characteristic of Argentine geopolitical thought, and one that has considerable significance in terms of international relations, is that it almost unanimously views Argentina as a country that has suffered geopolitical aggression from its neighbors (Chile and Brazil) as well as from outsider powers (Great Britain and the United States). In the case of the first two countries, there is a sense that Argentina gave up far too much territory in the nineteenth century; if there is no recovery or compensation for these territorial losses, Argentine geopoliticians fear that their nation will never regain the greatness of the Viceroyalty of the Rio de la Plata. Geopolitical writers speak of Argentina as a "país agredido geopoliticamente" (a country that has suffered geopolitical aggression) and one that has endured "mutilations" of its territory in the past. As General Villegas has put it: "It is painful to say it, but Argentina is perhaps the only country in the world which, throughout its history, from the moment of independence to our days, has given up territory, as a consequence of the fact that our ruling class has not considered space valuable as a power factor; it has not borne in mind that to diminish the space of a Nation is to reduce its power."[21]

This sense of geopolitical aggression against Argentina receives its strongest contemporary thrust in terms of the Malvinas/Falklands issue. There is a strong belief that geopolitical aggression was committed against Argentina by Great Britain not only in 1833 (the date when Britain took the islands by force), but also in 1806 and 1807 (when the British invaded Buenos Aires), and in the 1840s when the British blockaded the River Plate. The sense of geopolitical aggression by the United States is based on the perception that the United States assisted Great Britain in robbing Argentina of the Malvinas in 1832 and that the United States has had a basically unfriendly attitude toward Argentina throughout the history of their international relations. The events of 1982, of course, only served to heighten this sense of geopolitical, and now military, aggression against Argentina. This feeling of geopolitical mutilation has the potential, in the hands of a demagogic and irresponsible leader, of being a justification for aggressive posturing and even actions against perceived enemies. In recent years Argentine geopoliticians have stressed the theme that Argentina's old geopolitical enemies (Chile, Brazil, Great Britain, and the United States) have hostile designs on legitimate Argentine sovereign claims in the South Atlantic, and Southern Islands, and Antarctica.

Because of this strongly held perception of geopolitical aggression, there is an indignant, self-righteous, combative, and hostile tone to much of Argentine geopolitical writing. In recent years there has also been the need to find explanations for Argentina's decline in relation to Brazil, and for Argentina's seeming inability to get its internal house in order. Unfortunately, geopolitical writings sometimes give glib and easy answers to these questions. This in turn serves to shift attention to outsiders as the cause of Argentina's present and future problems. As one geopolitical writer put it, quoting the Bible: "If we do not concern ourselves with developments which are the essence of national security, then, as the Biblical precept says, 'one day the men of the jungle and of the mountains will descend to the plains and will take them'; as has occurred not a few times in history."[22] In the context of Argentine geopolitical thinking, there can be little doubt that the Bible here is speaking of Argentines as the men of the plains, Brazilians as those of the jungle, and Chileans as those of the mountains.

Major Themes

Historically, the major themes of Argentine geopolitical writers have been Brazil, Brazilian expansion, and the need for Argentina as the leader of Spanish-speaking South America to counter that expansion. However, since the Brazilian-Argentine rapprochement of the early 1980s, and the Malvinas/Falklands conflict, this old concern with Brazil has lost its primacy to a new geopolitical worry: that the British, in alliance with the United States and perhaps the Chileans, will work together to deny Argentina its destiny in the Malvinas, the South Atlantic, and Antarctica. These themes will be developed more fully when the individual conflicts are analyzed in Chapters 5 through 7 but will be identified briefly here.

Argentine geopolitical writers who analyze relations with Brazil[23] look back to the days of the early explorers and note how first Portugal, and then Brazil, have since 1494 been steadily expanding westward at the expense of Spanish-speaking South America. According to one colorful statement, the Brazilians will not be willing to end this expansionary process "until Portuguese-speaking feet can wash in the Pacific Ocean." Thus, the Argentines take a very negative view of the skillful diplomacy of Baron Rio Branco, of the Brazilian alliances with first Great Britain and then with the United States, and of the various Brazilian geopolitical doctrines dealing with frontiers, such as the Travassos doctrine and the concept of the natural and living frontiers. These concerns over Brazilian expansion focus on the buffer states of Bolivia, Uruguay, and Paraguay, on the international hydroelectric projects, and on Argentina's own exposed territory of Misiones. Figure 4 shows Argentine per-

CI-L7-2-9/76

Figure 4. Geopolitical projection of Brazil (as seen by Argentina).

ceptions of Brazilian geopolitical projection into the territory of its South American neighbors, into the Atlantic, and south to the Antarctic.

Argentine geopolitical perceptions of Brazil have been strongly influenced by the triangular relationship between Brazil, the United States, and Argentina. For many years Argentine geopolitical writers portrayed Brazil in pejorative terms as the junior partner or stalking horse of the United States in Latin America. The Argentines argued that Brazil eventually must choose between continuing to play this humiliating role or breaking away from the United States and rejoining Latin America. In this interpretation the United States is perceived to have a strategy of picking "key countries" around the world to act as U.S. surrogates: West Germany in Europe, Pakistan in South Asia, Israel in the Middle East, Japan in the Far East, and Brazil in South America. With the strained relations between Brazil and the United States in the Carter years, Brazil seemed to be following Argentina's advice, and from the perspective of Buenos Aires this was undoubtedly one of the circumstances that permitted the strengthening of Argentine-Brazilian relations that followed.[24]

Argentine geopolitical concern with Chile reached an intense level with the announcement of the Beagle Channel Islands arbitration award, which, in Argentina's eyes, was totally favorable to Chile and thus unacceptable. To many Argentine geopoliticians this was yet another example of geopolitical aggression, this time by the Chilean-British coalition, since the arbitration award was handed down by the British Crown. The intensity of feeling was such that Argentina actually began mobilizing for war (as did Chile) before the Vatican's intercession managed to defuse the issue temporarily. But the issue has not been solved and remains a potentially dangerous situation. The geopolitical thinking involved here is complicated but is based on the so-called bi-oceanic principle under which Argentina controls the South Atlantic approaches to the Strait of Magellan and Chile the Pacific. The problem becomes how to define the limit between the Atlantic and Pacific Oceans. Giving the Chileans sovereignty of the three Beagle Channel Islands pushes the oceanic limit too far east to be acceptable to Argentina. In fact, it begins to undermine seriously the treasured Argentine concept of a tricontinental Argentina, which flows uninterrupted from South American Argentina through Insular Argentina to Antarctic Argentina. Argentine geopoliticians regard Argentina's destiny in the area to be that of the "keeper of the doorway" from the Atlantic to the Pacific, and will not tolerate Chilean intrusion into the very sensitive area of the eastern approaches to the Strait of Magellan.[25]

As something of a parallel to Brazil's sense of *grandeza* and Manifest Destiny, Argentina has its own sense of national geopolitical destiny as the natural leader of the Southern Cone. This attitude is sometimes expressed in terms of restoring the glory of the Viceroyalty of the River Plate, which lasted from 1776 until independence in 1816. This concept is also sometimes expressed as the natural Argentine geopolitical domination of the Paraná-Plata

River and Estuary system. This was expressed to the author by a senior Argentine general (once head of the Geographic Commission and later the director of the Argentine Border Commission) as a manifestation of the "law of the orange." By this he meant that any floating object dropped in the entire area of the River Plate Basin would sooner or later drift by the port city of Buenos Aires and thus symbolically would come under Argentine geopolitical influence. At times this sense of Argentine geopolitical greatness and the glories of yesteryear become wrapped up in the excessive pride, and even arrogance and racism, that is the occasional dark side of the Argentine character. As expressed by one leading Argentine geopolitical writer:

> The exceptional historico-political formation of the Argentine nation has been made possible thanks to the marvelous conjunction of the most favorable geographic environment and the optimum ethnic conditions of the Argentine People, which probably cannot be found in any other country on earth. The spiritual currents of the human masses which make up the country — essentially and principally greco-latin — have produced a philosophical and political conception that distinguishes it with unique characteristics, which are humanitarian, with a universal transcendence, which have made of Argentina the recipient of the friendship and consideration of all the people of the Earth.[26]

Argentine geopolitical thinking has always had a very strong maritime thrust; in fact Admiral Storni's naval doctrines are acknowledged as the first original Argentine geopolitical ideas. Atencio, for example, notes that although Argentina is on the South American mainland, it really is primarily a maritime nation since it has such a long South Atlantic coastline and, if granted its Antarctic claim, the Malvinas, and the Beagle Channel Islands, is the guardian of the access from the Atlantic to the Pacific. He illustrates this by rotating a globe until the maximum exposure of water and the minimum amount of land is shown; this is the so-called oceanic hemisphere centered approximately on New Zealand. Using this perspective of the globe, Argentina (and its Antarctic claim) are in the "doorway" position to the Pacific Ocean.[27]

This idea has also been expressed in terms of the geographic continuity of tricontinental Argentina, as well as the recent concept of *Atlantártida*. This latter idea stresses the unity that the South Atlantic offers as the body of water between mainland Argentina and Antarctica, and that contains the geopolitically crucial islands: Malvinas, South Georgia, South Sandwich, Orcadas del Sur (South Orkneys), and South Shetland (see Figure 5). Apart from the emotional aspects of the Malvinas/Falklands claim, it is this perception that the continuity of tricontinental Argentina is being violated by the British (and potentially by the Chileans) that makes the islands so fundamentally important from a geopolitical and strategic viewpoint to Argentina. There is also a keen perception that without the islands Great Britain's own Antarctic claims are considerably weakened. Argentine occupation of the islands is thus a geo-

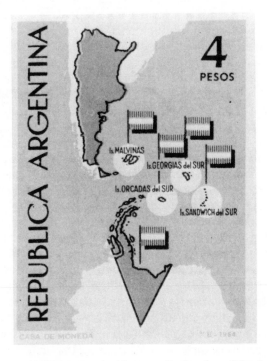

Figure 5. Stamp showing Argentine flags on the Southern Islands and the Antarctic claim. (Photo by the author.)

political imperative in order to neutralize the aspirations of both Britain and Chile.[28]

Although Argentina is practically self-sufficient in energy, there is a strong concern with energy in Argentine geopolitical thinking. In part this stems from the prestige of having a strong oil industry and from the implications of having the most advanced nuclear energy program in Latin America. There is also a sense of geopolitical energy competition with Brazil (with Paraguay and Uruguay playing classical buffer roles) for the hydroelectric resources of the upper Paraná River. The nuclear issue acquires even greater significance when one considers that there are no really effective safeguards on Argentina's nuclear programs, and there is little to stop the government from manufacturing an explosive device if it chose to; if this should happen, Brazil would be almost compelled to do the same. The temptation for Argentina to opt for nuclear weapons was heightened during the Falklands/Malvinas conflict, when it was assumed that the British had nuclear weapons in the battle area, although with no conceivable reason to use them. This produced a strong reaction among many Argentines and led some to comment that if Argentina had had nuclear weapons then perhaps Great Britain and the United States would have taken their country more seriously.

One group of Argentine geopoliticians has concentrated on something less dramatic: food, specifically the geopolitical implications of Argentina's almost unique potential for producing grain and meat. In an appropriately titled book (*El Poder del Pan* — "The Power of Bread") Rodríguez Zia makes this point, arguing that humanity will soon reach the moment when food will become the most sought-after (and possibly fought-after) resource. This situation, he warns, will be one of great opportunity for Argentina, but also one of great danger as other nations become tempted to seize Argentina's riches.

One last geopolitical theme of consequence in Argentine thinking is the seemingly eternal search for a grand "National Project" that would return to Argentina the sense of unity and direction it seems to have lost in recent decades. There are a variety of such National Projects embedded in the geopolitical writings of the Argentine school. Some are pragmatic and positive suggestions involving greater economic and political integration with neighbors; others take this same idea further by arguing that any such integration should naturally come under Argentine leadership (an outcome that would effectively kill the idea). Other National Projects are grandiose or bizarre schemes to unify river systems, create huge inland lakes, build vast new cities, and transfer large percentages of Argentina's population to its uninhabited areas, including inhospitable Patagonia.[29] Suffice it to say that there is little agreement on any of these National Projects; tragically, the one National Project that seemed to have unified Argentina (albeit very briefly) was the taking of the Malvinas/Falkland Islands in April 1982.

The Historical Development of Argentine Geopolitical Thinking

The historical development of geopolitical thinking in Argentina is not as clear as in the Brazilian case, since there is no succession of major figures who built upon their predecessor's work. It does seem clear that the Spaniards who settled in Argentina lacked the geopolitical instinct that the Portuguese *bandeirantes* seemed to have had. This lack of a geopolitical vision carried over into early national Argentina until the advent of Juan Bautista Alberdi, who is seen by many Argentine geopoliticians as having a well-developed sense of space and demography comparable to that of the early Brazilian geopoliticians. Their favorite Alberdi quotation used to illustrate this is his dictum "gobernar es poblar" (to govern is to populate), a concept that was the basis for the large migration into Argentina at the turn of the century.

As indicated previously, Admiral Segundo R. Storni was the first Argentine to lay out a coherent geopolitical doctrine, and his influence and ideas can in some ways be compared to those of Mahan in the United States. Writing in 1916, he emphasized Argentina's sea lines of communications and stressed the need for Argentina to recover the Southern Islands from Great Britain in order to assure the security of the South Atlantic and the approaches to the Strait of Magellan.[30]

Retired Army Colonel Jorge Atencio was the first Argentine geopolitical writer to chronicle the progress of geopolitical ideas in Argentina and to attempt to synthesize them and present them in a single text. He taught for many years at the University of Cuyo, and in his principal work, *¿Qué es la Geopolítica?*, he gave Argentine geopolitical writers both a textbook and a history of geopolitical influences in the country. He takes note of the strong influence of the Germanic school and states with some pride that at the end of World War II, when much of the world was attacking geopolitics as the "Nazi science,"[31] it was alive and well in Argentina.

It can be argued that Juan Domingo Perón was a geopolitician, especially if one considers his concept of "Gran Argentina,"[32] which was a contemporary revival of the Viceroyalty of the River Plate under Argentine leadership. However, the concept was strongly resisted by Uruguay and Chile, and only Bolivia and Paraguay went along with the idea, which died with the fall of Perón in 1955. Perón's writings did stress the need for a great and powerful Argentina but contain little in the way of explicitly geopolitical ideas or theories.

Contemporary Argentine geopolitical writings can be grouped around three individuals. Perhaps the best known is the recently deceased General Juan E. Guglialmelli, who edited the prestigious journal *Estrategia* from its founding in 1969 until his death in 1983; he was closely associated with the Instituto Argentino de Estudios Estratégicos y de las Relaciones Internacionales (INSAR). Guglialmelli was a prolific writer; however, his major contribution was to provide a forum and publication outlet for the "nationalistic" current of Argentine geopolitical ideas, harshly critical of Brazilian geopoliticians and extremely suspicious of the intentions of Brazil, Chile, and the United States.

The second group, as indicated previously, was less harsh in its attitudes toward Argentina's neighbors and acquired the label of *integrationist* because of its advocacy of closer ties with the other nations of the Southern Cone. Alfonso Bravo and Colonel Rattenbach are the main figures of this group, which publishes the journal *Geopolítica* and has acquired institutional identity in the form of the Instituto de Estudios Geopolíticos. Other significant figures in this group have been Nicolás Boscovich, Jorge T. Briano, Gustavo Cirigliano, Andrés Fernández Cendoya, Héctor Gómez Rueda, Carlos P. Mastrorili, Carlos Juan Moneta, and Osiris Villegas.

CHILE

Significance

The significance of geopolitical thinking in Chile can be easily summarized: the president of Chile since the 1973 coup that overthrew Salvador Allende is a geopolitician. The Pinochet regime has implemented a number of ideas that are geopolitical in nature; thus, an understanding of Southern Cone geopolitical thinking provides insight into the ideas and actions of President/General Pinochet. His notions of geopolitics have a strong emphasis on the organic theory of the state and on the existence of objective "laws" of geopolitics. Further, he feels that geopolitics has utility for the diplomat: "One of the objectives of geopolitics is to provide guidance on the possible application and use of these special laws in the foreign policy of the State and in its period of development."[33]

In his 1973 edition of *Geopolítica*, Pinochet lamented that, in contrast to Argentina and Brazil, there was no "school" of geopolitical thinking in Chile. Just a few years later, this was no longer true, since the basic elements of a Chilean geopolitical school now seem firmly in place, thanks to the efforts of the Pinochet regime. There are now, for example, a number of individuals who are writing and disseminating a prolific and reasonably coherent body of geopolitical doctrine. There is also now an Instituto Geopolítico de Chile, which was formally founded in August 1981 under the auspices of the Senior National Security Academy, and at the direction of the president himself. Pinochet, his defense minister, several senior military officers, and a number of other prominent geopolitical writers (including Colonel Julio von Chrismar and Navy Captain Luis Bravo Bravo) were all founding members. The instituto disseminates its ideas through the journal *Seguridad Nacional* published by the Senior National Security Academy. The final, and perhaps most significant, element of the Chilean geopolitical "school," is the manner in which geopolitical ideas are permeating the educational systems of the governing elite, the public schools, and the mass media.

The German geopolitical school has had an important influence on Chilean geopolitical thinking. This should not come as a surprise when one considers the strong Prussian and German presence in Chile, especially in the army, which was the first Latin American military institution to receive Prussian military training missions. Immigration is another factor that accounts for the influence of German geopolitical thinking and the general respect and admiration for things Teutonic. The ideas of Ratzel, in particular, are strongly evident in Chilean geopolitical thinking, especially his concepts of the state as an organic being, the flexible nature of the frontier, and his vision of international relations in Darwinian terms. Pinochet specifically relates Ratzel's ideas to the 1879–83 War of the Pacific, and notes that Chile was a strong and organized state at the time while Bolivia and Peru were weak and disorganized; thus, he says, Chile easily expanded its frontiers at the expense of its northern neighbors.[34]

Chilean geopolitical thinking has a quasi-fascistic flavor to it. There are strong currents of corporatism, authoritarianism, discipline, morality, militarism, and patriotism in the recent writings of individuals closely linked to the military regime in Chile since the September 11, 1973 coup.[35] There is also a very strong link to the concept of the national security state, a topic that will be explored in the following chapter.

A further reason why geopolitical thinking is significant in Chile stems from the extraordinary influence of geography in that country. Chile's shape, topography, and frontiers are unique; Chileans jestingly refer to their *loca geografía*. This sensitivity to the limitations and opportunities imposed by the physical medium is innate in every Chilean, and it is only natural that this feeling for geography should find a strong echo in geopolitical modes of analysis. Perhaps because their land has been so difficult, Chilean geopoliticians stress that the sea has been very generous to their country and that Chile should study, understand, and take full advantage of the geopolitical opportunities that the sea offers. Chilean sea power was decisive in the War of the Pacific and helped turn the southern Pacific into a Chilean sphere of influence; Chilean probes into the Atlantic, its Antarctic claim, and its suspected collaboration with Great Britain on the Falklands Islands issue are major factors in its relationship with Argentina. All of these geopolitical issues have a strong maritime component.

Major Themes

Historically the major theme in Chilean geopolitical thinking has been a defense of the territorial gains of the War of the Pacific. However, in the last few years, and especially since Argentina's rejection of the Beagle Channel Islands arbitration award and the Falklands/Malvinas conflict, Chile has shifted its geopolitical priorities so that now the principal emphasis is to the south and toward Argentina.

The War of the Pacific is a classical example of *Lebensraum* and the organic theory of the state; so it is not surprising that Chilean geopoliticians should stress these ideas as justification for their actions a century ago. Two quotes (the first from Pinochet) illustrate this attitude: "No matter how much one would like to think of law as an equalizing element among nations, it is always true that when countries face hard realities in border litigations, the country with the advantage is the one which is stronger militarily, economically, diplomatically, and demographically. Of this we have various examples in South America." The second quote is even more blunt (in reference to Bolivia): "An artificial country has no right to survive."[36]

A related major theme is the need for a strong Chilean presence in the

South Pacific; this idea was vividly expressed by a Chilean diplomat at the time of the War of the Pacific when he declared that this body of water should become "a Chilean lake."[37] This theme is so important that even army officers stress the maritime element as fundamental to Chilean geopolitical priorities (a situation not to be found in Brazil or Argentina, where only the navy defends this type of premise). Chilean geopolitical thinking mirrors the Argentine idea of the nation being the "keeper of the doorway to the Pacific." The Chilean Pablo Ihl Clericus, for example, uses the same concept of the *Oceanic Hemisphere* and the Antarctic claim to show how Chile dominates, at least cartographically, the Southern Passages (Strait of Magellan and the Drake Passage between Antarctica and South America). The South Pacific, and its entry points through the Beagle Channel and the Southern Passages, are seen by Chilean geopoliticians as a region subject to the geopolitical "law of valuable areas," which holds that if a nation does not fill, develop, and defend its valuable areas, another nation will. Accordingly, they stress the need to give this area a high priority and link their South Pacific presence to the Chilean Antarctic claim and the claim to the Picton, Lennox, and Nueva Islands at the eastern mouth of the Beagle Channel. Chilean geopoliticians also subscribe to an obscure geocultural theory which holds that the center of power and civilization in the world has been steadily shifting westward over time: civilization was born in the Fertile Crescent of the Euphrates, then moved to the Mediterranean, then Western Europe, and now to the United States. Chilean geopoliticians perceive the United States as being in a moral, economic, political, and military decline. Thus, the next logical location for the world cultural "center" is the Pacific Basin, and Chile will, according to its geopoliticians, come to play its rightful role and fulfill its "Manifest Destiny" in the process.

The "bi-oceanic principle," mentioned earlier in discussing Argentine geopolitical thinking, is an important element in Chilean thought as well. Even though Chileans accept the concept of "Argentina in the Atlantic and Chile in the Pacific," there is also a historical memory that Patagonia was once Chilean. Therefore, the line between the Atlantic and the Pacific should be drawn to favor Chile in terms of the Beagle Channel Islands and an arc running from them through South Georgia, South Sandwich, South Orkney, South Shetland, and the Chilean Antarctic sector. This concept, as we shall see when we discuss the Argentine-Chilean conflict, is anathema to Argentine geopoliticians (see Figure 8).

These considerations suggest that Antarctica is also a major theme in Chilean geopolitical thinking, a supposition that is amply borne out by the evidence. As was the case in Argentine geopolitical writing, in Chile there is also a theme of tricontinental Chile (mainland, insular, and Antarctic) and a strong feeling that the geographic continuity between the three must be maintained in order to protect the Antarctic claim. Chile is frequently portrayed as "the Southernmost country in the world,"[38] and maps and postage stamps are relentlessly used to bolster this self-image (see Figure 6).

Figure 6. Stamp showing Chile's Antarctic claim. The quotation is from the epic poem "I a Araucana" written by Alonso de Ercilla y Zúñiga during the conquest of Chile in the sixteenth century. The poem makes specific reference to Chile's location in "the famous Antarctic region." (Photo by the author.)

Because Chile is seen by its geopoliticians as being surrounded by hostile neighbors, an important theme in its geopolitical thinking is the search for allies in a delicate balance of power arrangement. This idea of a geopolitical balance of power will be analyzed more fully in Chapter 8 but can be sketched out here in terms of the geopolitical "theory of discontinuous borders." This theory argues that a country inevitably will tend to have poor relations with its immediate neighbors, but good relations with those nations that are reasonably close, but not contiguous;[39] thus, Chile's natural allies are Brazil and Ecuador. Beyond that, Chilean geopoliticians believe that "the enemy of my enemy is my friend," and there is thus also an interest in developing understandings with Great Britain and the United States as possible allies against Argentina.

Historical Development of Geopolitical Thinking in Chile

Bernardo O'Higgins, Chile's national independence hero, is frequently called the first Chilean geopolitician because of his interest in a Chilean presence in Patagonia, the Southern Islands and Passages, and even Antarctica. Pittman[40] traces the early evolution of Chilean geopolitical thought in terms of the competition between the O'Higgins tendency, which he labels "Americanist" (because of its interest in integrating and cooperating with other South American nations), and the "Nationalist" school of Diego Portales, which stressed balance of power relationships and the need for Chile to be strong in the South Pacific. These two currents, the cooperative and the conflictual, still exist in Chilean geopolitical thinking.

The first Chilean to write consistently on geopolitical themes, especially maritime ones, was General Ramón Cañas Montalva in the 1940s, who, along with Pablo Ihl Clericus formed the Terra Australis group. Their main concern was Chile's maritime role in the South Pacific, the Southern Passages, and Antarctica. Cañas Montalva had been the commander of Chile's Southern Military Region and was instrumental (along with Oscar Pinochet de la Barra) in bringing about Presidential Decree 1747 of 1940, which established Chile's Antarctic claim.

In the 1950s and 1960s the ideas of the Terra Australis group had begun to take root in the military academies and senior schools, where individuals such as Colonels Augusto Pinochet and Julio von Chrismar taught these themes to succeeding groups of military officers. Pinochet published his *Geopolítica* as an army text (Biblioteca del Oficial) in 1968, but it had little initial impact beyond purely military circles. The book is basically a geopolitical primer, with strong emphasis on the classical and Germanic schools and the organic theory of the state. The significance of the book, and its author, were greatly magnified on September, 11, 1973, when Pinochet as army commander led the coup against Salvador Allende and became the first Latin American president who explicitly considers himself a geopolitician. With Pinochet and the junta in power, Chilean geopolitical thinking received a considerable stimulus and has been an important factor in guiding the internal and external affairs of the regime.

Colonel Julio von Chrismar, a colleague and advisor of Pinochet, is probably the most significant geopolitical writer in Chile today. He holds an influential position in the National Senior Security Academy and is a thoughtful and prolific writer. Von Chrismar's emphasis is on the organic theory of the state and on the existence of objective geopolitical "laws" that can be identified, analyzed, and then applied to national development and relationships with other states.[41] In recent years he has also concentrated on defining Chile's vital national security interests and in establishing the relationship of geopolitics to national security. In this latter capacity he is one of the intellectual architects of the national security state as it has been constructed in Chile since 1973.

The long tenure of the Pinochet regime in Chile has permitted the dissemination of geopolitical ideas among both the ruling elite and a group of military and civilian intellectuals in the major universities in the country, principally the Catholic University. Among the most prominent and productive of these is Professor Emilio Meneses, who teaches geopolitics and political science at the Political Science Institute of the Catholic University as well as at the Army War Academy. Meneses has close ties to von Chrismar and the Chilean Geopolitical Institute; he has made lengthy analyses of Chile's geopolitical situation and has focused on the Argentine threat to Chilean interests in the South and Antarctic.

PERU

Significance

With Peru we move away from those South American countries that have geopolitical "schools" (Argentina, Brazil, and Chile) and begin to examine those that do not. What emerges from the countries without such a "school" is a pattern of individuals, usually military men, who publish sporadic articles and books on geopolitical themes and who probably exercise some influence on government policy, elite opinions, and mass media. Moreover, the military establishments of all the Spanish-speaking countries of South America have senior war or national security academies where lieutenant colonels, colonels, and their equivalents in the other services and government bureaucracies receive advanced instruction that usually includes a substantial dose of geopolitical topics. As an example, Gorman notes how, despite the lack of a "Peruvian geopolitical doctrine," geopolitics has in fact played an important role in shaping Peru's foreign policy.[42]

One other consideration is that there is considerable communication between mid- and upper-level military professionals in South America. At times this communication takes place through personal contacts at U.S. military installations or multilateral forums (such as the Inter-American Defense Board and the Inter-American Defense College); at other times it takes the form of exchange of doctrine, manuals, and military journals. Thus, a typical mid-level Peruvian officer is probably exposed to the major geopolitical themes that are prevalent in the professional literature of the Brazilian, Argentine, and Chilean militaries. Further, when one of these geopolitical themes published in the ABC countries strikes a sensitive nerve (in the Peruvian case it could be something to do with Chile and the War of the Pacific), there is usually a response in the form of a letter to the editor, a comment in the local media, or even an official statement. All of these considerations suggest that despite the lack of a geopolitical "school" geopolitical thinking is a factor to be considered in Peru and the remaining countries of South America.

Major Themes

The major themes of Peru's geopolitical writings reflect its principal foreign policy concerns, especially as they relate to the neighboring states of Chile, Ecuador, and Brazil. With Chile the theme is of Chilean geopolitical aggression during the War of the Pacific, a topic that has dominated the principal journal of Peruvian geopolitical thinking, the *Revista* of the Instituto Peruano de Estudios Geopolíticos (IPEGE). A theme that sometimes emerges in the context of the War of the Pacific is the need for a Pacific coast alliance (usually meaning Peru and Bolivia, and sometimes including Argentina as an outside ally) in order to counter Chilean power. These themes dealing with Chile reached a peak in 1979 with the centennial of the War of the Pacific. There were, in fact, serious concerns that there might be an outbreak of fighting near the anniversary, a fear that seemed justified in light of the massive amounts of Soviet weapons purchased by the Peruvian military regime.

By contrast, Peru devotes far less attention to Ecuador in its geopolitical writing, since it is Peru's view that there is no unsettled border issue with Ecuador. As Peru sees it, the 1942 Rio Protocol is valid, the border is settled, and the only problem is that the Ecuadoreans are trying to stir up trouble. However, in the 1940s, immediately after the short war between the two countries, there were numerous books and articles written in Peru with a geopolitical theme that attacked Ecuador and its claims.[43]

Since the late 1960's, Peru has embarked on an aggressive campaign in ocean claims and in 1970 joined eight Latin American governments in declaring claims to a 200-mile territorial (not merely economic) sea. This was followed up with an energetic effort to limit foreign fishing within that zone, an effort that caused severe diplomatic strains with the United States. This issue of ocean claims has shown up in Peruvian naval geopolitical writings, as it has in the naval journals of other Latin American nations.

A contemporary geopolitical theme in Peru is the need to develop and populate its Amazon area on the eastern slope of the Andes — *la marcha para la selva* (the march to the jungle). There appear to be two motivations behind this concern. One is the hope that such a colonization effort will reap an important economic benefit and will relieve population pressures in the coastal plain and central highlands. The other motivation concerns the geopolitical "law of valuable areas." This "law" argues that if Peru does not fill this empty Amazon Basin, then Brazil will do it as it expands its living frontiers to the west. This concern is frequently fueled by Argentine geopolitical writings, which are followed quite closely by Peruvian military leaders and have an impact because of the traditional belief that Argentina and Peru are natural allies when it comes to problems involving either Brazil or Chile. The operational aspect of this Peruvian geopolitical concern for the Amazon Basin takes the form of an ambitious road network. Ironically, the moving force behind this road construction project (known as the *carretera marginal de la selva* — the marginal jungle road) is not a military geopolitician but a civilian president who is also an architect: Fernando Belaúnde Terry, removed by the military in 1968 and returned as the elected president in 1980. Belaúnde Terry has long had a fascination for the Amazon and has felt the need for projects that would not only develop Peru's Amazon, but also integrate it into similar programs in other Amazonian nations.[44] Peru's military geopolitical thinkers are ambivalent about Belaúnde Terry's project; on the one hand, they support the idea of Amazon Basin development, but they also clearly do not trust Brazil. Peruvian military offices have expressed concern that developing the area will increase its attraction for Brazil and that roads in the area will make it easier for Brazil to complete its penetration of the Amazon.[45]

One favorite theme of the Peruvian military in the 1968 to 1980 period was the idea of "integral security," which includes a few geopolitical concepts. Basically, "integral security" dealt with the need to coordinate development efforts with security requirements; the two fields of security and development were often described as being inseparable. In this sense the Peruvian concept is similar to the Brazilian idea of *segurança e desenvolvimento* (security and development) but differs in that the Peruvians' is far less authoritarian and focuses more on social development than the Brazilian. The Peruvian concept has been laid out in some detail by General Edgardo Mercado Jarrín in his book, which also includes a rather harsh attack on the United States and on what he considers to be the excessive U.S. domination of the Inter-American Military System.[46]

The Peruvians have taken note of the Brazilian frontage theory of Antarctic sectors and have published maps and written about the sector that would correspond to Peru if the frontage theory were implemented. However, to date there has been no serious consideration of Peruvian activities in the Antarctic. The issue has the potential of further exacerbating relations between Peru and Chile since, as a Peruvian geographer has noted,[47] the Peruvian frontage sector includes part of the Antarctic sector claimed by Chile.

ECUADOR

There is even less evidence of geopolitical thinking in Ecuador than in Peru, but what little there is focuses on areas of conflict that Ecuador has had in the past and may have in the future. Ecuadorean geopolitical writers emphasize that Ecuador was "mutilated" by Peru in both the 1941 war and the subsequent 1942 Rio Protocol, which greatly favored Peru. Perhaps as compensation, Ecuadorean geopolitical thought promotes a "greater Ecuador." This involves the recovery of the lost Amazonian territories, the idea that Ecuador is a Pacific nation with an important oceanic sovereign area extending out to the Galapagos Islands, and even an interest in the Antarctic sector that frontage theory would give it. A recent geopolitically oriented book spoke of Ecuador as being "Janus-like" in that it must, like the Roman god of two faces, look geopolitically in two directions: toward the Amazon and toward the sea.[48] While there is no journal devoted to geopolitical thinking in Ecuador, geopolitically oriented articles appear in military journals and in the *Revista Geográfica*.

COLOMBIA

Like Ecuador, Colombia has little in the way of published geopolitical writings, although it can boast of one very prolific author: General Julio Londoño. His work deals more with political geography than geopolitics, and his focus has been on physical and descriptive geography, borders, and political units. He has made a comprehensive study of border "triple points" (that is, places where three sovereignties meet), but his analysis does not go into the power politics that are considered, for the purposes of this book, to be the essence of geopolitics. In Londoño's writings on cultural geography, he has included topics such as the impact of civilization on geography and the geographical distribution of folklore and music in South America.[49]

The lack of geopolitical writings in Colombia is curious, since that nation also suffered "geopolitical aggression" with the loss of Panama in 1903. Colombia also has ongoing disputes with both Nicaragua and Venezuela, which would presumably have given impetus to geopolitical analysis.

VENEZUELA

Although Venezuela has no geopolitical "school" in the sense of the ABC countries, there are strong indications that geopolitical thinking has some influence in high-level decisions and in military thinking. It should be noted, however, that the geopolitical currents that can be observed in Venezuela are much more in the United States mold, rather than the Germanic or classical mold of the Southern Cone. The evidence that geopolitical concepts are having an impact shows up in presidential statements in which the term *geopolitics* is used and in the way military and media commentators apply such ideas when discussing problems with their neighbors. These include the border disputes with Colombia and Guyana (and to a lesser extent Trinidad and Tobago) and the concern with Brazilian expansion and Cuban influence in the Caribbean. There is another dimension to Venezuelan geopolitical thought:

the geopolitics of energy (that is, oil). This dimension views Venezuela as an emerging nation that should use the power derived from its oil to play a significant role in the Caribbean and Central America. In this context the contemporary policy relevance of geopolitics in Venezuela is indeed significant, as Ewell has brought out in a recent article.[50]

In that article Ewell identifies the major themes of Venezuelan geopolitical concerns, to include the security of its oil resources, the recovery of territory lost to neighbors, the need to populate and develop its empty areas, and to somehow lower the level of tension in the Caribbean so as to protect its maritime trade. Like many of the South American nations examined thus far, Venezuela also has a geopolitical vision of past greatness that could be repeated in the future: its specific vision is the zenith of Bolivarian prestige and influence from 1810 to Bolívar's death in 1830. This was a period in which Caracas was a major power center in the area and had a greatness that was slowly lost in the civil wars and disorder that followed. There is in present Venezuelan geopolitical writings a sense that, if its oil income is invested wisely and secured from the designs of greedy outsiders, Venezuela has a chance of restoring this nineteenth century period of power and prestige.

Specific Venezuelan geopolitical concerns involve disputes with its neighbors, Colombia and Guyana. The less serious one, with Colombia, is nevertheless significant because the area in contention (parts of the Gulf of Venezuela) is close to the Maracaibo oil basin. It is therefore of great sensitivity to Venezuelans, and of great interest to Colombians, who are not self-sufficient in energy. Venezuelan geopolitical writers such as Carpio, who has done the most extensive work on the geopolitical implications of Venezuela's border disputes, note that Venezuela has already give up far too much of its territory to Colombia. The arguments suggest that Venezuela, like Argentina, is a geopolitically dissatisfied nation and one that sees itself as having been the victim of aggressions in the past. The parallel with Argentina is emphasized in Venezuela, particularly since the Malvinas/Falklands conflict.

In the Caribbean, Venezuela is seeking foreign policy objectives that are the natural offshoot of its increasing economic and political power. These objectives do not seem to be the result of any sense of *Lebensraum* or geopolitical expansion of a living frontier at the expense of any other nation. There is concern over the very real military power of Cuba, backed by the Soviet Union, and the recent decision to make a major purchase of advanced U.S. fighter planes by Venezuela can be seen as a realistic response to Cuban military power, including the potential threat posed by the airfield in nearby Grenada prior to October 1983. Beyond the immediate Caribbean area lies the Central American cauldron, and here too, as a member of the Contadora group, Venezuela has emerged as a regional power with geopolitical responsibilities.

Geopolitical writings in Venezuela also focus on the special nature of Venezuelan relations with Brazil and the United States. Both are seen with ambiguity. In some ways Brazil seems very far away geopolitically because of the vast empty expanses of the Orinoco and Amazon Basin that separate the two nations. But Venezuelan geopoliticians read the material published by their Brazilian counterparts and are well aware of the road-building program that is filling the previously empty Amazon Basin; they are also keenly sensitive to Brazil's great need for energy resources. The geopolitical ambiguity toward the United States stems from a sense of historic subordination to Washington on strategic matters coupled with a feeling that the United States is no longer the power it once was in the Caribbean. This has led to the belief that Venezuela had better be more prepared to defend itself than in the past.

Like the United States, Venezuela has a strong interest in protecting its sea lines of communications, with special emphasis on the routes taken by the oil tankers. Once again the threat posed by Cuba is significant in geopolitical terms and helps justify the expensive Venezuelan air and naval modernization program.

The historical development of Venezuelan geopolitical thinking is well documented by Ewell. She notes that it was rather passive through World War II and received a strong impetus during the period of strains in Venezuela over Cuban support for its subversive movements. The most prolific period of geopolitical writings in Venezuela is the present one, especially in terms of the disputes with Colombia and Guyana, and the Falklands/Malvinas conflict.

THE BUFFER STATES (URUGUAY, PARAGUAY, BOLIVIA)

In general, there is little independent and original geopolitical writing in Uruguay, Paraguay, and Bolivia, with the important exception of Quagliotti de Bellis in Uruguay. There is considerable awareness of geopolitical ideas and of the publications and discussions that take place in Brazil, Argentina, and Chile, but the lack of originality is understandable in light of the subordinate status of these three nations in the larger power arrangements of the Southern Cone. A further reality that limits their geopolitical production is the more modest size of their military establishments, whose emphasis on academic and theoretical matters is less than in the ABC countries.

The most sophisticated geopolitical production in the three buffers is clearly taking place in Uruguay. The closeness to Buenos Aires, and the constant looming presence of Brazil, have given geopolitical writers in Uruguay a keen sense of what can be called the "geopolitics of the buffers" (for a candid assessment of this line of thought, see the works of Methol Ferré, especially *Geopolítica del Cuenca del Plata*). There are occasional brave attempts by Uruguayan geopolitical analysts to speak of their country as a "hinge" around which important developments will take place, rather than a "buffer," which has a subordinate role. Despite these attempts there is an almost fatalistic resignation that Uruguay, created as a buffer between two powerful neighbors, will always be just that.

The important exception to this frame of mind is the extraordinary contribution of one man, Bernardo Quagliotti de Bellis. Almost singlehandedly he has created an integrationist geopolitical current in the buffer states. He also has established influential journals and associations with a potential for effectively promoting the cause of Southern Cone geopolitical integration in general, and of the buffers in particular. Quagliotti de Bellis heads the Instituto Uruguayo de Estudios Geopolíticos (IUDEG), which publishes the journal *Geopolítica* (not to be confused with the Argentine journal of the same name). Quagliotti de Bellis is also the driving force behind the Asociación Sudamericana de Estudios Geopolíticos e Internacionales (ASEGI), which publishes the journal *Geosur*. Both serve as vehicles for the integrationist thrust, and for Quagliotti de Bellis's concept of URUPABOL: the embodiment of cooperative efforts by Uruguay, Paraguay, and Bolivia.[51]

Uruguayan geopolitical writing also has a maritime and even an Antarctic component, although both reflect its buffer status. Any projects in either of these two directions, the writings reveal, would have to be taken in coordination with Brazil or Argentina. Despite this realistic understanding, Uruguayan naval officers have frequently been early proponents of ideas such as the South Atlantic Treaty Organization.

The production of geopolitical writings and ideas in Paraguay is very limited. Articles by Paraguayan authors occasionally appear in *Geosur* and *Geopolítica*, especially if they support the integrationist thesis, but there is no indication of a Paraguayan geopolitical journal nor of significant published books. There is an institute of geopolitics in Paraguay, but its activities appear to be limited to what comes through its affiliation with ASEGI and *Geosur*. Apart from the integrationist issue, Paraguayan geopolitical writing is principally concerned with the hydroelectric energy issue (mainly Itaipú) and its role in the River Plate Basin.

Bolivian geopolitical output is considerably more prolific and focuses on one issue that almost becomes an obsession: the loss of the outlet to the sea and ways of getting it back. This theme is the major issue in Bolivia's foreign relations, and the government supports geopolitical analysis in this area. A second theme of interest is an application of Mackinder's heartland thesis: that, since Bolivia occupies the heartland of South America, it is destined to someday achieve "greatness." Bolivian geopoliticians relate this theme to the loss of the sea outlet in the following way: Bolivia is not only the heartland, but is also the nerve center and balancer of geopolitical currents in South America since it sits at the point where the three major geopolitical units of South America (Plata, Amazon, and Pacific Basins) converge. With the loss of the sea outlet, Bolivia can no longer effectively play this role, and as a result the development of South America has been thwarted by Chile's aggression; the resultant latent state of tension will remain until the day when Bolivia regains its outlet.[52]

Bolivia has two geopolitical institutes (at La Paz and Santa Cruz); both produce material related to the sea outlet theme as a primary focus. They also consider other topics such as integration, and tensions with Paraguay that still remain from the Chaco War of the 1930s.

THE GUIANAS

There is no identifiable geopolitical writing emerging from Guyana or Suriname (to say nothing of French Guiana). In Guyana there is a considerable volume of material dealing with the dispute with Venezuela, but no indication that this stems from a doctrinal base that could be considered geopolitical.

NOTES

1. *Latin American Research Review* 14 (Summer 1979).

2. Howard T. Pittman, "Geopolitics in the ABC Countries: A Comparison," Ph.D. dissertation, American University, 1981, chap. 15.

3. "Declaración de Montevideo," *Geosur* no. 8 (March 1980): 1.

4. See, for example, Bernardo Quagliotti de Bellis, "Estrategia y Geopolítica en el Atlántico Sur," *Geopolítica* no. 5 (April 1978): 23.

5. *Clarín* (Buenos Aires), September 5, 1980 in *Foreign Broadcast Information Service (FBIS)*, September 11, 1980, p. B-3.

6. Bernardo Quagliotti de Bellis, *Geopolítica del Atlántico Sur* (Montevideo: Fundación de Cultura Universitaria, 1976), p. 19.

7. Therezinha de Castro, *Atlas-Texto de Geopolítica do Brasil* (Rio de Janeiro: Capemi Editores, 1982); Rubén Carpio Castillo, *Geopolítica de Venezuela* (Caracas: Editorial Ariel-Seix Barral Venezuela, 1981), pp. 190 and passim.

8. Ruben de Hoyos, *The United States and Latin America: Geopolitics and Political Development*, paper delivered at the Congress of the International Political Science Association, Rio de Janeiro, August 1982, pp. 15–16.

9. *O Estado de São Paulo*, April 29, 1983, in FBIS, May 5, 1983, p. D-4.

10. "The Brazilian Connection," *Washington Post*, January 6, 1964, p. B-3; *O Estado de São Paulo*, April 30, 1983, in *FBIS*, May 13, 1983, p. D-3.

11. Carlos de Meira Mattos, *A Geopolítica e as Projeções do Poder* (Rio de Janeiro: José Olympio, 1977), pp. 111–13; Therezinha de Castro, "El Atlántico," in *Geopolítica y Relaciones Internacionales*, ed. Luis Dallanegra Pedraza (Buenos Aires: Pleamar, 1981), p. 99. Carpio Castillo, *Venezuela*, pp. 186–87.

12. Julio J. Chiavenato, *Geopolítica, Arma do Fascismo* (São Paulo: Global Editores, 1981), pp. 73–80.

13. Jack Child, "Strategic Concepts of Latin America: An Update," *Inter-American Economic Affairs* 34 (Summer 1980): 61–82.

14. Nelson Freire Lavenere-Wanderley, "Atlántico Sur: Tres Visiones de una Estrategia," *Geopolítica* no. 5, (April 1978); de Castro,"El Atlántico," pp. 63–64.

15. Professor de Castro's ideas are presented in her *Rumo a Antártica* (Rio de Janeiro: Freitas, 1976). See also Pericles Azambuja, "Antartida: Derecho que Tiene Brasil," *Geosur* no. 23 (July 1981): 36–40.

16. This section draws from the author's "Geopolitical Thinking in Latin America," *Latin American Research Review* 14 (Summer 1979): 90–92.

17. Mario Travassos, *Projecão Continental do Brasil* (São Paulo: Edit Nacional, 1935), esp. pp. 19, 30–31, 41, 126, 130. For analysis, see Hector María Balmaceda, "Tendencias

Geopolíticas en el Atlántico Sur," in *Geopolítica y Política del Poder en el Atlántico Sur*, ed. Carlos J. Moneta (Buenos Aires: Pleamar), 1983, pp. 64–67. For critical views, see Carlos P. Mastrorilli, "Geopolítica del Brasil: Historia y Doctrina," *Estrategia* nos. 19–20 (November 1972–February 1973): 20–21. See also Chiavenato *Arma do Fascismo*, p. 41.

18. Golbery do Couto e Silva, *Aspectos Geopolíticos do Brasil* (Rio de Janeiro: Biblioteca do Exército, 1957), pp. 137–38; Golbery do Couto e Silva, *Geopolítica do Brasil* (Rio de Janeiro: Editorial José Olympio, 1967), pp. 137–38. Mastrorilli, "Geopolítica del Brazil," pp. 26–28.

19. Carlos de Meira Mattos, *Brasil: Geopolítica e Destino* (Rio de Janeiro: Biblioteca do Exército, 1975), p. 58. Interviews with General Meira Mattos, Washington, D.C., September 1976, October 1979, and September 1981.

20. Pittman, "ABC Countries," p. 752 and passim.

21. Osiris G. Villegas, "Imperium Jurisdiccional," *Geopolítica* no. 21 (March 1981), p. 7.

22. Osiris G. Villegas, "Puntos de Vista para una Geopolítica Nacional," *Geopolítica* nos. 3–4 (March–June 1976): 14.

23. For example, Juan E. Guglialmelli, "Argentine-Brasil: Enfrentamiento o Alianza para la Liberación," *Estrategia* no. 36 (September 1975): 1–29; Florentino Díaz Loza, "Geopolítica del Brasil," *Estrategia* no. 29 (July 1974), pp. 30–40.

24. See, for example: Vivian Trias, *Imperialismo y Geopolítica en América Latina* (Buenos Aires, Editorial Jorge Alvarez, 1969) pp. 175–76; Juan E. Guglialmelli, "Golbery do Couto e Silva: El "Destino Manifiesto Brasileño y el Atlántico Sur," *Estrategia* no. 39 (March 1976): 5–24; Augusto B. Rattenbach, "Venta de Armas de los Estados Unidos a la América Latina," *Estrategia* no. 28 (May 1974): 81–90; Arturo E. Barbieri, "Análisis de los Factores Geopolíticos Nacionales y sus Vinculaciones con el Proyecto Nacional," *Estrategia* nos. 64–65 (May–August 1980): 24; Raul Mason Lugones, "Plan Externo para una Subordinación de Argentina al Brasil," *Estrategia* nos. 64–65 (May–August 1980): 10.

25. Osiris G. Villegas, "Paz, Soberanaía e Integridad Territorial," *Geopolítica* no. 18 (June 1980): 5; Oscar Montes, "Errores, Omisiones y Excesos del Laudo Arbitral," *Geopolítica* no. 21 (March 1981): 19; Raul Rey Balmaceda, "Otra Cuestión de Limites con Chile?" *Estrategia* no. 69 (1981): 106.

26. Jorge T. Briano, *Geopolítica y Geoestrategia Americana* (Buenos Aires: Pleamar, 1966), pp. 338–39. For a commentary on the restoration of the Viceroyalty of the Rio de la Plata, see Vicente Palermo, "Geopolítica del Virreynato del Rio de la Plata," *Geopolítica* nos. 5–6 (July–December 1976): 19. Also Pittman, "ABC Countries," pp. 675–92.

27. Jorge E. Atencio, *¿Qué es la Geopolítica?* (Buenos Aires: Pleamar, 1965), p. 339.

28. Osiris G. Villegas, "El Petróleo como Arma en el Campo Económico," *Geosur* no. 13 (September 1980): 27; See also Luis Sartori, "Malvinas: Visita de Ridley y Perspectivas," *Estrategia* nos. 67–68 (November 1980–February 1981): 114–22; Armando Lambruschini, "Disertación del Comandante en Jefe de la Armada," *Estrategia* no. 69 (1981): 131–37. Ernesto J. Fitte, *La Disputa con Gran Bretaña por las Islas del Atlántico Sur* (Buenos Aires: Emece, 1968); Fernando A. Milia, *La Atlantártida: Un Espacio Geopolítico* (Buenos Aires: Pleamar, 1978).

29. Osiris Villegas, *Tiempo Geopolítico Argentino* (Buenos Aires: Pleamar, 1975); Gustavo Cirigliano, *La Argentina Triangular* (Buenos Aires: Humanitas, 1975).

30. Juan E. Guglialmelli, "Argentina Insular o Peninsular?" *Estrategia* nos. 40–41 (March–August 1976): 5; Lewis A. Tambs, "The Changing Geopolitical Balance of Latin America," *Journal of Social and Political Studies* (Spring 1979): 27–29.

31. Atencio, *Geopolítica?*, pp. 122–25.

32. Carlos Berraz Montyn, *Ensayo Sobre el Justicialismo y la Unión Americana* (Santa Fe, Argentina: Universidad Nacional del Litoral, 1954), pp. 64–65.

33. Augusto Pinochet, *Geopolítica* (Santiago: Editorial Andrés Bello, 1974), p. 21.

34. Ibid, pp. 175–76.

35. See, for example, Julio von Chrismar, "Geopolítica y Seguridad Nacional," *Seguridad Nacional* (Chile) no. 21 (1981): 36–43. Mario Barros van Buren, "Política Exterior y Seguridad

Nacional," *Seguridad Nacional* no. 21 (1981): 45–49. Hugo Tagle Martínez, "Seguridad Nacional y Matrimonio," *Seguridad Nacional* no. 21 (1981): 83–92.

36. Pinochet, *Geopolítica*, p. 165; Miguel Lastarria Servat, *El Espacio Vital* (Santiago: Editorial Simiente, 1944), p. 135.

37. Quoted in Robert N. Burr, *By Reason or Force: Chile and the Balancing of Power in South America, 1830–1905* (Berkeley: University of California Press, 1965), p. 184.

38. Ramón Cañas Montalva, "Reflexiones Geopolíticas," *Revista Geográfica de Chile* 1, (September 1948): 27–40. Ramón Cañas Montalva, "Chile: El Pais más Austral de la Tierra," *Geosur* no. 23 (July 1981): 22–35.

39. Armando Alonso Pineiro, "El Equilibrio Geopolítico Sudamericano," *Estrategia* no. 30 (September 1974): 6.

40. Pittman, "ABC Countries," pp. 1250–54.

41. Julio von Chrismar, *Leyes que se Deducen del Estudio de la Expansión de los Estados* (Santiago: Biblioteca del Oficial, 1968).

42. Stephen M. Gorman, "Geopolitics and Peruvian Foreign Policy," *Inter-American Economic Affairs* 36 (Autumn 1982): 65.

43. See, for example, Alfonso Benavides Correa, "Esquema para una Interpretación Geopolítica," *Revista de América (Bogota)* (July 1948): 115–23.

44. *Washington Post*, April 17, 1966, p. E-2; *Washington Post*, July 31, 1983, p. A-17; *New York Times*, August 11, 1983, p. A-2.

45. *Latin American Weekly Report*, December 12, 1980.

46. Edgardo Mercado Jarrín, *Seguridad, Política, Estrategia* (Lima: Ministerio de Guerra, 1974).

47. Arnaldo Zamora Lazo, "Proyección Peruana a la Antártida," *Geosur* no. 23 (July 1981): 41–43.

48. Jorge García Negrete, "Esquema para una Interpretación Geopolítica," *Revista Geográfica* (Quito) no. 7 (May 1972): 27–58.

49. Julio Londoño, *Suramérica: La Geografía como Destino* (Bogotá: Imprenta del Ministerio de Guerra, 1948); Julio Londoño, "Nueva Geopolítica de Colombia: Sus Fronteras," *Geosur* no. 28 (December 1981). For a recent commentary on geopolitical thinking in Colombia, see Juan Diego Jaramillo, "Colombia y la Geopolítica Universal," *El Siglo* (Bogota), September 25, 1983, p. 12.

50. Judith Ewell, "The Development of Venezuelan Geopolitical Analysis Since World War II," *Journal of Inter-American Studies and World Affairs* 24 (August 1982): 295–316.

51. For an example, see *Geosur* issue for January 1980.

52. Bolivia, Ministerio de Relaciones Exteriores, "El Encierro Geográfico de Bolivia," *Geosur* no. 22 (May 1981): 52.

4

GEOPOLITICAL THINKING AND THE NATIONAL SECURITY STATE

In previous chapters occasional references have been made to the national security state and the national security doctrine, suggesting that there was a link between these concepts and geopolitical thinking, at least in the Southern Cone of Latin America. Such a link is important in understanding both the internal and external behavior of South American nations that subscribe to geopolitical doctrines and accept the national security state as a basic organizing concept. This topic has been explored in considerable depth by Comblin and Arriagada, whose ideas form the basis for much of the criticism directed against the national security state as it exists in the Southern Cone.[1] This chapter examines the relationship between geopolitical thinking and the national security state before continuing with an analysis of the specific conflict case studies in South America.

THE NATIONAL SECURITY STATE

The national security state employs a unique concept of the state as an organic entity, a view that is also used by geopoliticians. The nation-state is seen in terms of the ideas brought out by Ratzel in the nineteenth century: that it is a dynamic, living organism struggling to survive in a frequently hostile environment in which the only real law is political Darwinism. Organic concepts of the state in Latin America are not new. As Crahan notes, the Estado Novo of Getulio Vargas of Brazil in the 1930s was an important and extensive experiment with organic state ideology.[2] It is perhaps no coincidence that this was also the time that Southern Cone (and especially Brazilian) geopoliticians were beginning to absorb and discuss the organic ideas of Ratzel and the German geopolitical school.

Apart from the implications that this aggressive and Darwinian vision of the state has for foreign relations, it has an important impact on the way the individual is seen in relation to the state. Organic state theorists argue that the state and not the individual is the most important element, since the individual, like a particular cell in an organism, can be replaced if it dies. This in turn suggests that if some individuals are seen as enemies of the state, those individuals should be shown why they are wrong and convinced to change their views; if this fails, then the state in its own defense must expel or destroy the individuals who have gone wrong. To apply a medical analogy to the organic theory, individuals who oppose the organic state are like cancer cells, and if the cancer cannot be cured the malignant cells must be surgically removed or destroyed. It is interesting to note that the military officers who took power in most of the Southern Cone nations in the 1960s and 1970s frequently spoke of the need to "extirpate" (that is, surgically remove) the "cancer of Marxism" that had infiltrated the nation-state. The implications of this vision of the state for the protection of individual political and human rights should be readily apparent.

Those who view the state as a living organism also tend to see it constantly threatened by a variety of forces, physical and ideological, internal and external. Part of the duty of the defenders of the organic state (that is, the military and security apparatus) is to be constantly alert for these vulnerabilities, interferences, and threats. As expressed by Colonel von Chrismar (the Chilean geopolitician mentioned in the last chapter), the detection of these dangers involves "not only an action of permanent control by the nation-state of all the negative effects (internal or external) which affect its security, but also a complete and profound study of all the past, present and future circumstances of the nation-state, oriented towards the scientific analysis of the causes which generate such circumstances, be they geographic, geohistoric, political, juridical, social, economic, ethnic, etc."[3]

THE CONCEPT OF NATIONAL SECURITY

If one can temporarily set aside these darker implications of the organic theory of the state, the national security doctrine can be seen as a logical process by which the nation-state seeks to provide for its legitimate defense. This process involves defining national objectives and interests, identifying threats to those interests, evaluating the available elements of national power that the state can mobilize, and then searching for a strategy for action. In effect, this is the national security planning process that almost all nations in the world employ; it is nothing more than an adaptation of classical problem-solving techniques: define the problem, propose possible solutions, test the solutions, and implement the best one.[4]

The definition of national interests and objectives can range from the very general to the quite specific. At the general level, these interests would include such elements as the survival of the state, protection of its sovereignty, and assuring the welfare of its citizens. More specific national interests are derived from these and tend to focus on concrete geographic, economic, and political problems, such as how to encourage the settlement of empty frontier areas, how to reduce excessive dependency on foreign energy imports, how to defend a particular border against a presumed enemy, and so forth. The identification of threats to these national interests is basically a function of the state's intelligence apparatus in both the external and internal dimensions. The way in which threats are defined frequently produces a self-fulfilling prophecy. Intelligence organizations told to be on guard for a particular threat have a vested interest in finding just that kind of threat and have little incentive for finding other kinds of threats or for reporting that no threat exists.

Attempts to measure the available elements of national power have absorbed a great deal of attention and energy. There is general agreement regarding the kinds of things that make up a nation's power: territory, population, economic capability, military strength, national strategy, and national will. Difficulties arise when one tries to quantify these elements and arrive at some kind of formula that will allow a comparison of national power or that will permit the allocation of national power on a priority basis to solve certain national security problems. Cline, for example, has proposed a formula that would quantify the elements of national power listed above and would permit a ranking of the world's nations by their numerical power units.[5]

As can be seen from this sketch of the national security planning process, the concept of power is central to the concerns of the national security state. The analysis of state power is generally accomplished by considering four general fields of power: economic, political, military, and psychosocial. These four fields are the organizing framework for many strategic analyses, and the curricula of most of the senior war colleges and geopolitical institutions are organized around these fields of power. It is also common to find the academic departments of these institutions structured bureaucratically on the basis of these four fields of power, with an office assigned the responsibility for organizing studies at the internal, national, continental, and global level for each one of the four fields.

Although in a sense the national security concepts sketched out above are universals, the United States' influence in presenting these ideas to the Latin American military establishments has been very strong. The United States National War College (and the individual army, navy, and air force war colleges) have been the models for their counterparts in Latin America, with the exception of those countries in which the pre–World War II Prussian or French staff model has left a strong legacy. The Brazilian Escola Superior de Guerra (ESG) was copied from the U.S. National War College, as was the Inter-American Defense College in Washington.

THE NATIONAL SECURITY DOCTRINE

Those rather innocuous and somewhat universal concepts of national security become less innocent when they come together to form a coherent operational "doctrine." This is especially true when they are linked to the organic concept of the state, to the geopolitical frameworks of some of the Latin American military establishments, and to the particular ideological mind-sets and institutional needs of the Southern Cone militaries. Comblin (as well as the Brazilian Chiavenato) have suggested that what emerges from this mix is not merely a doctrine but an ideology that provides its adherents with a full explanation of the world, its problems, and the action necessary to correct them. As Comblin states:

> This ideology has no official name, but I call it the national security ideology because it is the ideology of the national security system, the new political system of today. This ideology has not yet been philosophically elaborated by its disciples, but since it covers virtually all individual and social activities of the nation and gives a new meaning to all human existence, it is universal and totalitarian enough to exclude any inference by another philosophy.[6]

It seems clear that this national security state and its doctrine have gone far beyond what the United States intended when it offered its National War College as a model for the Latin Americans within the context of an Inter-American Military System. The United States had created the Inter-American Military System in the early days of World War II in order to eliminate the remaining German and Italian influence among the Latin American military establishments. At the end of the war, this system was institutionalized when the organizations that had been created on an ad hoc basis during the war were given a permanent status. These included the Inter-American Defense Board, the Military Assistance Program, and the training of Latin American military officers in the Panama Canal Zone and the United States.

In the early postwar period, these institutions of the Inter-American Military System were justified on the grounds that they contributed to "Hemisphere Defense" against an outside threat, which had been the Fascist Axis in World War II but was soon to become the Soviet Communist threat during the cold war. Thus, a cold war anti-Communist orientation was part of the model that U.S. military leaders taught their Latin American counterparts. When Fidel Castro's revolution triumphed in January 1959, the operational thrust of this cold war anticommunism went in the direction of counter-insurgency in what the United States military called the "IDAD" concept (for internal defense and development). The concept was that in a guerrilla war the military had to make a contribution to a nation's internal development as well as to its defense; thus, new programs were implemented such as the civic action plan under which the Latin American military would initiate road building, school construction, well drilling, and other projects that would hopefully contribute to national development and "win the hearts and minds of the people." There was also an optimistic assumption that by absorbing the military's energy it would be less likely to become involved in politics.[7]

In retrospect, it now appears that by presenting the Latin American military with the IDAD concept, the United States opened a Pandora's box. After the early guerrilla movements were contained and defeated in most of the Southern Cone nations, the militaries in these countries discovered a new rationale and justification for their existence: they would now play a role in national development at the upper levels of the state apparatus and not just simply at the tactical level fighting guerrillas in the hope of winning peasant hearts and minds. The national security doctrine provided a theoretical justification for this new role by merging the United States' IDAD concept with indigenous ideas about the organic nature of the state and geopolitics.

This process was especially evident in Brazil, which was closely tied to the United States in the 1960s, and had almost slavishly copied the National War College model. However, at the same time the influence of Brazil's geopolitical thinking was making itself felt, and the Brazilian military began to evolve its own concept of *segurança e desenvolvimento*. The evolution of the Brazilian national security doctrine has been well documented by Selcher and has been articulated and explored by a number of official and critical sources in Brazil itself.[8]

The pervasive and open-ended nature of the national security state and its doctrine was best captured (perhaps only partially in jest) by a senior Chilean intelligence officer when he said: "National security is like love. There is never enough."[9]

THE INSTITUTIONS OF THE NATIONAL SECURITY STATE

The institutions of the national security state in South America in many cases bear the same name as their U.S. counterparts. Frequently, however, they have functions that go considerably beyond their U.S. models, defined by the legislation that set up the U.S. national security institutions in the late 1940s.

The central coordinating institution is the national security council (NSC), which in most Latin American nations consists of the president, the senior military or defense ministers, the head of the intelligence organ, and the interior minister. The 1947 U.S. legislation that created the National Security Council also established the Central Intelligence Agency, and the Defense Department as a single agency that would integrate the military services. Whereas in the United States the National Security Council has remained firmly under the control of the civilian president, in many of the South American nations the national security council arrangement has served to increase the military's power and the effectiveness of its coordination, thus reducing the already tenuous civilian control of the military. Where the president is a military officer (a frequent occurrence in the Southern Cone), the national security council performs this function all too well.

A second key institution of the national security state system is the war college or senior security academy. Most of the Latin American military establishments have a complex educational system consisting of preparatory academies, low- and mid-level training schools, and, at the apex, a senior service college (army, navy, or air force). The concept of a single security academy at the national level above the individual service academies is a relatively new one. It was copied from the U.S. model of a national war college that would focus more on national problems, would integrate representatives from the three military services, and would be above the service colleges in prestige and focus. However, the Latin American military establishments, especially the Southern Cone ones, took the concept considerably farther: they gave their senior security academies a key role in three new and different dimensions.

The first dimension was as a policy-influencing instrument in the sense that members of the military establishment worked very closely with the national security council and frequently had some of their officers serving on the NSC staff. Secondly, they functioned as "think tanks" in that they addressed major problems in national development, strategy, and policy, which are roles that in the United States would be filled by special study groups or by independent think tanks like the Brookings Institution, the Hudson Institute, the Rand Corporation, or the Hoover Institution. Third, they went considerably beyond the U.S. model in the educational role in that the courses were longer, paid more attention to major national problems, and enrolled a far greater percentage of civilians than did their U.S. counterpart. This latter point is a revealing one, since it suggests that one function of the Southern Cone security academy is to "militarize" a key civilian ruling elite and educate it in the military approach to national problems and their solutions. The Southern Cone war colleges have one further unique activity, that of their alumni organizations, which maintain the bonds forged during the academic period and continue to disseminate the academy's doctrine to their military and civilian graduates long after they leave the institution. As a senior Brazilian military officer put it, the ESG is a "laboratory of ideas"[10] — but it is also a creator, indoctrinator, and disseminator of them.

The intelligence apparatus of the national security state is a key element in the system. In the United States the Central Intelligence Agency was created as the principal foreign intelligence organization in 1947. Its record in the functioning democracy that is the United States is an instructive one: it has often been difficult to control and limit the functions of the agency. Similar organizations in a Southern Cone environment, with ineffective or nonexistent legislatures and judiciaries, have frequently been guilty of great excesses. To compound the problem the Southern Cone intelligence apparatuses were frequently given both internal and external security functions; thus the U.S. equivalent would not simply be the CIA, but the CIA plus the FBI and the National Security Agency and a local police force. The end results in the Southern Cone were institutions such as the Brazilian SNI (National Intelligence Service) and the Chilean DINA (National Intelligence Directorate).

The last important institution of the national security state system has been the geopolitical or strategic studies and international relations institution. These have been either attached to the security academies, as in the Chilean case, or have been semi-independent, as in Argentina. In the latter case they would typically be headed by a retired senior officer and would include on their board of directors, and as frequent contributors, a number of active duty and retired military officers. It is the publications of these geopolitical institutions that provide some of the most valuable insights into the thinking of key personalities in the national security states of the Southern Cone.

THE NATIONAL SECURITY STATE AND GEOPOLITICAL THINKING

By now the close links between geopolitical thinking and the national security state in the Southern Cone should be increasingly evident. At one level geopolitics is clearly the geography of the national security state; but it is far more than that. It is also the geography of the organic state and in many ways the pseudoscience that serves as a justification for the organic state's very existence and the justification for its expansionary drives. The organic state exists to survive and increase its power, and geopolitical thinking serves this purpose well by suggesting to the diplomat ways in which this can be achieved. To quote the Chilean von Chrismar, "Since the growth of national power is the fundamental basis of National Security, one can say that geopolitics is one of the disciplines which most contributes to the growth of National Security."[11]

Many of the geopolitical thinkers of the Southern Cone have a tendency to make geopolitics the central organizing discipline of their mind-set so that all the other branches of knowledge become related to the *geo* part of the geopolitics and become subordinated to geopolitics as the higher discipline. Thus, we have geostrategy as the military science of planning for war using geopolitical principles; we have geoadministration as the bureaucratic process used to implement geopolitical concepts; we have geohistory, geo-medicine, and so on.

THE INTERNAL IMPACT

The internal impact of the linking of geopolitical thinking with the national security state must be seen in relation to the authoritarian, corporatist, and militaristic state systems that have been so evident in the Southern Cone of South America. The internal structures of these nations are characterized by strong centralized governments with a widespread security apparatus to detect and control any signs of political or social unrest. The concept of security is applied not only at the national level, but at the community and individual level as well.[12] The most comprehensive application of this approach has been in Brazil and Chile, with Uruguay imitating some aspects of the model. Argentina's internal security has been shaped more by the special nature of the Peronista populist forces that have opposed their country's military regimes, and by the much more brutal responses of the government security apparatus.

The Chilean model of the national security state shows some special characteristics. As noted previously, its proponents have placed a strong emphasis on the need for order, discipline, and morality (for example, one recent article in *Seguridad Nacional* was titled "National Security and Marriage"). This type of an attitude suggests that what has emerged is very close to fascism, complete with geopolitics as its pseudoscientific justification; or, as one author has succinctly put it, "geopolitics is the geography of fascism."[13]

As Pittman has extensively documented (and as Barros in Brazil has corroborated), one of the concerns of the national security state in the Southern Cone is to educate the current generation of youth so as to remove (*extirpate* is the verb frequently used) the last vestiges of Marxist thinking. As a result of this concern, one can observe in the publications of the geopolitical institutes a strong interest in preparing geopolitical materials for use in the primary and secondary schools as well as in civilian institutes of higher learning. The geopolitical journals frequently print model curricula and offer seminars and short courses on geopolitics. Pittman has observed that this process has had considerable success, most notably in Argentina, where it is wrapped in highly patriotic exhortations, especially as it pertains to the Malvinas or the disputes with Chile. Some of the suggestions are original: maps should use projections that show Argentina at the center; they should always (by law if necessary) show Argentina's Antarctica as an integral part of the map, not as a reduced footnote; the Argentine sea should be shown as national territory, not just as a body of water; the use of "upside down" maps should be encouraged so as to implant the idea that Antarctic territory and surrounding waters are valuable.[14]

NOTES

1. Joseph Comblin, "Latin America's Version of 'National Security,'" *America* 134 (February 21, 1976): 137–39; Joseph Comblin, *The Church and National Security* (Maryknoll, N.Y.: Orbis Books 1981); Genaro Arriagada, *Seguridad Nacional y Bien Común* (Santiago: Talleres Gráficos Corporación, 1976); *Washington Post*, February 9, 1984, p. DC-11. For a response to Comblin and others who attack the national security state, see General Carlos de Meira Mattos, "Desinformação Histórica e Seguranca Nacional," *O Estado de São Paulo*, May 6, 1979.

2. Margaret E. Crahan, *The State and the Individual in Latin America: Some Implications for Human Rights* (Washington, D.C.: Woodstock Theological Center, October 1979), p. 21.

3. Julio von Chrismar, "Geopolítica y Seguridad Nacional," *Seguridad Nacional* (Chile) no. 21 (1981): 30.

4. Alfonso Littuma, *Doctrina de Seguridad Nacional* (Caracas: Biblioteca del Ejército, 1967), p. 143; Brasil, Escola Superior de Guerra, *Manual Básico* (Rio de Janeiro: Escola Superior de Guerra, 1972); José Alfredo Amaral Gurgel, *Segurança e Democracia* (Rio de Janeiro: José Olympio, 1978), p. 73 and passim.

5. Ray S. Cline, *World Power Trends and U.S. Foreign Policy for the 1980s* (Boulder, Colo: Westview Press, 1980).

6. Comblin, *National Security*, p. 65.

7. For a more detailed analysis, see Jack Child, *Unequal Alliance: The Inter-American Military System, 1938*–1978 (Boulder, Colo.: Westview press, 1980), esp. chap. 5.

8. Wayne A. Selcher, "The National Security Doctrine and the Policies of the Brazilian Government," *Parameters* 7 (1977): 10–24. Amaral Gurgel, *Segurança e Democracia*; Julio J. Chiavenato, *Geopolítica, Arma do Fascimo* (Sào Paulo: Global Editores, 1981).

9. *Times of the Americas*, March 28, 1984, p. 5.

10. Antonio Jorge Correa, "Escola Superior de Guerra: Laboratorio de Ideias," *A Defesa Nacional* no. 667 (May–June 1976): 23–34.

11. Von Chrismar, "Seguridad Nacional," p. 42.

12. Amaral Gurgel, *Segurança e Democracia* pp. 136–38, 141–42.

13. Quoted by Amaral Gurgel, *Segurança e Democracia* rear cover. For an example of this moralistic view, see Hugo Tagle Martínez, "Seguridad Nacional y Matrimonio," *Seguridad Nacional* no. 21 (1981): 83–92.

14. See "Comentarios," *Geopolítica* nos. 3–4: 60–61.

PART THREE
GEOPOLITICS AND
CONFLICT—CASE STUDIES

INTRODUCTION TO PART THREE

The following three chapters examine specific case studies of conflict situations in South America in an attempt to discover how geopolitical thinking is related to these conflicts. The conflicts will be organized in three categories, each corresponding to a chapter: the Southern Cone conflicts (Chapter 5), the South Atlantic-Antarctica conflicts (Chapter 6), and the South American-Caribbean conflicts (Chapter 7).

Each conflict will be analyzed using the following format:

- Introduction: parties to the conflict, summary, and geography.
- Historical background of the conflict.
- Recent developments (in the period of the last two to three years).
- The type of conflict: classification using the typology developed in Chapter 1. A brief assessment will also be made of the military factors involved, such as the tactical theater of operations, tension levels, and implications for arms purchases.
- Relationship to other conflicts.
- Relationship to geopolitical thinking: using some of the geopolitical ideas analyzed in Chapters 2 and 3, this section will explore the possible relationship between the conflict and forms of geopolitical thinking prevalent in the countries involved in the dispute.

5

THE SOUTHERN CONE CONFLICTS

THE SOUTHERN ANDEAN CONFLICT: ARGENTINA-CHILE (BEAGLE CHANNEL ISLANDS)

Introduction: Parties, Summary, and Geography

The dispute between the two southernmost nations of Latin America[1] involves the possession of three normally uninhabited and seemingly unimportant islands at the eastern entrance to the Beagle Channel, south of Tierra del Fuego: Nueva, Picton, and Lennox (the so-called NPL Islands). Three smaller islands (Evout, Barnevelt, and Deceit) also figure in the dispute. Although the immediate parties to the conflict are only Chile and Argentina, Great Britain is also involved since it was the British Crown that passed down the crucial arbitration award in 1977. Great Britain is involved as well via the Falklands/Malvinas conflict since the Argentines strongly suspect that the Chileans were sympathetic to the British cause and assisted them during the actual fighting.[2]

As unlikely as it may seem, in late 1978 Argentina and Chile almost went to war over these islands. The popular press and geopolitical journals in both countries, but especially Argentina, were full of talk of hostilities in 1978. An Argentine admiral, writing in 1982, recalls the seriousness of the situation in 1978 and suggests that the tension remained beyond that date: "We all know the gravity of the consequences of a war, and we realize that even when one is victorious all objectives are not accomplished. No one wants it, but perhaps, in the absence of other possibilities, there could be hostilities such as in the case of Peru and Ecuador [January 1981] which were fortunately stopped in time. And we also know how close we were to that alternative towards the end of 1978."[3]

Among the most vocal and aggressive spokesmen in both countries were some noted geopolitical thinkers, especially those who were also military men. The words of retired General Osiris Villegas illustrate this bellicose attitude:

> If they take the sovereignty of the southern Islands [the Beagle Channel Islands] away from us, we will have lost sooner or later, our rights in the South Atlantic and will have compromised our revindication of the Antarctic Sector, and the corresponding rights to ocean bottom riches and their exploitation, and even our claim on the Malvinas Islands. Then we will have ceased to be what we should be and we will be nothing.
>
> A Santiago newspaper, clearly of the official line, has already published an editorial affirming that the question of the future of the Malvinas cannot be a matter of indifference to the foreign policy of Chile, because it could damage its rights in the Southern region. England, continuing its historic support to the expansionism of the rapacious Andean country [i.e., Chile], looks with approval on this latent pretension.[4]

It seems clear that such views and the real possibility of war stem from causes much deeper than three rather useless islands. In fact, the hostilities are rooted in Chilean-Argentine tensions that go back to their independence and that have flared up over a number of border and territorial issues in the Southern Andes. They also stem from Chile's perceptions that it was cheated out of Patagonia and from Argentine fears that Chile might be tempted to do something to rectify that situation. Many Argentines firmly believe that Chile is already engaged in a "silent invasion" of semi-empty Patagonia through migration. The Beagle Channel conflict also involves resources (or at least the perception of resources), as the quote from Villegas suggests, and is linked to the Malvinas/Falkland Islands and competing Antarctic claims. The role of Great Britain and the clash of Argentine and Chilean geopolitical thinking further exacerbate the situation.

The geography of the conflict area is complex and the environment forbidding. Figure 7 shows the general location of the NPL islands and Tierra del Fuego. The map shows the center line of the Beagle Channel the way the Chileans interpret it, which also is the way the 1977 arbitration award defined it: the line of the channel is north of the islands, and the islands thus are Chilean. The geopolitical implication of this seemingly simple finding is profound. With these three islands Chile now has a clear outlet to the Atlantic Ocean, and in Argentine eyes this violates the fundamental bi-oceanic principle of "Chile in the Pacific and Argentina in the Atlantic." It also means that Argentina's much valued concept of a continuity between the three sections of Tricontinental Argentina is threatened.

The issue of how to define the line between the South Atlantic and the South Pacific is one that has long caused problems in Argentine-Chilean relations. Figure 8 illustrates the worst Argentine nightmare and reflects what Argentine geopoliticians believe Chile's true intentions are in pushing the Beagle Channel Islands claim. The map shows the Chilean "thesis," as inter-

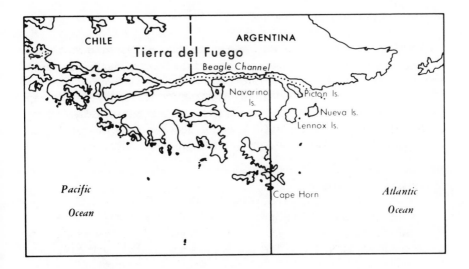

Figure 7. The Beagle Channel Islands: Picton, Lennox, Nueva. The dotted line passing to the north of the islands represents the 1977 arbitral award, which awarded the islands to Chile.

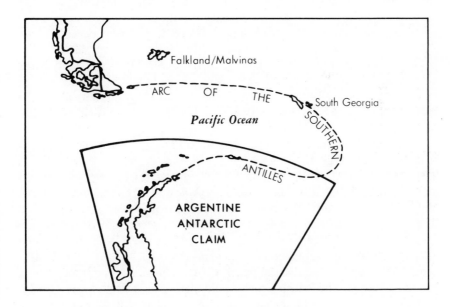

Figure 8. Argentine perception of Chile's goals in the South Atlantic. The Argentine concern is that the Chileans intend to define the line between the Atlantic and Pacific Oceans along the "arc of the Southern Antilles" as shown. Although this would preserve the "bi-oceanic principle" (Argentina in the Atlantic, Chile in the Pacific), it would severely weaken Argentina's claims in the Southern Islands and Antarctica.

preted by Argentina, that the Pacific-Atlantic dividing line follows the "arc of the Southern Antilles." This arc runs from the Beagle Channel Islands to South Georgia and then to the South Sandwich, South Orkney, and South Shetland Islands, and ultimately to the Antarctic Palmer Peninsula. The map strikingly illustrates why Argentines are so adamant about the Beagle Channel Islands; their possession by Chile would indeed severely weaken Argentina's whole elaborate structure of South Atlantic and Antarctic claims.

Historical Background

Current aspects of the dispute must be seen against the fact that Argentina and Chile have had difficulties over border problems ever since they became independent nations. Burr has pointed out that these early Argentine-Chilean rivalries became an integral part of the nineteenth century balance of power arrangement to the extent that whenever Argentina had a problem with Brazil it had a tendency to soften its position toward Chile on border issues.[5] Chile, in turn, frequently took advantage of the situation to make territorial or diplomatic gains.

In 1881 a general agreement was reached between the two countries under which the boundary would be the "highest peaks" of the Andes; however, differences remained for many years over just what these highest peaks were. That same 1881 treaty also clarified the status of Patagonia, giving it to Argentina, and divided the island of Tierra del Fuego between the two countries. The British Crown was given arbitration power over details under a 1902 treaty and through the years has further refined the sovereignty issues in the Southern Islands. Unfortunately, the limits of the Beagle Channel were never clearly defined, and as a result there were always doubts about the ownership of the Beagle Channel Islands and the easternmost point of Chilean sovereignty.

The British role as arbiter between Argentina and Chile has always been a sore point for Argentina. This feeling intensified during the first Perón era (1945–55) when Argentina became increasingly aggressive over the issue of the Malvinas/Falkland Islands. Argentina was quite frank in stating that it doubted the neutrality of Great Britain in light of the Malvinas/Falkland Islands controversy and suspected that there were secret understandings between the United Kingdom and Chile. As a result, in 1971 Argentina insisted that the arbitration arrangement be changed so that the actual judgment would be made by an impartial panel of five members of the International Court of Justice. The British Crown could then either accept or reject the arbitral decision but would not have the power to change it. The arbiters, an American, a Nigerian, a Frenchman, a Swede, and an Englishman, spent a six-year period studying the treaties, logs, maps, documents, and lengthy position papers submitted by Argentina and Chile. The findings were released in early 1977 and came down heavily on the side of Chile. The net result was to reject the Argentine contention that the bi-oceanic principle should take priority over evidence that suggested that the Beagle Channel ran north of the islands, as Chile argued. Argentina then took the most unusual step of rejecting the arbitration on the grounds that the award went beyond the strictly defined issues that had been laid before the arbitral board. This in turn provoked strong reactions from Chile, which argued with some logic that an arbitration award is binding and cannot be rejected if one does not like the result.

Argentina's formal rejection of the arbitral award in January 1978 was followed by attempts to negotiate the issue bilaterally, but little progress was made, and both nations prepared for war during the year. The war hysteria reached a fever pitch in December 1978 when troop movements signaled that mobilization was underway in both countries. A report that Peruvian forces were also moving along their southern border with Chile raised the specter that the conflict might extend beyond the two countries. As Christmas approached and tensions continued to rise, Chile called for a Meeting of Consultation under the OAS Rio Treaty; Argentina in turn proposed that the matter be negotiated by Pope John Paul II. Chile accepted and the Meeting of Consultation was cancelled. The Pope named Cardinal Antonio Samore as his personal representative, and early indications were that the Vatican's approach to a compromise would involve giving Chile possession of the islands, but somehow limiting any possible Chilean thrust out into the Atlantic. One of the suggestions was for a "sea of peace" that would extend from Nueva Island to Cape Horn; this would be a demilitarized zone in which control would be shared between Argentina and Chile.[6]

Recent Developments

The most significant developments in the Argentine-Chilean relationship are those stemming from the Falklands/Malvinas conflict. Chile was one of only two Latin American nations to abstain in key OAS votes that supported Argentina, and Argentines strongly suspected that Chilean public opinion and the Pinochet government supported Great Britain. This suspicion was based in part on history but also on the idea that if Argentina were weakened by a defeat against the British the Argentines would have a diminished capacity to pressure or go to war with Chile. There was also the uncomfortable feeling in Chile that the Argentine "recovery" of the Malvinas/Falkland Islands was but the beginning of a long process of Argentine aggressive actions in the south. This concern was fueled when General Galtieri of Argentina, in a moment of euphoria after taking the islands, declared that the Malvinas recovery was "only the beginning of the reaffirmation of Argentina's right to assert territories."[7]

Another current of opinion held that the Galtieri regime would really have preferred to go to war with Chile to take the Beagle Channel Islands, but that the Vatican's role prevented them from doing so; thus, they had to settle for the Falklands/Malvinas conflict instead.[8] During the fighting the Argentine press strongly criticized Chile's neutral stand and constantly played the theme of secret British-Chilean understandings linked to control of the South Atlantic and the Antarctic. Tensions were further increased when a British helicopter crashed in Chilean territory near the Argentine border on Tierra del Fuego; to many Argentines the presence of this aircraft was clear evidence of Chilean-British collusion.

There seemed to be a great deal of pessimism in Chile during the Falklands/Malvinas conflict, along with a tendency to expect the worse. If Argentina won it would be even more arrogant and emboldened to try and take the Beagle Channel Islands; if Argentina lost it might move to take them in order to salve its hurt pride.

After the Falklands/Malvinas war ended, there was renewed attention to the Vatican's mediation effort, but new proposals dealing with variants of the "sea of peace" idea were rejected by Argentina.[9] In the forefront of the opposition to any compromise were Argentine "hardliners," generally retired military officers, who have frequently written or spoken on strategic and geopolitical issues in the past. One of the most outspoken of these is Admiral Isaac Rojas, the former vice-president, who argued in early 1983 that if Chile got the Beagle Channel Islands "the defense and security of Patagonia would be seriously compromised" and that the "future strategic movements to recover the Malvinas would be hampered by the Chilean spearhead on the Atlantic side of Tierra del Fuego."[10]

Argentina's rearmament program after the Falklands/Malvinas war has concerned Chile, since there seems little prospect of any successful Argentine action against the reinforced British garrison on the islands, and many Chileans wondered if these weapons might be used against them. Tensions eased with the transition to an elected civilian president in Argentina, and in mid-1984 there were hopes that Vatican diplomacy could find a solution acceptable to both Chile and Argentina.[11]

Type of Conflict and Military Implications

Fundamentally this is both a territorial and resource conflict because the area in contention (land and sea) is believed to have important economic and strategic value. The strategic value is far greater for Argentina than Chile because of the link to the Malvinas/Falkland Islands and the Antarctica claim. However, the conflict is also a border one in terms of the tensions stemming from the frontier itself; this is especially true in the southern Patagonia region. Lastly, there are some aspects of migratory conflict because of the large numbers of Chileans in Patagonia who have given the Argentines reason to worry about effective possession of parts of the area.

The military aspects involved in this conflict are complex and considerable. Both Argentina and Chile have impressive military establishments, by Latin American standards. The 1978 mobilization gave an indication of how many troops, ships, aircraft, and other equipment could potentially be involved in a conflict between these two countries. The military geography of the area tends to favor Argentina for a number of reasons, the principal one being that Argentina has more military bases closer to the Beagle Channel area than Chile. Should hostilities involve attacks on each nation's heartland, Argentina again has a very significant advantage in that Chile's Central Valley heartland lies quite close to Argentine bases in the west (mainly in Mendoza), while the Argentina heartland of Buenos Aires is far from Chilean bases.

Both countries would be hard-pressed to manage a confrontation with each other if they were already engaged in another conflict. Chile, in particular, would have a classic worst-case situation if it were required to mobilize against a Peru-Bolivia coalition to the north, face Argentina in the Patagonia-Beagle Channel area, and at the same time defend its Santiago-Valparaiso-Concepción heartland. Argentina's corresponding worst-case scenario would involve a Chilean attack while Argentina was involved with Great Britain over the Malvinas/Falkland Islands or Antarctica. This possibility weighed very heavily on the Argentines during the 1982 conflict. They were not amused or reassured by the Chilean government's statements that Argentina did not have to worry about its back since "Chile was guarding it." The overall advantage to Argentina has led some analysts to suggest that it would be to Chile's strategic advantage to launch a quick preemptive strike, especially at a time when Argentina was distracted elsewhere. In Latin American military circles, this is known as the "Israeli Tactic" of making a rapid advance and then holding terrain while an international organization or other mediator attempts to find a political solution.[12]

On the naval side the advantages also lie with Argentina. Argentine naval power is greater than Chilean, bases are closer, and Argentine naval aviation (the aircraft carrier *25 de Mayo* equipped with A4 Skyhawks and Entendards) is impressive in regional terms. In this connection the Falklands/Malvinas conflict again is relevant. It is true that after Argentina lost the cruiser *ARA Belgrano* to a British nuclear submarine the Argentine navy stayed in port or very close to shore and thus did not particularly distinguish itself. On the other hand, this was a rational strategy, for to have faced the Royal Navy head on would have been little short of suicidal. Argentine naval aviation did distinguish itself, and one should remember that it was an Exocet missile fired from an Argentine naval Entendard that sank the *HMS Sheffield*. In the context of Chilean-Argentine naval power balance, the most important element seems to be the aircraft carrier (Argentina has one, Chile has none; the only other Latin American nation with one is Brazil). Thus, when reports circulated in mid-1983 that the Chilean navy was interested in purchasing the British light carrier *HMS Hermes*, which had been the Royal Navy's flagship in the 1982 Malvinas/Falklands war, the Argentines were outraged, suspicious, and more than a little concerned.

No assessment of the military factors involving Argentina could be complete without a consideration of the impact of interservice rivalries. This is a factor that was also important in weakening Argentine military power during the Falklands/Malvinas conflict. There is strong suspicion that the 1978 crisis over the Beagle Channel Islands was stimulated by the Argentine navy, and in particular its Commander in Chief Admiral Massera, as a vehicle for promoting internal political goals at the expense of the Argentine army.[13]

Relationship to Other Conflicts

The Beagle Channel dispute is clearly linked to a number of other South American conflicts:

The Falklands/Malvinas conflict through Argentine suspicions of Chilean-British collusion.

The Argentine-Brazilian rivalry due to Argentine suspicions of a Chilean-Brazilian understanding.

The Central Andean conflict through Chilean suspicions of Argentine-Peruvian cooperation.

The Antarctic dispute because of conflicting Argentine, Chilean, and British claims.

South Atlantic tensions because of the bi-oceanic principle and Argentine concerns over Chilean influence in the area.

The Essequibo dispute between Venezuela and Guyana because of the strong Venezuelan support to Argentina during the Falklands/Malvinas conflict and because both Argentina and Venezuela see parallels between the situations. The parallels include the fact that Venezuela considers the 1899 arbitration (which gave the Essequibo region to what was then British Guiana, now Guyana) to be just as null and void as the Argentines consider the 1977 Beagle Channel arbitration award.[14]

Relationship to Geopolitical Thinking

As noted in Chapter 3, geopolitical thinking is well established in both Argentina and Chile. Thus, it should come as no surprise that this geopolitical thinking has paid a great deal of attention to Chilean-Argentine problems in general and to the Beagle Channel dispute in particular. The Beagle Channel dispute readily lends itself to analysis by both classical and indigenous Argentine-Chilean geopolitical thinking. The issues of expansion, struggle for resources (real or imagined), and the perception of a hostile world in which states are either enemies or temporary allies suggest that there are strong relationships between this conflict and geopolitical thinking. During the 1978 crisis geopolitical thinkers in both countries were extremely active in publicly analyzing the conflict in geopolitical terms. This was especially true in Argentina, where the journal *Estrategia* was a major outlet for this highly nationalistic and aggressive current of Argentine geopolitical thinking.

As was noted previously, Argentine geopolitical thinking has a strong maritime focus that links the validity of Argentine claims to the Malvinas/ Falkland Islands, the Southern Islands, the Antarctic, and the Beagle Channel Islands. A fundamental element in this current of geopolitical thinking is the bi-oceanic principle, under which Argentina controls the Atlantic and Chile the Pacific. Any Chilean incursion (real or perceived) into the South Atlantic is seen as a threat to this principle and as a weakening of the whole structure of Argentine claims and of tricontinental Argentina. In Argentine geopolitical writings, Chile is frequently portrayed as an expansionist and aggressive nation strongly influenced by the organic state concept. Argentina sees Chile's strategy as one of probing and pushing for every weakness and possible advantage in its attempts to increase its influence and territory at the expense of its neighbors, Argentina, Bolivia, and Peru. Argentine geopolitical thinking thus stresses the vulnerability of Patagonia, the Southern Islands, and Antarctica, and attempts to alert Argentines against the threat of a Chilean-British or Chilean-Brazilian entente that might be used as a weapon against Argentina.

Chilean geopolitical thinking also has a strong maritime current. This has caused its geopoliticians to focus on its status as a South Pacific power, its Antarctic claim, its role in controlling the Strait of Magellan, and the absolute need to keep Argentina out of the Pacific. This last point is Chile's own version of the bi-oceanic principle, and the Chileans are rather flexible in defining the boundary between Pacific and Atlantic when there is a possibility of pushing that boundary east past the meridian of Cape Horn. It is to Chile's advantage to keep the dividing line as far eastward as possible, and a favorable Beagle Channel award would raise the possibility of establishing a 200-mile exclusive economic zone into the South Atlantic at the expense of Argentina.

THE CENTRAL ANDEAN CONFLICT: CHILE-BOLIVIA-PERU

Introduction: Parties, Summary, and Geography

The west coast area of the central Andes where Chile, Bolivia, and Peru meet has long been a zone of tension and was the scene of one of Latin America's major conflicts a century ago: the War of the Pacific, 1879–83, in which Chile decisively defeated Bolivia and Peru.[15] One of the principal results of the war was that Peru lost southern territories and Bolivia lost its outlet to the sea. Neither country (but especially Bolivia) has fully accepted this outcome, and relations with Chile will probably never be normal until Bolivia's psychological (and, to a lesser extent, economic) need for a sea outlet is satisfied. Any settlement satisfactory to Bolivia is complicated by a provision in the Treaty of Ancón, which settled the War of the Pacific, but gave Peru a veto power over any arrangement involving territory it once possessed. Chile is reluctant to give up any territory without concessions in return and in any case is unlikely to give Bolivia territory that would create an isolated Chilean enclave along the Peruvian border.

The conflict has been aggravated by a slow decline of Chilean military and economic power since the turn of the century, by Chile's sense of isolation after the fall of Salvador Allende, and by the psychological impact of the centennial of the War of the Pacific. This was especially significant in Peru and Bolivia, where a common nationalistic slogan swears that these countries will not let a hundred years pass without recovering the lost territories. During the period of the Peruvian military regime (1968–80), tensions were further raised when the Peruvians made major arms purchases of tanks, artillery, and aircraft from the Soviet Union. To any Chilean the explanation was obvious: these weapons would be used to retake Peru's southern territories before the centennial. However, the passing of the centennial in a peaceful manner (despite the efforts of some Peruvian and Bolivian geopolitical nationalists), and the transition from military to civilian governments in Peru and Bolivia, tended to ameliorate tensions somewhat in the early 1980s.

The geographic area concerned is the central west coast of South America, specifically the present-day Chilean regions of Arica and Tarapacá (which were Peruvian until the War of the Pacific) and of Antofagasta (which had been Bolivian until the war). It was the Antofagasta area that provided Bolivia with its sea coast, and it was its loss that has made it a land-locked country. The region as a whole is known as *Atacama*, or the *Atacama Desert*; it is indeed one of the driest regions on earth, and for many years no rain at all falls in the area. Topographically it consists of the western slopes of the Andes and a very narrow sandy coastal plain occasionally cut by deep ravines with short-lived streams (see Figure 9).

Historical Background

Even in the colonial period, there had been strains between the various jurisdictions in this area. These strains increased shortly after independence, when Chile successfully broke up a Bolivian-Peruvian coalition that it saw as a potential threat. Mutual suspicion, threats, and fears have been a constant in the relations of Bolivia and Peru with Chile ever since.

Figure 9. Territorial losses in the War of the Pacific, 1879–83.

By the middle of the nineteenth century, the Atacama desert had begun to acquire economic significance despite its barren and inhospitable appearance. What made the difference were mineral deposits, mainly nitrates, which were used for gunpowder and fertilizer. Chile, as the best organized and most economically advanced nation in the area, was quick to exploit these minerals. Bolivia soon found that sections of its coastal region were being occupied by Chilean miners and small companies eager to take advantage of a resource that the Bolivians apparently were incapable of exploiting. Growing increasingly alarmed at Chile's aggressiveness, the Peruvians and Bolivians signed a secret mutual defense treaty in 1873, but the treaty did not remain secret for long. A few years later the Bolivians attempted to raise taxes on Chilean nitrate operations in the Antofagasta area, and the Chileans used their knowledge of the treaty to refuse the tax increase and occupy the area, declaring war on Peru and Bolivia in April 1879. The Peruvian-Bolivian coalition was numerically superior, but no match for the better trained and equipped Chileans, who had recently acquired modern battleships and quickly controlled the sea. In January 1881 a Chilean force landed at Chorrillos near Lima, easily took the capital city of Peru, and began a two-year occupation of Lima, which has never been forgiven or forgotten. To this day Peruvians will recount stories of the Chilean occupation, telling how the Chileans stole the books from Lima's libraries, the statues from the museums, and the animals from the zoo. In response, Chileans comment on how the two-year stay of their army in Lima "helped improve the ethnic stock of the Peruvian mestizos."

The 1883 Treaty of Ancón supposedly settled the war by awarding Tarapacá and Antofagasta outright to Chile and placing the provinces of Tacna and Arica under Chilean rule until a plebiscite was held to determine the final settlement in ten years. However, the plebiscite was continually delayed, friction increased, and the issue was not settled until 1929 when Tacna was returned to Peru and Arica was awarded to Chile. The 1929 Washington Protocol contained a provision that no territory originally belonging to Peru (i.e., Arica and Tarapacá) could be ceded by Chile to any third party (i.e., Bolivia) without Peru's approval. It is this provision that has vastly complicated Bolivia's quest for a corridor to the sea by making Peru a third party to any Chilean-Bolivian negotiation for territorial transfer in the Arica-Tarapacá area.

The historical legacy of bitterness left by the War of the Pacific and its settlement remains to this day. Not only is this legacy a major factor in the geopolitical thinking of these three countries; it is also an important element in the perceived missions of their armed forces and in the substantial percentages of their national budgets that go for weapons and military expenses. Further, many historians believe that Bolivia's loss of a Pacific outlet was a major reason for its drive to achieve an Atlantic Ocean outlet through the Paraná-Plata River system; this in turn led to the disastrous Chaco War with Paraguay, 1932–35. Gorman notes that the perception (held in the period from the 1920s through the 1950s) that the Atacama issue had faded into the past was probably due to the fact that Peru and Bolivia both had other serious border problems in this period that diverted them from focusing on Chile.[16] Once these two problems and their resultant wars (the Chaco War for Bolivia and the 1942 Ecuadorean war for Peru) faded into the background, then the old concerns over the War of the Pacific began to acquire new significance, especially when nationalistic revolutions emphasized them in Bolivia after 1952 and Peru after 1968.

Hershkowitz observes that the issue of the sea outlet is taught to every Bolivian schoolchild and becomes wrapped up in intense nationalism to the point that it is one of the few things that can unite all Bolivians.[17] Slogans, rallies, postage stamps, speeches, and publications keep alive the Bolivian resentment of the Chileans and the Bolivian hope that one day the coast will once again be theirs: "Mar para Bolivia," "Antofagasta es y será Boliviano," and "Hacia el Mar." For the rulers of poverty-stricken and unstable Bolivia, the issue has consistently provided a dramatic focus with which to draw attention away from domestic problems and failings. One could almost suggest, in this vein, that the worst thing that could happen to Bolivia would be to receive the sea outlet, for then it would have lost the diversion and the excuse for a number of Bolivian failures that have little to do with an opening to the Pacific Ocean.

As complicated as Chilean-Bolivian-Peruvian strains over the Atacama are, they are further complicated by the involvement of two other actors: Argentina and Great Britain. The latter country enters the picture because of a considerable interest (and investment) in the Chilean nitrate operations in the nineteenth century and because of a long British association with Chile. In fact, there is evidence that the British may have encouraged Chilean aggression in 1879. Argentina is involved because of the Chilean concern that a Peruvian-Argentine alliance could cause Chile problems with both neighbors simultaneously. For example, diplomatic historians note that at the time of the War of the Pacific Chile was having serious strains with Argentina over Patagonia.[18]

In 1973 the old fears of a replay of the War of the Pacific began to take on new meaning when the revolutionary Peruvian military government made major arms purchases from the Soviet Union. This acquisition came after the United States turned down their request for high-performance jet aircraft. In the mid-1970s there were a flurry of proposals and counterproposals that would in one way or another give Bolivia the sea outlet it so ardently desired without leaving Chile feeling that it had made too many concessions and without further injuring Peru's sensibilities. The Chilean proposals would have granted Bolivia a strip to the ocean, but Chile demanded land and sea concessions from Bolivia in return. A Peruvian proposal made in November 1976 suggested that a Bolivian corridor extend to Arica, which would have a trinational government. Little progress was made, and in early 1978 Bolivia broke diplomatic relations with Chile over the delays. As the centennial approached tensions were raised between Chile and Peru with the constant arrival of Soviet arms and a series of incidents in which each side accused the other of spying and provocations. However, the centennial passed quietly, and with the coming to power in Peru of civilian President Fernando Belaúnde Terry in 1980 the situation seemed calmer for the moment.

Recent Developments

As was the case with Argentine-Chilean tensions, the Falklands/Malvinas conflict had an impact on Central Andean strains. Especially significant were reports in June and July of 1982 that the Argentines had made a secret agreement with the Peruvians (and possibly also the Bolivians) to support each other in case they were attacked. According to a Mexican newspaper, the agreement would acknowledge Argentine hegemony in the South Atlantic and the interoceanic passages (Magellan, Beagle, and Drake), while Argentina would recognize Peruvian influence in the Pacific as far north as Ecuador and the southern coast of Colombia. Both Argentina and Peru would recognize Bolivia's right to access to the Pacific. The existence of any such agreement was quickly denied by the Peruvian ambassador to Chile, but the denial could hardly seem very convincing to Chileans at the time of considerable tension between Chile and Argentina over the Falklands/Malvinas conflict.[19]

In early 1984 there were continuing indications that strains still remained. Editorials in Santiago fretted about Soviet and Communist bloc fishing boats engaging in espionage activities near Chilean waters from bases in southern Peru; at the same time they expressed concern over arms purchases in both Argentina and Peru. Editorial commentary from Bolivia stressed the old Bolivian theme of the sea outlet and called for renewed efforts of the democratic nations of Bolivia and Peru to work together to persuade Chile to make concessions.[20]

Type of Conflict and Military Implications

The Central Andean conflict contains territorial, resource, and possibly ideological elements. For Peru and Chile the dispute is essentially territorial, although it once involved very significant resources (nitrates and other minerals). The significance of these resources has now practically disappeared, and neither country really needs additional desert seacoast. For Bolivia things are different: the issue is simultaneously territorial, resource, and possibly ideological. The resource is the outlet to the sea that is seen as being crucial for Bolivia's economic development. The possible ideological component relates to the intensity of Bolivian feelings about the lost seacoast and the strong resentment held against Chile for its actions a hundred years ago and its perceived intransigence since then. The national obsession with the sea outlet unifies Bolivia, gives it a national purpose, and in this sense can be interpreted as serving some of the functions of a political ideology.

Military factors involved in the conflict stem from the general perception that the old balance of power based on clear Chilean military supremacy no longer holds. For many years after the War of the Pacific, the basic factor for stability in the area was the well-founded belief that Chilean superiority in military equipment, training, and experience meant that any combined Peruvian-Bolivian military adventure against Chile would be a repeat of the 1879–83 disaster. But since the late 1960s, this perception has been eroded by Chile's isolation in the world, by its internal problems, and by the impressive buildup of Peruvian weapons. There is now a rough parity between the Chilean and Peruvian military establishments, with Chile holding the advantages in training, maintenance, and morale, and Peru the upper hand in quantity and quality of weapons, especially the Soviet tanks, aircraft, artillery, and surface-to-air missiles. The major unknown factor is how well the Peruvian soldiers can operate, maintain, and logistically support these large quantities of relatively sophisticated modern equipment. The Chileans have a military tradition of being winners, while the Peruvians and Bolivians have the psychological burdens of being losers. In this context there was a perhaps apocryphal anecdote making the rounds in 1973 to the effect that the main reason the Peruvians sent a battalion to join the United Nations UNEF I peace-keeping force in the Middle East was finally to learn how to fight in the desert.

The military geography of the conflict area favors Chile as the defender against a Peruvian tank or air attack. The desert is essentially an open area, but the coastal strip is narrow, there are deep ravines, and it would be relatively easy for the Chilean defenders to channel Peruvian armor to chosen killing grounds. Further, the Chilean heartland is a long way from the border area, while the Lima-Callao Peruvian heartland is within range of aircraft stationed in northern Chile. In the final analysis distances and logistics would probably grind any Peruvian advance to a halt long before any vital Chilean areas were threatened, although Peruvian tanks and aircraft could probably recover enough terrain to symbolically claim victory. At the same time the Bolivians could, with Peru's acquiescence, establish their corridor to the sea behind the protection of Peruvian forces.

The likelihood of such a scenario occurring has diminished considerably since the passing of the centennial. The issue is no longer as important to Peru and Chile as it seemed only a few years ago, and tensions have eased. For Bolivia the dream of a sea outlet can never disappear, but for the immediate future the dream is likely to remain nothing more than that.

Relationship to Other Conficts

The Central Andean conflict is closely linked to other Southern Cone tensions:

The Northern Andean conflict (Peru-Ecuador) because of Peruvian concerns over a Chilean-Ecuadorean understanding that would force it to face adversaries on two fronts.
The Southern Andean (Argentine-Chilean) strains due to Chilean fears of a Peruvian-Argentine agreement that, in a similar fashion, would force it to deal with two enemies at the same time.
Other Chilean-Bolivian bilateral issues, such as the Lauca River dispute.

Relationship to Geopolitical Thinking

Many geopoliticians, most notably those of the Germanic school in the 1920s, often cite the Chilean victory in the War of the Pacific as a pure and classical case of *Lebensraum*. However, the contemporary relationship between geopolitical thinking and conflict in the Central Andean disputes seems somewhat weaker than in the Argentine-Chilean case. This is true in part because of the lower volume and lesser sophistication of geopolitical writings in Peru and Bolivia than in Chile and Argentina. It is also due to the fact that Chile's geopolitical priorities have in recent years focused more on the Beagle Channel, Argentina, and the Antarctic claim. Chilean geopolitical thinkers generally take condescending and even contemptuous attitudes toward their counterparts in Peru and Bolivia. This feeling parallels Chilean attitudes toward these two Indian countries that can fairly be described as arrogant and, at times, even racist. Chilean geopoliticians implicitly, and sometimes explicitly, explain the War of the Pacific in terms taken directly from the Germanic geopolitical school's ideas on the organic state and *Lebensraum*. This perception argues that in 1879 Bolivia and Peru had resources in the desert coastal strip but were too backward to develop them; Chile in effect did humanity a service by taking these territories and developing the mining industry. Chile was a well-organized and strong nation that acted in response to its natural need to grow and expand. To these ideas we must add the Chilean geopolitical notion that the South Pacific must be a Chilean lake, if Chile is to achieve its tricontinental destiny.

Understandably, Peruvian and Bolivian geopolitical thinkers view the issue differently. Although there is not a great deal of geopolitical writing emanating from Bolivia or Peru, the literature that does emerge emphasizes the War of the Pacific and the theme of revindication of the losses to Chile. In Peru the centennial brought forth a new geopolitical institute and a rash of articles and commentaries on the geopolitical significance of the war and its centennial. In the Bolivian case the main theme, and indeed the obsession, of geopolitical thinking is the outlet to the sea. A related theme is the negative impact that the Chilean theft of that outlet has had not only on Bolivian development, but also on the development and integration of all of Latin America. A related Bolivian geopolitical theme is that of the "frustrated heartland" noted in Chapter 3, which suggests that Bolivia fulfills the same function for South America that central Europe did for Mackinder's heartland. Thus the Chileans, by blocking Bolivia's outlet to the sea, are perversely frustrating the normal balance and flow of history in South America.

THE NORTHERN ANDEAN CONFLICT: PERU-ECUADOR

Introduction: Parties, Summary, and Geography

The significance of the Northern Andean conflict between Peru and Ecuador[21] is emphasized by the fact that a recent flare-up in January 1981 was the bloodiest border conflict on the South American mainland since the early 1940s, when the Peruvians and Ecuadoreans fought a brief but even more sanguinary war. The dispute involves some 100,000 square miles of essentially unpopulated Amazonian jungle. The results of the fighting in 1941 were overwhelmingly in Peru's favor, and in the 1942 Rio Meeting of Consultation of Ministers of Foreign Affairs (which was meeting for a far more important reason: World War II) Ecuador was forced to sign a protocol that ratified Peru's conquest. During the war years and shortly thereafter, it appeared as though Ecuador would quietly accept the settlement, but this has not been the case. Rising tides of nationalism in Ecuador have focused on what is popularly known in Ecuador as the "Protocol of Sacrifice," and there is great resentment over the way the Rio Protocol was forced on a prostrate nation.

Ecuador sees itself as a small country that had its possibilities for greatness taken away by the force of arms. If the Bolivian obsession is to regain the outlet to the sea, then the Ecuadoreans have a similar feeling that they could again be an "Amazonian power" if the lost territories were regained. As the foreign minister put it recently, "Ecuador's permanent objective can be summarized in one word: Amazon."[22] The territory at issue may be unpopulated, but it lies near Ecuador's oil-producing area, and there are fairly good reasons to believe that significant oil deposits may yet be found in the region. The dispute is also a part of the larger Southern Cone conflict scenario because of rumors of an informal Ecuadorean-Chilean "understanding" directed against Peru, as well as indications of historical Ecuadorean-Brazilian cooperation in policies that Peru regards as less than friendly.

The geographic area involved is the so-called Amazonian Triangle between the eastern slope of the Andes, the Ecuadorean-Colombian border, and the Marañon River (see Figures 10 and 11). The 1942 Rio Protocol confirmed the cession of territories that removed Ecuador's possible access to the Amazon. The protocol also meant that Ecuador no longer had a boundary with Brazil, making it the only country in South America besides Chile in that category. As we shall see in Chapter 8 when we develop the geopolitical theory of "discontinuous borders," this fact is of considerable importance in the geopolitical thinking of the Southern Cone.

Historical Background

The basic dispute, which involves almost the whole length of the Ecuador-Peru boundary, is rooted in the ambiguities and uncertainties of the colonial divisions between the Audiencia de Quito and the Viceroyalty of Peru. The dispute simmered throughout the nineteenth century and the first decades of the twentieth, with both sides presenting de jure arguments and Peru exercising de facto control of most of the area under contention. In the late 1930s a series of border skirmishes led to attempts by outside arbiters (chiefly Argentina, Brazil, and the United States) to reach a peaceful settlement, but

Figure 10. The Peru-Ecuador border dispute: Ecuadorean stamp. "Ecuador has been, is, and will be, an Amazonian nation." (Photo by the author.)

Peru discouraged these efforts. Peru was basically eager for a fight with Ecuador, not only to affirm its hold on the territories, but also because the Peruvian military was still suffering from the "psychology of defeat" as a result of the decisive loss to the Chileans in the War of the Pacific. A quick and easy victory over Ecuador, as one Peruvian put it, "had the undeniable merit of serving as a national tonic."[23]

In July 1941, with the nations of the Western Hemisphere distracted by the rising tide of the world war, the conflict broke out with a series of border clashes in which the Ecuadorean forces were quickly routed. The Peruvian army moved quickly to secure large areas of Ecuadorean territory in the coastal province of El Oro (which was not one of the areas in dispute) as well as in the disputed Amazon region. In late 1941, with the Peruvians now advancing toward the key coastal city of Guayaquil, a hastily arranged truce left the Peruvians in a strong position. Six months later, in January 1942, with the Peruvians still occupying these areas and threatening to take more of Ecuador's territory, the foreign ministers of the hemisphere nations met in Rio de Janeiro in response to Japan's attack on Pearl Harbor. The United

States and other Western Hemisphere nations (notably Brazil) wanted to settle the Peru-Ecuador issue quickly and in effect persuaded Ecuador to accept Peru's terms on the Amazonian claim as the price for Peru's withdrawal from the coastal provinces.

In 1955 Ecuador invoked the Inter-American Treaty of Reciprocal Assistance (the 1947 Rio Treaty) claiming that Peru was preparing to invade again. The Organization of American States mounted a peace-observing team using military attachés stationed in Lima, who were not able to find any evidence of the Peruvian invasion force. Legal, cartographic, and geographic

Figure 11. The Peru-Ecuador border dispute: Peruvian stamp. "These lands and these rivers have been, are, and will be, Peruvian. Frontier fixed by the Rio de Janeiro Protocol of 1942." (Photo by the author.)

technicalities permitted the Ecuadoreans to keep the dispute alive in the 1950s until they formally declared the 1942 Rio Protocol null and void in 1960. This action was rejected by Peru, which claims that the issue was settled permanently at Rio in 1942 and that there is no border problem other than the difficulties Ecuador is now trying to stir up.

In the 1970s both Ecuador and Peru intensified their search for oil on the eastern slope of the Andes, with Ecuador having more success. The significance of the finds was that there was a geographic and geologic continuity between the proven oil area and the area in dispute; thus, there seemed to be reasonable grounds for believing that the territories may in fact possess a valuable resource.

Like Chile, Ecuador has viewed the Peruvian arms buildup with concern and has spent a substantial amount of its oil revenues in an attempt to keep up with the Peruvian efforts, although on a much more limited scale. A plan to buy Kfir aircraft from Israel was blocked by the United States on the technical grounds that since the engines were U.S.-made the United States had the right to veto this arms transfer, much to the annoyance of the Ecuadoreans. In response, in 1977 they purchased advanced French Mirage F-1 aircraft, which, along with Jaguar fighters, gave their air force an impressive capability for its size. In the period since then there have been a series of minor border shooting incidents involving soldiers and civilians from both countries.

Recent Developments

The most serious outbreak of fighting since 1941 occurred in January 1981 when, in a somewhat confused incident involving a Peruvian helicopter and an Ecuadorean outpost, there was shooting and mutual recriminations. The incident quickly escalated, and in five days of fighting the Peruvian forces dislodged Ecuadorean troops from at least two separate positions. The Peruvians made heavy use of helicopters, air strikes, and commandos with jungle training. A total of 200 were believed killed in the fighting.[24]

The area involved was a 78-kilometer stretch of the so-called Cordillera del Condor sector of the border, which had never been adequately marked. The 1981 fighting involved the somewhat bizarre report of a "false" outpost named Paquisha, which the Peruvians claimed the Ecuadoreans had moved and reconstructed, placing the false outpost in what used to be Peruvian territory. New, but less serious, fighting broke out in February 1981. The actions of the four guarantor powers of the 1942 Rio Protocol (Argentina, Chile, Brazil, and the United States) were able to get a cease-fire and establish a demilitarized zone, but not before the peace-keepers themselves lost a helicopter with three U.S. crewmen aboard.

In early 1983, and again in January 1984, shooting incidents involving patrols from both countries occurred, suggesting that the basic issue was still not resolved and that this level of tension and incidents could be expected to continue. The Peruvian position remains adamant: there is no issue or problem beyond the final demarcation of the boundary and the placing of markers along the 78-kilometer section in the Cordillera del Condor area. The Ecuadoreans argue that there is the broader issue of the validity of the 1942 Protocol, and they are not particularly anxious to see the Cordillera del Condor area marked out since they feel the current level of tension is garnering attention for their position from the rest of the hemisphere.

Type of Conflict and Military Implications

The conflict is fundamentally territorial in nature, but the probable presence of oil also makes it a resource conflict. This is especially true for Peru, whose oil reserves are far lower than Ecuador's (Ecuador, an OPEC member, is an oil exporter, while Peru is not). For Ecuador there is also the perception that an outlet to the Amazon is an important economic and strategic resource.

The military geography of the area is formidable. There are few roads through the jungle area, and transportation is generally by foot, by boat where the river system permits, or by air. The current military advantage is on the Peruvian side, as it has been historically, although the Ecuadoreans are much better prepared for war than they were in 1941. Their use of oil income to buy advanced aircraft has significantly reduced Peru's advantage and might permit retaliatory attacks on Peruvian industrial installations, including the oil refineries on Peru's north coast. In the broader context of regional Southern Cone tensions, the Ecuadoreans would not be at too much of a disadvantage if the Peruvians at the same time had to face a real or perceived threat from the Chileans to the south.

Relationship to Other Conflicts

Although the basic issue is a bilateral Peruvian-Ecuadorean one, it clearly has linkages to other Southern Cone conflicts, especially the Central Andean conflict, if the rumors of an Ecuadorean-Chilean or a Chilean-Brazilian or an Ecuadorean-Brazilian understanding have any validity. The Ecuadorean argument that the 1942 Rio Protocol is null and void has broader implications as well. The Ecuadoreans have made a conscious effort[25] to relate their views on the 1942 Protocol to parallel feelings on analogous situations by other nations, such as the Argentine position on the 1977 Beagle Channel arbitration and the Venezuelan perception of the 1899 Essequibo decision.

In a broader sense the Peru-Ecuador conflict also reflects a conflict over one edge of the last great remaining empty space in the South American continent: the Amazon Basin. We will return to the topic of a possible Amazon

Basin dispute when we examine the role of Brazil in the buffer states and in the context of the Argentine-Brazilian rivalry.

Relationship to Geopolitical Thinking

As noted in Chapter 3, geopolitical thinking is not particularly advanced in Ecuador, and the volume of writings on the subject is rather limited. However, what is produced tends to concentrate on the significance of the Amazon (and thus the territories lost to Peru) and the importance of an Amazon outlet to the Atlantic. As noted previously, Ecuador's geopoliticians argue that their country must develop a "Janus geopolitical base," meaning that like the Roman god of two faces, Ecuador must look geopolitically in two directions. The first is toward the sea and the Galapagos Islands, and the second is toward the continent, the Amazon, and ultimately the Atlantic.

On the Peruvian side, there is a similar focus on the need to develop its Amazon territories contested by Ecuador, especially in light of the oil resources that may exist there. In the best tradition of the organic theory of the state, Peruvian geopolitics also stresses a sense of being surrounded by hostile neighbors. As a senior Peruvian general officer explained to this author when he attempted to justify Peru's massive weapons purchases: "We Peruvians must buy many weapons because, like Israel, we are surrounded by enemies: Chile to the south wants to refight the War of the Pacific; Ecuador to the north wants to steal our Amazon territory and our oil fields; Colombia to the northeast has not forgotten the 1932 Leticia episode; and then there is Brazil — Brazil, which like the United States of a hundred years ago, believes she has a Manifest Destiny to occupy the continent and reach the Pacific. And in South America, Peru is California."[26]

THE ARGENTINE-BRAZILIAN RIVALRY

Although not a "conflict" in the same military sense as the previous three, the Argentine-Brazilian rivalry[27] is fundamental to an understanding of the international relations of the Southern Cone. This is due to the fact that it involves not only the two principal states, but also the three buffers (Uruguay, Paraguay, and Bolivia) and the other state actors in the subcontinent.

The theme of Argentine-Brazilian rivalry and struggle for influence in South America is the oldest of all the Latin American conflicts. Indeed, it is sometimes viewed as the contemporary manifestation of the Spanish-Portuguese rivalry of five centuries ago. Or, as some Argentine geopolitical analysts have put it, the rivalry represents the continuing struggle of the Spanish-speaking world, led by Argentina, to contain the expansion and westward movement ("la marcha al oeste") of the Portuguese-speaking world. Further, inhabitants of this Portuguese-speaking world, led first by Portugal and then Brazil, are viewed as acting as surrogates for their English-speaking masters (first England and later the United States). The argument continues that, ever since the 1494 Treaty of Tordesillas divided the New World into Portuguese and Spanish domains, the Portuguese-Brazilians have by diplomacy, pressure, and stealth steadily pushed the dividing line to the west at the expense of the Hispanic world. Not surprisingly, Brazilian geopolitical writers tend to have a much more relaxed view of the Argentine-Brazilian rivalry. However, Brazilian geopoliticians occasionally express concern over the Argentine dream of restoring the viceroyalty of the Rio de la Plata, a restoration that would be partially at Brazil's expense and would tend to polarize the Southern Cone.[28]

In the nineteenth century the rivalry took a variety of forms. These ranged from the war over the "Banda Oriental" of Uruguay (1825–28), the attempt to bring down Argentine dictator Rosas in the early 1850s, competition in Paraguay after the 1865–70 War of the Triple Alliance, and a series of less dramatic confrontations over borders and territories. In the twentieth century the rivalry continued with support for different sides in both the Chaco War and in World War II, when Argentina was frankly pro-Axis and Brazil was a close U.S. ally. The slow decline of Argentina's fortunes and the dramatic rise of Brazil's in the postwar period have in some ways only intensified the rivalry (at least from the Argentine perspective), as the balance tilted steadily toward Brazil.

Despite this long-lasting rivalry, an outright military clash between Argentina and Brazil is not likely.[29] But the rivalry is real and has important implications for conflict and the international relations of the Southern Cone. The rivalry also is of special interest because of the strong element of geopolitical thinking that sustains it.

If the hypothesis of diminished U.S. influence in South America is valid and continuing, one of the possible international arrangements to emerge in the area is a new balance of power realpolitik. Argentine-Brazilian tensions might be the centerpiece of the new power politics of the region, and geopolitics one of its driving forces. The interlinked nature of conflicts and tensions in the Southern Cone suggests that an international clash may involve as many as eight nations of the region. An alternative arrangement, which would also have geopolitical bases, would involve a cooperative Argentine-Brazilian condominium or shared power approach.

The rivalry has important echoes in the domestic and international politics of the three buffer states of Uruguay, Paraguay, and Bolivia. The echoes have to do with several categories of Argentine-Brazilian competition, a competition that is usually low-key and even cordial, but is nevertheless a present and constant factor. One important aspect of the rivalry is competition for the arms market in the buffers. Both Brazil and Argentina have arms industries and export their products to the buffers; in recent years Brazil's industry has moved far ahead of Argentina's, but the sense of competing for the markets in the buffers, and the influence that accrues from the sales, continues.

The Argentine-Brazilian rivalry has also been expressed in terms of subregional arrangements or blocs, which are reminiscent of the geopolitical idea of the pan-region. One could postulate, as a number of geopolitical thinkers in the area have, the emergence of four such blocs in the hemisphere: a Caribbean-Central American one, an Andean bloc, an Amazon Basin one (under Brazilian leadership), and a River Plate Basin arrangement (under Argentine leadership). The last two blocs would represent yet another manifestation of the Argentine-Brazilian rivalry.

In recent years the rivalry has included competition for resources such as Paraguayan hydroelectric energy and, to a lesser extent, Bolivian oil, gas, and iron ore. Brazil's awakening interest in the South Atlantic and Antarctica makes these regions new theaters for the Argentine-Brazilian rivalry. The Falklands/Malvinas conflict brought Brazil into the tangled Argentine-British-Latin American relationship in some interesting ways, and it seems clear that Brazil will continue to have a keen interest in developments in the area. An ominous nuclear dimension is also present in the rivalry since Argentina and Brazil both possess a capability to construct nuclear weapons or peaceful nuclear explosives.

Historical Background

The colonial and early independence roots of Argentine-Brazilian rivalry have been exhaustively studied elsewhere. A particularly relevant analysis of nineteenth century South American international relations is provided by Burr.[30] In his seminal work Burr shows that two separate balance of power systems evolved in South America in the past century: the Pacific System, involving Chile, Peru, and Bolivia, and the River Plate/Atlantic System, involving Argentina, Brazil, Uruguay, and Paraguay. After the War of the Pacific, these two systems slowly merged into one power politics system dominated by Argentina, Brazil, Chile, and Peru. This system had a tendency to align itself along two "diagonal alliances" between Brazil-Chile and Argentina-Peru. The balancing of power implicit in these alliances brought a remarkable measure of stability to the area. This stability was to endure until the old balance of power system was replaced by U.S. influence and eventually the hegemony of Pax Americana.

Bailey provides another interesting perspective on the Argentine-Brazilian rivalry with his analysis of the struggle for subparamountcy in South America.[31] He argues that Latin America has always been dominated by a paramount power (Spain and Portugal, then Great Britain, and later the United States) and that the conflicts in the region have been over subparamountcy. Thus, the War of the Pacific was the culmination of the long struggle for South Pacific subparamountcy that was settled when Chile defeated Peru and Bolivia. The Argentine-Brazilian rivalry can be seen as another struggle for subparamountcy, which has over time included: the dispute over the "Banda Oriental" of Uruguay (1817–28); continuing meddling in Uruguay in the "Long War" (1836–52); and rivalry in Paraguay after the War of the Triple Alliance (1865–70). The competition for subparamountcy also involved Argentina's concern over Brazil's skillful diplomacy in the second half of the nineteenth century when Brazil expanded its borders at the expense of almost all its neighbors; and Brazil's concern over Argentina's economic, industrial, and military growth in that same period.

A key point in the Argentine-Brazilian rivalry was reached around World War II. For a variety of reasons, Argentina and Brazil found themselves on opposite sides of the conflict, with Brazil forging a close political, military, and economic alliance with the United States, and Argentina observing a studiously aloof neutrality that, in fact, leaned toward the Axis. The rise to power of Juan Domingo Perón in Argentina brought a new dimension to the conflict as Perón spoke of creating a "new Argentina" that would consist of a bloc of Southern Cone nations under Argentine leadership.[32] The tension between Argentina on the one hand, and the informal Brazilian-U.S. alliance on the other, was exacerbated by the large amounts of U.S. economic and military aid that flowed to Brazil during World War II and shortly thereafter. This aid was a significant factor in Brazil's postwar growth, its moving past Argentina, and its progress toward its "destiny."

The nuclear aspects of the Argentine-Brazilian rivalry pose deeply disturbing questions because both countries are "threshold nations" that could develop a nuclear explosive device in the near future (less than five years). Argentina's nuclear program is the oldest and most sophisticated in Latin America. It dates back to the 1950s, when the Perón government gave the first impetus to the program, staffing it with German scientists who came to Argentina at the end of the war. Argentina has consistently held to a policy of nuclear autonomy and has based its program on slower methods using natural uranium. However, since it has ample uranium supplies, Argentina is, in effect, self-sufficient in all the materials and technology required for nuclear energy programs, for the development of peaceful nuclear explosives (PNEs), and for military devices. Brazil's program is making swift progress, especially after the important 1975 agreement with the Federal Republic of Germany. The transfer of both full fuel cycle plutonium reprocessing and uranium enrichment technology will eventually also give Brazil all the components it needs. Presently both Argentina and Brazil have adequate aircraft delivery systems and probably will have missile delivery systems by the year 2000. Neither country is effectively bound by the Nuclear Non-proliferation Treaty or the Treaty of Tlatelolco.

Because of its perception that it is steadily falling behind Brazil on various counts, Argentina has perhaps the greater incentive for detonating a nuclear device. Argentine strategic and geopolitical doctrine has always (and inevitably) stressed the merits of "Argentine quality" (higher cultural level, literacy rates, racial "whiteness," arms sophistication, and military training) over "Brazilian quantity" (sheer physical size, population, and gross national product). In this context the possession of a nuclear device must appear to Argentine planners to be the ultimate "quality" weapon, the great equalizer that would once again put Argentina at its rightful place ahead of Brazil. Argentine disincentives for developing nuclear weapons would include the problems of provoking Brazil, of initiating an arms race, of generating world opprobrium, of cost, of diverting resources, and of destabilizing the balance of power in the Southern Cone.

Brazil's incentives are fewer than Argentina's because of its secure position in the rivalry, its relative stability, and its economic progress when compared to Argentina. Brazil can afford not to be concerned with obtaining an "equalizer" for the simple reason that it is far ahead of Argentina. And yet there are incentives for Brazil also. Brazil must consider the dangers of Argentina going nuclear first, and, while it can tolerate the possibility of an Argentine "first," Brazil probably would not accept a long-lasting situation where Argentina is nuclear and Brazil is not. Thus, Brazil feels the need to be ready to go nuclear as a reaction to Argentina or, possibly, to preempt its southern neighbor. Leaving Argentina aside, there is also the feeling in Brazil that an advanced nuclear program would make it more likely that it would be taken seriously as an emerging major power; thus, pride and nationalism alone are also incentives. Brazil's disincentives are similar to Argentina's, with cost probably being a lesser consideration. It is clearly more to Brazil's advantage than Argentina's for both to remain nonnuclear. A possibility for both countries is the so-called Israeli option[33] under which both countries would move close to having an explosive device but would not cross the detonation threshold. Just how close, and what ingredients were missing, would be a closely held secret. This option also affords ample opportunities for denials, psychological warfare, and bluffing. Another option, begun somewhat haltingly in 1982, is a cooperative effort in which both countries would collaborate in their nuclear programs, possibly in cooperation with other countries (Chile and Peru have been mentioned, along with South Africa). However, even under the closest of cooperative programs, both nations will probably hold back certain essential elements and plans considered crucial for the development of military applications.

In conclusion it appears that both nations will move a great deal closer toward the threshold but will not actually take the last step unless provoked. There will continue to be a heavy emphasis on nuclear power and nuclear technology, and on the need to remain unhindered by nonproliferation restrictions imposed by the superpowers. There appears to be little prospect of development of nuclear devices for strictly military purposes, although psychological and diplomatic considerations will continue to keep this point ambiguous. Talk of peaceful nuclear explosions and "the peaceful uses of the atom" will be used as thinly veiled code words. The danger of irrational actions by an unstable government in either country will also be present, as will the possibility that future tensions will upset the delicate balance between these two threshold nuclear powers.

Recent Developments

Among the more significant developments to affect Argentine-Brazilian relations in the past few years were a series of economic, political, and military agreements between the two countries, including one that would start a joint nuclear program.[34] These cooperative agreements followed the historic moment in the late 1970s when Brazil moved away from its traditional close relationship with the United States. Argentine geopoliticians described the change differently, calling it the moment when Brazil quit being Uncle Sam's stalking-horse and returned to Latin America. How significant these agreements will be in practice, and whether they will withstand changes in the political system in both countries, remain to be seen. For the moment, though, they appear to be an important factor in ameliorating the historic Argentine-Brazilian rivalry.

The Falklands/Malvinas conflict caused strains in the Brazilian-Argentine relationship. Polls taken during the conflict indicated that Brazilian public opinion tended to favor the British, and many Brazilians tauntingly referred to the islands by their English name, Falklands. However, after some fence-sitting, the Brazilian government decided that moderate support for Argentina was probably the best course of action in view of the way the Argentines were able to line up fairly strong Latin American support. Brazil voted in support of Argentina's positions in key votes in the Organization of American States and even supplied Argentina with two reconnaissance aircraft. However, Brazilian support was never enthusiastic. As one Brazilian diplomat put it, "we are supporting our Argentine cousins," a statement that was in marked contrast with those of other Latin American nations that were "supporting their Argentine brothers." The Brazilian position in the conflict was shaped by strong ties to Great Britain, fundamental coolness toward Argentina, and a concern that Brazil's own interests in the South Atlantic and Antarctica might not be served by an aggressive and victorious Argentina in control of the Malvinas/Falkland Islands. Brazil was especially critical of the way in which Argentina resorted to force to resolve a territorial issue, a method that went against the tradition of Brazilian foreign policy. Nevertheless, Brazil recognized the wisdom of not siding with Great Britain and the United States against most of Latin America, and thus the Brazilians gave their grudging support to Argentina. A long-scheduled trip by Brazilian President Joao Figueiredo to the United States was held in May of 1982 but was scaled down in length and scope due to the crisis. Shortly afterward, the Brazilian foreign minister commented that the Falklands/Malvinas conflict had not caused any fundamental change in Brazilian-U.S. relationships.[35]

The Falklands/Malvinas conflict also had an impact on the nuclear issue. Although the British have not admitted it, it seems probable that several of their ships carried nuclear weapons on board. In a very pointed comment, the head of Argentina's National Atomic Energy Commission, an admiral, said that because of the presence of these weapons and because the British used a nuclear submarine to sink the cruiser *ARA Belgrano*, "Argentina is free to make use of its nuclear development for military purposes."[36] The Argentines were deliberately vague as to what the admiral had in mind, but subsequent reports indicated that the Argentines were referring to the possibility of building a nuclear power submarine, which would be a formidable, expensive, and not especially useful project.

Type of Conflict

The Argentine-Brazilian rivalry is basically an influence conflict (the most obvious of this type in Latin America), but it also has elements of a resource conflict in terms of the competition for energy and mineral resources in the buffer states. The rivalry could also acquire an ideological tone if the two political systems were to diverge sharply (as occurred in the Quadros-Goulart period of 1962–64).

No detailed assessment of the military geography will be made here, since there is not even a remote possibility of an armed clash involving these two countries. Some authors have in fact made these assessments, and one Argentine, Pablo Sanz, has presented complex war hypotheses involving Argentina against Brazil with different alignments of the buffers, Chile, Peru, and Ecuador.[37] There are also indications that the national war colleges and general staffs draw up similar war hypotheses and engage in war games in which military confrontations take place. In general, the strategic geography is believed to favor Brazil because of its greater depth and the fact that its national heartland is not concentrated almost exclusively in one city, as is the case in Argentina.

Relationship to Other Conflicts

Although the Argentine-Brazilian rivalry is not likely to lead to an armed confrontation between these two countries, it is related to all the other Southern Cone conflicts because of the way the relationship between these two nations influences the international relations of this region.[38]

Relationship to Geopolitical Thinking

The Argentine-Brazilian rivalry is one of the most important and most discussed themes in South American geopolitical writing, certainly from the Argentine perspective. The literature, as we have noted in Chapter 3, is somewhat skewed, with the Argentines paying a great deal more attention to the rivalry than the Brazilians. Perhaps a more accurate description of the theme is not so much one of Argentine-Brazilian rivalry as it is one of Brazil's search for its destiny and Argentina's response to the perceived expansionism implied in that search.

At present it seems that some of the cooperative agreements between the two countries are toning down the Argentine-Brazilian rivalry. It also appears that the cooperative aspects of the relationship are overcoming the conflictual ones to the extent that the integrationist geopolitical tendency may come into its own. And yet it is hard to believe that the long period of Argentine-Brazilian rivalry and the extensive volume of geopolitical writings that have noted and fed the rivalry are now irrelevant. It seems more likely that the two currents, rivalry and cooperation, will continue to coexist and that the period of agreements and apparent convergence of interests in the early 1980s may give way to the more traditional strains.

In any case, the conflictual elements in the relationship are reflected in the geopolitical literature, especially on the Argentine side. As Pittman's research has indicated, these themes do have an influence in decision-making circles and are beginning to be found in the educational curricula.[39] A recent study by a Brazilian political scientist[40] makes use of Argentine and Brazilian geopolitical writings to explore conflict studies and perceptions in these two countries with conclusions similar to the ones suggested above.

The themes in Brazilian geopolitical writing that are most closely linked to the Argentine-Brazilian rivalry are those that deal with Brazil's projections beyond its borders in the search for *grandeza*. This includes the idea of the "march westward" and the need to fill the continental heartland of the Bolivian "magic triangle" of Travassos before the Argentines do. The Argentines are also very sensitive to Brazilian geopolitical thinking that deals with a greater Brazilian role in the South Atlantic and the Antarctic, as well as competition for energy resources. The Argentine geopolitical writings concerned with Brazil's role as a subordinate "key country" for the United States have diminished as Brazil and the United States have grown more distant. On the other hand, there is now a new geopolitical concern in Argentina: that Brazil is becoming powerful enough in its own right to achieve its expansionary goals without the need for U.S. assistance.

TENSIONS IN THE BUFFER STATES

Before going on to consider the South Atlantic/Antarctic conflicts in the next chapter, brief mention will be made here of some areas of dispute between the South American buffer states of Uruguay, Paraguay, and Bolivia. In Chapter 3 the point was made that there is not much geopolitical writing in these three countries and that much of what does exist is the product of geopolitical currents emanating from Brazil, Argentina, and Chile. This situation is due in part to the small and relatively unsophisticated military establishments in these three countries. Further, as buffer states, these nations tend to react rather than act and tend to develop foreign policies and military plans as a function of their subordinate status in relation to Argentina and Brazil. The Argentine-Brazilian rivalry, and the geopolitical thinking that is behind that rivalry, are of far greater influence in these countries than any geopolitical ideas generated locally.

The aspects of this Argentine-Brazilian rivalry that affect the buffer states are economic, military-strategic, diplomatic, and cultural. The economic ones concern competition for resources, especially energy ones, and the search for markets.[41] Military-strategic competition involves selling arms and equipment, providing military advisors, and awarding scholarships for cadets from the buffer states to attend military academies and schools in Argentina and Brazil. Both countries maintain military missions in the buffers, and the rank and status of the military attachés in the capital cities are considered to be significant. On the issue of security, both Argentina and Brazil have historically been concerned that political systems in the buffers should not provide a potential focus for a subversive threat to them. Given the recent predominant role of military-dominated governments in the Southern Cone, this has meant that both Brazil and Argentina are prepared to work (together if necessary) to insure that the governments in Montevideo, Asunción, and La Paz are not too far to the left. Much attention has focused on Bolivia, and here the record shows that there was Argentine and Brazilian involvement in the fall of several Bolivian governments (such as that of General Torres and Lidia Gueiler) that were seen as potentially dangerous to right-wing Southern Cone interests. An Argentine general put it succinctly: "We are not so stupid as to allow a Nicaragua in the Southern Cone."[42]

Despite the overwhelming significance of the Argentine-Brazilian rivalry in the geopolitics of the buffers, there are some issues in which national geopolitical thinking is of importance. One of these is the legacy of the Chaco War of 1932–35, a second concerns Paraguayan and Uruguayan geopolitical thinking on hydroelectric projects, and a third is the integrationist current among the buffers themselves. Each will be briefly considered below.

The Legacy of the Chaco War

Even after half a century, bitterness remains in Paraguay and Bolivia (especially the latter) over the Chaco War and continues to make relations between these two nations difficult. Not only does this bitterness provide a theme for geopolitical thinking in these two countries, but it also explains why both countries station substantial military strength on their common border and continue to consider the other country as a possible opponent in a future conflict.

The basic roots of the conflict lie in the familiar pattern of vague frontier delimitations and ill-defined jurisdictions of the colonial and early national periods. However, the Chaco War (and its legacy of bitterness) was also the product of the two major nineteenth century wars discussed previously: the War of the Triple Alliance and the War of the Pacific. The first conflict devastated Paraguay and left it with a sullen resentment and desire to regain lost prestige. The second conflict cost Bolivia its ocean outlet and caused it to seek the Atlantic outlet through the eastern river system as an alternative. Tambs notes that Bolivian statesmen, driven by geopolitical considerations, attempted to seek an opening to the outside world through a policy of revindication;[43] the result was the Chaco War. Resource considerations were also important in the Chaco War as a result of rumors that there were important oil discoveries made there in the late 1920s by foreign firms.[44]

The war itself was preceded by arms buildups, construction of border fortifications, and frequent shooting incidents on the frontier in the late 1920s. Large-scale fighting broke out in 1932 and continued for three years until both sides reached the point of military, physical, and economic exhaustion. The net result was to give Paraguay about 80 percent of the disputed Chaco area, which ironically has not produced any significant economic benefits. In a very real sense, there was no victor in the war since both sides took heavy losses from disease, exposure, and starvation as well as combat.

Although the issue was supposedly settled at the 1936 Buenos Aires Peace Conference, the conflict lives on in fundamental antagonisms between the two countries and, although dormant, has the potential of being revived. Tensions between Paraguay and Bolivia emerge from time to time in press statements, nationalistic demagoguery, and patriotic exhortations on both sides. Any plans for development projects near the border area, or on any of the rivers in the region, are viewed with much suspicion. New indications of oil deposits near the present border area have also reawakened some of the old sense of competition for resources, which was one of the causes for the original conflict. Further, there is an unfulfilled provision in the 1936 treaty that could give Bolivia an excuse to renew demands for an ocean outlet if it fails in its bid to get one from Chile: the provision called for Paraguay to provide port outlet facilities for Bolivia, but it has not complied.[45]

Both Paraguay and Bolivia now have geopolitical institutes whose output, while not voluminous, concentrates on issues related to the Chaco. Should the perception of oil resources in the area become more salient, then the geopolitical "law of valuable areas" might come into play once more and heighten tensions. About the time of the centennial of the War of the Pacific, the Bolivian Institute of Geopolitical Studies warned that Paraguay might be tempted to attack and take Bolivian petroleum-producing areas near the border if a conflict broke out on the west coast of South America.[46] This type of analysis suggests the existence of linkages between the Bolivia-Paraguayan tension and the Central Andean conflict.

The Hydroelectric Energy Issue

The issue of hydroelectric energy has been a major theme in Argentine geopolitical thinking and, to a lesser extent, in Brazilian. The topic also appears frequently in the Uruguayan and Paraguayan geopolitical literature, although from a slightly different perspective. This view is an optimistic one, stressing the advantages that will accrue to Uruguay and Paraguay from development of these resources. There is even occasionally a statement that the two larger powers (i.e., Argentina and Brazil) badly need the cooperation of the two smaller states because many of the proposed dam projects cross international rivers and thus are binational in nature. A recent Paraguayan article went so far as to boast that the massive Itaipú project would cost Paraguay nothing because it would be built with Brazilian funds (obtained from the international banking community) and that Paraguay's only contribution would be its geography. Somewhat more realistic assessments stress that these massive projects are yet another form of penetration into the buffer states, and one more arena for Argentine-Brazilian rivalry.[47]

The Integrationist Current in the Buffer States

In discussing geopolitical thinking within the buffer states in Chapter 3, mention was made of the ideas of Quagliotti de Bellis concerning the integration of the buffers in a scheme he called URUPABOL (an acronymn for the names of the three countries involved). URUPABOL never really had much of a chance because of the Bolivian-Paraguayan rivalry and a feeling in Uruguay that it did not have very much in common with the other two countries. In late 1982 Paraguay pulled out of URUPABOL, arguing that Bolivia was acquiring weapons, which implied a hostile attitude toward Paraguay; little has been heard from URUPABOL since.[48]

NOTES

1. For further information on the controversy, see "The Beagle Channel Affair," *American Journal of International Law* 71 (October 1977): 733–40; Hugo G. Gobbi, "Problemas Australes Argentino-Chilenos," *Estrategia* no. 48 (September 1977): 27–36; Andres Ruggieri, "Canal de Beagle. Algunas Reflexiones sobre el Laudo Austral," *Estrategia* no. 45 (March 1977): 48–61; Juan E. Guglialmelli, "Patagonia," *Estrategia* no. 59 (July 1979); pp. 5–36. Chile, Ejército, *Memorial* no. 395 (May 1977) and no. 399 (Sept. 1977); *El Mercurio* (Santiago), November 19, 1978 (statements by Fabio Vio Valdieso, ex-director of the Chilean Boundary Commission); Chile, *Controversia en la Región del Canal Beagle* (Santiago: Editorial Jurídica de Chile, 1982); Juan E. Guglialmelli, "Cuestión del Beagle," *Estrategia* nos. 49–50 (November 1977–February 1978); pp. 5–22. German Carrasco, *El Laudo Arbitral del Canal Beagle* (Santiago: Editorial Jurídica, 1978); Sergio Villalobos, *El Beagle: Historia de una Controversia* (Santiago: Editorial Andrés Bello, 1979); Alberto Marín Madrid, *El Arbitraje del Beagle y la Actitud Argentina* (Santiago: Editorial Universitaria, 1978).

2. For Argentine concern over Chilean coordination with the other nations, see Vicente Palermo, "La Argentina y la Antártida," *Geosur* no. 23 (July 1981): 17. For Chilean concern over Argentine coordination with the others, see "Argentine-Soviet Friendship," *El Mercurio* (Santiago), April 3, 1983 in *Joint Publications Research Service (JPRS)*, April 27, 1983.

3. Jorge Alberto Fraga, "Beagle: Hablar con Claridad al Sumo Pontífice," *Estrategia* no. 69 (1981): 63.

4. Osiris G. Villegas, "No Ataco—Impugno," *Estrategia* no. 23 (December 1981): 11.

5. Robert N. Burr, *By Reason or Force* (Berkeley: University of California Press, 1965), pp. 112–13.

6. For a useful summary, see *Washington Post*, March 27, 1981, p. A-27.

7. *New York Times*, June 17, 1982; *AFP, Paris*, May 13, 1982, in *FBIS*, May 13, 1982, p. E-1.

8. Robert Cox, "Argentina's Dream," *The New Republic*, May 12, 1982, p. 17.

9. *Noticias Argentinas*, January 17, 1983, in *FBIS*, January 20, 1983, p. B-7.

10. *La Prensa*, February 10, 1983 in *JPRS*, March 17, 1983.

11. *New York Times*, January 5, 1984, p. A-16; *Washington Post*, January 12, 1984, p. A-28.

12. Stephen M. Gorman, "The High Stakes of Geopolitics in Tierra del Fuego," *Parameters*, June 1978, pp. 53–54; Florentino Diaz Loza, "Geopolítica de Chile," *Estrategia* no. 48 (September 1977): 61; Geoffrey Kemp, "The Prospects for Arms Control in Latin America: The Strategic Dimension," in *Military Rule in Latin America*, ed. Philippe C. Schmitter (Beverly Hills: Sage, 1973), pp. 211–13; Kenneth Nolde, "Arms and Security in South America: Towards an Alternate View," Ph.D. dissertation, University of Miami, 1980, pp. 233–34.

13. Gorman, "Tierra del Fuego," pp. 50–51; Daniel Waksman Schinca, "El Proyecto de la OTAS," *Nueva República* 2 (April–September 1977): 344.

14. Jorge Villacrés Moscoso, "Laudos Arbitrales Nulos," *Geopolítica* no. 21 (March 1981): 25.

15. For further historical background, see Jack Child, *Peru: A Country Study* (Washington, D.C.: American University Foreign Area Studies, 1980), esp. chap. 1; David P. Werlich, "Peru: The 'Lame Duck' Revolution," *Current History*, 76 (February 1979): 106–17; Norman D. Arbaiza, *Mars Moves South: The Future Wars of South America* (Jericho, N.Y.: Exposition Press, 1974), pp. 17–19; Edgardo Mercado Jarrín, "La Política y la Estrategia en la Guerra del Pacífico," *Estudios Geopolíticos y Estratégicos* (Peru) no. 2 (April 1979); Mariano Baptista Gumucio, *En Lugar del Desastre: Bolivia y el Conflicto Peruano-Chileno* (La Paz: Editorial Carla, 1975); Luis Antonio Morzone, *La Mediterraneidad Boliviana ante el Derecho Internacional* (Buenos Aires: Depalma, 1979); Jaime Ponce Caballero, *Geopolítica Chilena y Mar Boliviano* (La Paz: Ponce Caballero, 1975); Gonzalo Romero, "Bolivia: La Cuestión Marítima," *Geosur* fasciculo no. 8 (March 1980); Alfonso Vazquez, "Bolivia y su Salida Hacia el Pacífico," *Geopolítica* no. 23 (December 1981); Jorge Escobari, *El Derecho al Mar* (La Paz: Escobari, 1979).

16. Stephen M. Gorman, "Present Threats to Peace in South America," *Inter-American Economic Affairs* 33 (Summer 1979): pp. 51–71.

17. Patricia A. Hershkowitz, "The Border Dispute over the Pacific Seaboard Between Bolivia and Chile," paper presented at the Second Annual Meeting of the Middle Atlantic Council of Latin American Studies, Philadelphia, April 1981.

18. "Remembering the War of the Pacific," *Latin American Political Report*, April 13, 1979.

19. *Excelsior* (Mexico), July 5, 1982; *Paris AFP*, June 1, 1982 in *FBIS*, June 4, 1982.

20. *El Mercurio* (Santiago), March 24 and 30, 1983, in *JPRS* 3348/310 and 3348/312; *La Paz Cadena Panamericana*, March 23, 1983, in *FBIS*, March 24, 1983; *AFP La Paz*, March 17, 1983, in *FBIS*, May 18, 1983.

21. For further historical background, see Bryce Wood, *The U.S. and Latin American Wars, 1932-1942* (New York: Columbia University Press, 1966); David H. Zook, *Zarumilla-*

Marañón: The Ecuador-Peru Dispute (New York: Bookman, 1964); Georg Maier, "Ecuadorian-Peruvian Boundary Dispute," *American Journal of International Law* 63 (January 1969): 28–46; Carlos Palacios Saena, *La Guerra del 41: El Protocolo de Río no Demarcó Fronteras Definitivas* (Guayaquil: Ediciones Ara, 1979); Bolívar Lópes Herman, *El Ecuador y su Problema Territorial con el Perú* (Quito: Biblioteca Militar Ecuatoriana, 1961); Otavio A. Achoa, *Tragedia Ecuatoriana 1941* (Quito: Ochoa, 1976); Luis Alberto Rosero, *Memorias de un Veterano de la Guerra del 41* (Quito: Editorial Casa de la Cultura Ecuatoriana, 1978); Miguel Monteza Tafur, *El Conflicto Militar del Perú con el Ecuador* (Lima: Editorial Arica, 1976); F. de la Barra, *El Conflicto Peruano-Ecuatoriano y la Vigorosa Campaña de 1941 en las Fronteras de Zarumilla* (Lima: Procer, 1969).

22. *Voz de los Andes* (Quito), July 18, 1982, in *FBIS*, July 22, 1982.

23. Monteza Tufar, *Conflicto Militar*, p. 11.

24. *Times of the Americas*, February 4, 1981; *Washington Post*, March 13, 1981.

25. Villacrés Moscoso, "Laudos Arbitrales Nulos."

26. Interview with a senior Peruvian general, Lima, November 1973.

27. For Argentine and Brazilian commentary, see Juan E. Guglialmelli, "Argentina: Política Nacional y Política de Fronteras," *Estrategia* nos. 37–38, (November 1975–February 1976); Leopoldo González Aguayo, "Las Zonas de Influencia Latinoamericanas," *Cuadernos Americanos*, November–December 1973; Oscar Camillón, "Relaciones Argentino-Brasileñas," *Estrategia* no. 21 (March 1973); Carlos P. Mastrorilli, "Historia y Desarrollo de la Geopolítica Brasileña," *Estrategia* No. 19-20. (November 1972–February 1973); Luis Dallanegra Pedraza, ed., *Geopolítica y Relaciones Internacionales* (Buenos Aires: Pleamar, 1981); Ruben Oscar Moro, "Historia de un Expansionismo Geopolítico," *Geopolítica* nos. 3-4 (March-June 1976); Raul Bottelho Gosalvez, *Proceso del Subimperialismo Brasileño* (Buenos Aires: Maity, 1977); Ruben Carpio Castillo, *Geopolítica de Venezuela* (Caracas: Seix Barral Venezolana, 1981); Fernando A. Milia, ed., *La Atlantártida: Un Espacio Geopolítico* (Buenos Aires: Pleamar, 1978); Jorge Nelson Gualco, *Cono Sur: Elección de un Destino* (Buenos Aires: Fabril Editores, 1972); Nicolás Boscovich, *Geostrategia de la Cuenca del Plata* (Caracas: El Cid Editor, 1979).

28. Jack Child, *Unequal Alliance: The Inter-American Military System, 1938-*1978 (Boulder, Colo.: Westview Press, 1980), p. 50; Juan E. Guglialmelli, "Itaipú-Corpus," *Estrategia* no. 61 (November 1979); Stanley E. Hilton, *Brazil and the Great Powers, 1930-1939* (Austin: University of Texas Press, 1975), p. 14.

29. For an analysis of possible scenarios and war hypotheses between Argentina and Brazil, see Pablo E. Sanz, *El Espacio Argentino* (Buenos Aires: Pleamar, 1976), pp. 335-52.

30. Burr, *By Reason or Force*; also his article "The Balance of Power in 19th Century South America: An Exploratory Essay," *Hispanic American Historical Review* 35 (February 1955): 37-60.

31. Norman A. Bailey, *Latin America in World Politics* (New York: Walker, 1967), pp. 55-60.

32. See documentation cited by Child in *Unequal Alliance*, chap. 4.

33. Onkar Marwah, *Nuclear Proliferation and the Near-Nuclear Countries* (Cambridge, Mass: Ballinger, 1975), pp. 288-89; Sanz, *El Espacio Argentino* p. 351; *Washington Post*, August 31, 1982, p. A-14; February 3, 1983, p. A-29; *New York Times*, September 17, 1983.

34. For details, see *International Herald Tribune*, October 1982 (special issue on "Latin American Nuclear Technology").

35. *Folha de São Paulo*, April 18, 1982, in *FBIS*, April 20, 1982; *Jornal do Brasil*, April 3, 1982, in *FBIS*, April 7, 1982; *Jornal do Brasil*, April 24, 1982 in *JPRS*, May 28, 1982; *Times of the Americas*, July 21, 1982.

36. *AFP, Buenos Aires*, June 24, 1982, in *FBIS*, June 25, 1982.

37. Sanz *El Espacio Argentino*; Kemp, "Arms Control," pp. 209-11.

38. Armando Alonso Pineiro, "El Equilibrio Geopolítico Sudamericano," *Estrategia* no. 30 (September 1974).

39. Howard T. Pittman, "Geopolitics in the ABC Countries: A Comparison," Ph.D. dissertation, American University, 1981.

40. Alexandre S. C. Barros, "Conflict Studies in Higher Education: The Case of South America with Emphasis on Argentina and Brazil," unpublished paper, July 1980.

41. Leopoldo Gonzalez Aguayo, "Las Zonas de Influencia Latinoamericanas," *Cuadernos Americanos* (November 1973): 116-17.

42. *Buenos Aires, Noticias Argentinas*, November 19, 1982, in *FBIS*, November 23, 1982.

43. Lewis A. Tambs, "Geopolitical Factors in Latin America," in Bailey, *Latin America*, p. 45.

44. Julio Laborde, "Imperialism and Border Conflicts," *World Marxist Review* (November 1978): 95-96.

45. Adrian English, "Latin American Power Balances and Potential Flash Points," *International Defense Review* 14 (1981): 1273-81.

46. *La Paz, Radio Cruz del Sur*, May 24, 1977, in *FBIS*, May 26, 1977.

47. For a discussion of the hydroelectric issue, see Rubén de Hoyos, "South American Geopolitics and the La Plata River Basin," paper delivered to the International Political Studies Association, Edinburgh, August 1976.

48. *Asunción AFP*, September 1, 1982, in *FBIS*, September 2, 1982.

6

THE SOUTH ATLANTIC CONFLICTS

This chapter analyzes three closely interrelated conflict situations whose significance was dramatically illustrated by the tragic Anglo-Argentine war of 1982: the Malvinas/Falklands conflict, the competition for influence in the South Atlantic, and the search for control of Antarctica. These conflict situations are also important because they involve outside actors, including the superpowers.

THE MALVINAS/FALKLANDS CRISIS

Introduction: Parties, Summary, and Geography

The complexity of the issues involved in this conflict, and the considerable volume of writings on the topic, make it impossible to do anything more in this section than briefly highlight some of the background of the conflict and then concentrate on its relationship to underlying themes of geopolitics in Argentina.[1] For Argentina the conflict has deep roots in geopolitical and strategic thinking. The books and journals that are outlets of this thinking in Argentina have devoted innumerable pages to the geopolitical importance of the islands and their relation to Argentina's ambitions in the South Atlantic and Antarctica. Some of these writings specifically called for military action to recover the islands and in retrospect can be seen as an unheeded warning that Argentina was in fact prepared to go to war to recover them at some point.

The Malvinas/Falklands Islands (see Figure 12) consist of two main islands (East Falkland/Soledad and West Falkland/Gran Malvina) and some

Figure 12. Argentine stamp showing "Islas Malvinas." (Photo by the author.)

200 smaller ones located about 300 miles east of the Argentine Patagonian city of Rio Gallegos. Their surface area is of some 6,400 square miles, which is approximately the same as the state of Hawaii. Before the Argentine invasion of April 2, 1982, their population was about 1,900 British subjects, of whom 1,100 lived in the capital, Port Stanley, later named Puerto Argentino by the Buenos Aires government.

The islands have a historic geopolitical significance in that they were one of the many original outposts of the British Empire selected because of their proximity to maritime "choke points," which permitted the Royal Navy to project its power at key sites with maximum effectiveness. The islands were the site of an important World War I naval engagement and played a role in the World War II defeat of the German pocket battleship *Graf Spee*. Their contemporary geopolitical and strategic significance lies in their relationship to the South Atlantic and Antarctica, since whoever possesses the islands is in a strong position to project power into these areas and strengthen any claims of sovereignty and influence in the region.

In the aftermath of the 1982 Anglo-Argentine war, the Falklands/Malvinas have also acquired a symbolic and political significance that far outweighs the inherent importance of the islands themselves. For a brief period their recovery provided a powerful unifying cause for all Argentines, a feat that has been difficult to achieve in that sometimes disunited nation. With defeat came a sense of bitterness and disillusion that was quickly directed against the nation's military rulers and was an important factor in Argentina's return to democracy in December of 1983. For the British, and especially for the Conservative government of Prime Minister Margaret Thatcher, the Falklands war was an equally important rallying point, which served to boost national pride, relive some of the glories of the lost empire, and eventually greatly improve the Conservatives' performance at the next election.

The 1982 conflict also affected U.S. relations with Latin America and further undermined the credibility of the Organization of American States and its principal juridical instrument for peace keeping and peace making, the 1947 Inter-American Treaty of Reciprocal Assistance (the Rio Treaty). Further, the 1982 fighting has not resolved the fundamental issue and has tragically set back a series of rather promising moves toward greater integration of the islands into mainland Argentina, which might have provided the ultimate peaceful solution to the Malvinas/Falklands issue. On both sides deep emotions, patriotism, nationalism, and a conviction that the heroic dead must not be betrayed by compromise now make a solution vastly more difficult. Even the return to civilian government in Argentina, and the growing British realization that the costs of maintaining a major garrison on the islands are prohibitive, have not yet led to a significant movement to resolving the conflict. Although no serious observers are predicting another outbreak of fighting, the tense relations between the two countries, the amounts of military equipment in the area, and the links to South Atlantic and Antarctic matters make this one of the more serious conflict situations in South America.

Historical Background

The early history of the islands[2] is complicated and ambiguous, making it difficult to establish any clear priority to the British or Argentine claims. The complications begin with two different sixteenth century discovery dates: 1520 by a Spanish member of Magellan's expedition, according to Argentina, and 1592 by an English navigator, according to Great Britain. Exploration and settlement in the seventeenth and early eighteenth centuries were sporadic, with no permanent inhabitants and many visits by whalers, sealers, and explorers passing through the Strait of Magellan. Spain, France, and Great Britain all established settlements of one kind or another in this early period, which ended when Argentina gained independence from Spain in 1810 and the Spanish abandoned the islands shortly afterward. A few years later, in 1820, representatives of the United Provinces of the Rio de la Plata landed and formally took possession of the islands. This early Argentine settlement was destroyed by a U.S. naval vessel in 1832 after a series of incidents between the settlers and U.S. sealers. A year later the British expelled the remaining Argentines and began their long period of effective control, which was rudely interrupted by the Argentine invasion of April 2, 1982.

In that period of almost a century and a half of British rule, there were few notable events in the island's history beyond the role in two naval engagements in the world wars. Argentina made periodic protests over British actions, but these protests were largely ignored, and the dispute was considered to be essentially dormant through the early part of the twentieth century. The highly nationalistic regime of Juan Perón in Argentina (1945–55) seized on the Malvinas/Falklands issue as a patriotic rallying point and linked it to Argentine claims in Antarctica and to a geopolitical version of a "greater Argentina." Argentina was able to appeal to the decolonization sentiment that swept through the Third World after World War II, and it was successful in obtaining a United Nations resolution that led to Anglo-Argentine talks over eventual resolution of the issue. In the late 1960s and 1970s, these talks produced a series of measures that brought the islanders into a closer logistical and human relationship with Argentina, and seemed to offer promise of slow but steady progress toward an eventual transfer of sovereignty.

In the mid-1970s this optimistic development received a setback when both countries began to perceive an economic benefit in terms of possible major oil deposits as well as other resources. In 1976 there was a shooting incident involving the British oceanographic vessel *Shackleton* (named after the Antarctic explorer who is buried on South Georgia) and the Argentine Navy destroyer *ARA Almirante Storni* (named after the father of Argentine naval geopolitical thinking). This incident seriously strained relations between the two countries and led to a withdrawal of ambassadors and a basic revaluation of options on the part of the Argentines.[3]

This revaluation apparently included contingency planning for the eventual recovery of the islands by force if negotiations with Great Britain did not yield favorable results in a fairly short period of time. The year 1976 also marked the beginning of a seven-year period of military governments, whose leaders felt they could take arbitrary actions on internal security and international relations without having to consult any civilian constituency. In this period (1976–83) there appeared a strong current of aggressive and bellicose themes in Argentine geopolitical and military journals. Much of this was directed against Chile and dealt with Argentine claims on the Beagle Channel Islands. Much of it, however, also addressed the Malvinas/Falklands question, and one distinct feature of these writings was that if negotiations and peaceful measures failed or were dilatory then Argentina must be prepared for more drastic solutions. As General Guglialmelli, editor of *Estrategia*, put it:

The negotiations, if they are renewed, will be slow and vexatious. Great Britain may insist upon not returning the islands or may embroil the problem with the same objective. However, it will have to play against time, since time is in our favor. In any event, Argentina should not lower its guard. It must insist on a peaceful solution, without dismissing the extreme alternative.[4]

An Argentine military journal was more specific, calling for Great Britain to return the "usurped Argentine national patrimony" before the one hundred fiftieth anniversary of the "treacherous affront" (that is, by January 3, 1983). If Great Britain refused, then "the Argentine Nation would be morally, spiritually and materially free to act with any political, economic or military means it deemed advisable."[5]

In 1981 official Argentine army magazines ran a series of articles calling for a realistic Argentine foreign policy based on power politics, and accompanied this call with a thinly veiled "international relations simulation" involving the taking of the Malvinas Islands as a conflict hypothesis.[6] Later that same year the Argentine army's commander in chief, Lieutenant General Leopoldo Galtieri, visited the United States and laid the basis for increasingly close cooperation with the Reagan administration on a range of matters that included Argentine diplomatic and military support of U.S. policies in Central America. General Galtieri also brought up the subject of closer cooperation in the South Atlantic and appears to have received the impression that the United States would in turn support (or at least not interfere with) Argentine attempts to recover the Malvinas/Falklands Islands.[7] Shortly after his Washington visit, General Galtieri removed the ineffective President Viola and assumed the presidency himself.

The Galtieri regime was initially characterized by a flurry of diplomatic activity and a sense that something had to be done soon to resolve the Malvinas and Beagle Channel questions, by diplomacy or by military means. In January and February of 1982, major Buenos Aires newspapers not only speculated on this possibility, but openly called for military action to take the islands by force. Writing in the prestigious *La Prensa* in late January, a columnist laid out the scenario: in the very near future Argentina would present Great Britain with its last demand for a negotiated solution leading to a return of the islands to Argentina. The columnist added that this step was linked to both the Beagle Channel issue as well as to concerns over protecting Argentine interests in the South Atlantic and Antarctica; should this Argentine demand not be met, then "Buenos Aires will take over the islands by force this year." The columnist concluded that the United States would understand and even support Argentine initiatives.[8] Exactly one month before the invasion, the headlines of the important daily *La Nación* read: "New Policy for the Islas Malvinas: the Government hardens its attitude as it reserves the right to take other measures if the proposed monthly meetings do not produce results to truly accelerate the negotiations to the limit."⁹ The stage was set for the fateful events of April 1982.

Recent Developments

The Malvinas/Falklands war produced a flood of accounts and analyses; no attempt will be made here to go over that well-covered ground. This section will merely note some recent developments, especially as they relate to the possibility of future conflict in this area.

Chilean neutrality in the conflict was greatly resented and suspected by Argentina during and after the fighting phase. In the postwar period, these Argentine concerns have focused on possible Chilean purchases of aircraft and ships from Great Britain, including some that fought in the Malvinas/ Falklands conflict, which would thus deliver a highly symbolic message to Argentina.[10] The Argentine press has also consistently reported news and rumors of joint Chilean-British maneuvers and military cooperation in the Strait of Magellan area. This has sustained speculation on the existence of a broad secret understanding between these two nations that would be counter to Argentine interests not only in Malvinas/Falklands, but also in the Antarctic and the Drake Passage.[11]

In the face of overwhelming and decisive military defeat on the islands, Argentina during the postwar period has focused its energies on the political and diplomatic fronts in an attempt to continue to pressure Great Britain. Argentina was able to gain considerable support in the Organization of American States and the General Assembly of the United Nations in this process. The November 1982 U.N. vote was especially gratifying for Argentina, and annoying for the Thatcher government, since the United States and several NATO allies supported Argentina's call for new negotiations.[12] Within the Inter-American System, Argentina was able to marshall continued support for its claim of sovereignty and negotiations, although there was still muted criticism over its use of force to settle a political issue. Colombia, which had remained neutral during the conflict, shifted its diplomatic position and supported Argentina when a new administration came into office in August 1982. Even the United States made a number of conciliatory gestures toward Argentina in an attempt to repair some of the damage caused by its strong support of Great Britain.

Recent developments within Argentina suggest that the 1982 conflict may well represent a turning point in Argentine political history. The most significant postwar development has been the internecine squabbling within the military, its great loss of prestige, and the return to an elected civilian government in December of 1983. Even as the Argentine combat efforts on the ground around Port Stanley were collapsing in mid-June 1982, there was a scramble among senior Argentine military officers to insure that they would not become scapegoats in the inevitable postwar search for explanations and blame. This process was exacerbated by traditional Argentine interservice rivalries and splits within each service, which had made it so difficult for the military to reach decisions and coordinate joint action during the war. Junior officers were disgusted over the self-serving actions of their seniors, and civilians and enlisted soldiers were outraged at the way many officers on the islands had neglected their troops while securing their own comforts. As the Argentine military lost prestige and moral authority to govern in late 1982 and 1983, the problem of the "disappeared ones of the dirty war" of the late 1970s came back to haunt them and accelerated the process of a return to a democratically elected civilian regime.[13]

Prospects for Anglo-Argentine negotiations on the islands and an eventual resolution of the conflict have been enhanced by this return to a civilian regime in Argentina, although President Alfonsin could not afford to be overly conciliatory to the British. The new president stated during his campaign that his civilian administration would be more effective than a military one in peacefully recovering the islands and that Argentina would continue to apply diplomatic pressure to extract British concessions. The Argentines also feel that they have time on their side as the British begin to fully understand the long-range costs of maintaining a large force on the islands. In this process it is especially important for Argentina to maintain both the appearance and reality of Latin American diplomatic solidarity. At the logistical and tactical level, the Argentine military believes it is essential that the British be denied access to Brazilian and Chilean territory for refueling aircraft and obtaining supplies. Another major concern of Argentina is that the British may seek NATO support as a way of relieving their burden of maintaining the Falklands garrison.[14]

Type of Conflict and Military Implications

The Falklands/Malvinas conflict is both territorial and resource in nature. The land itself is hardly impressive in terms of area or inherent economic value, and neither Argentina nor Great Britain particularly needs the territory as such. The economic resources that might be at stake are questionable and consist of possible oil and gas fields and krill. Their effective exploitation is possible by Great Britain only if it has Argentine cooperation; Argentina has no particularly urgent need for the resources. These territorial and resource considerations do not begin to explain the interest and commitment involved in the conflict. A fuller explanation of the type of conflict must include the strategic resource that the islands represent, especially as they relate to the geopolitical concept of a tricontinental Argentina.

Beyond the strategic and geopolitical explanations for the conflict lie profound emotions and nationalism, which almost make the conflict an ideological one. It is impossible to exaggerate the depth of feeling regarding the islands that Argentines of all political persuasions hold. The Malvinas claim also forms a part of the very special historic love-hate relationship that Argentina has had with Great Britain. That relationship includes the British invasions of the River Plate in the early nineteenth century, the role that British investors and settlers had in the economic and social development of Argentina, and the sense that British (and U.S.) opposition to Argentina has somehow deprived it of the greatness that is its destiny. The Argentines also attempted, with mixed results, to portray the 1982 conflict as a North-South one, which pitted a technologically superior but spiritually decadent British-U.S. Anglo-Saxon alliance against a Third World nation with considerable international support. For the British the conflict also acquired deep emotional elements once the Argentines took the islands by force. A sense of outrage and injured pride, coupled with matters of principle (self-determination and nonuse of force), fueled the British response.

The military significance of the conflict has been the subject of numerous studies on the part of the British, the Argentines, the Americans, and a number of others.[15] The conflict has been characterized as a slow-motion nineteenth century conflict fought with some very deadly high-technology twentieth century weapons. The high-performance weapons used in combat for the first time included the French Exocet missile, the British Harrier jump jet, the nuclear submarine, and a variety of surface-to-air and air-to-air missiles. Much of the military analysis, especially from the British and U.S. side, dealt with the performance of these new weapons systems, albeit in a unique environment that was unlikely to occur again. These high-technology sophisticated weapons made an impact of another kind among the military leaders of the larger nations of Latin America, who were impressed by the way in which a relatively cheap missile could severely damage the most modern warships afloat. These weapons seemingly had the capability of making the superpowers take the larger Latin American military establishments more seriously than they had in the past. This particular type of analysis ignores the fact that the British task force did not have the kind of air cover that could have kept the Argentine aircraft, with their Exocet missiles, from getting within range of the ships. The analysis also tends to ignore the reality that what ultimately won the war for the British was not so much the sophisticated weapons at the high-technology end of the scale as much as elementary military leadership, training, morale, endurance, psychological warfare, and surprise, especially at the lower tactical levels.

A major problem facing the Argentine military after the war was how to replace the equipment lost during the conflict. Major losses included a cruiser and a submarine, over 100 aircraft and helicopters, several complete radar systems, and the ground equipment for three army brigades. Despite attractive offers from the Soviet Union, the Argentine military opted for its traditional suppliers (West Germany, France, and Israel), as well as Brazil.

Their principal stated needs after the war were fighter-bomber aircraft with adequate range, maritime patrol aircraft, air defense weapons, and transport helicopters. Argentina's severe economic problems and unprecedented external debt made resupply more difficult, and military leaders were anxious to complete their major arms purchase before the transfer of power to a civilian regime in late 1983. Although Brazil, and especially Chile, watched Argentina's rearmament with more than passing interest, this rearmament did not go substantially beyond the expected replacement of lost material and did not lead to an arms race in the Southern Cone.[16]

The Malvinas/Falklands conflict also raised some disturbing questions regarding nuclear weapons and technology. Argentina argues that several British ships that entered its territorial waters carried nuclear depth charges in violation of Protocol I of the Treaty of Tlatelolco, which Great Britain has signed. The Argentines also hold that the use of a British nuclear-powered submarine in the conflict is a further violation of the treaty. Argentina's arguments ring somewhat hollow since a nuclear-powered submarine is hardly a "nuclear weapon" and Argentina itself has not ratified the treaty. Speculation on the true nature of Argentina's nuclear program was further stimulated when the director of its Atomic Energy Commission announced in late 1983 that Argentina now had the technological capability to control the full fuel cycle for uranium.[17] This meant that Argentina could develop and detonate a nuclear explosive outside of international controls. Such action might be favored by a humiliated and highly nationalistic military in Argentina, which could see a nuclear explosion as a means of restoring prestige. It would presumably also serve as a psychological weapon in Argentina's power relationships with Chile and Brazil, although it might also lead the latter country to develop its own device quickly.

Relationship to Other Conflicts

The Malvinas/Falklands conflict was the most significant Latin American armed clash since the Chaco War in the mid-1930s and affected almost all the other conflict situations in the Western Hemisphere to some degree. After April 2, 1982, even the most dormant of Latin American border disputes was seen in a slightly different light; nations involved in such conflicts could not escape considering the Argentine action as a precedent of some sort. As a result, the positions taken by most of the hemisphere nations on the Malvinas/Falklands issue were also affected by their own potential conflict situations. A notable example was the case of Venezuela, which feels that it has been a victim of British aggression much like Argentina, and whose president said in early May 1982 that the outcome of Venezuela's territorial dispute with Guyana would depend largely on the precedent of the Malvinas/Falklands case.[18] A diametrically opposed example was the case of Colombia, whose neutrality in the Malvinas/Falklands situation was based not only on principle, but also on its concern that there was a close parallel between Argentina's claim on the Malvinas and Nicaragua's claim on the islands of San Andrés and Providencia.[19] The ultimately disastrous outcome of the conflict for Argentina can be seen as a lesson for any government that might be tempted to follow the same path, but the experience left the Inter-American System with a disquieting feeling that major outbreaks of interstate conflict now seemed less unlikely than before.

The conflict most directly and immediately linked to the Malvinas/Falklands was the Beagle Channel dispute between Argentina and Chile. In referring to this theme, a noted Argentine geopolitical analyst argued that, in awarding the Beagle Channel Islands to Chile, Great Britain was "not only seeking to establish the presence of Chile in the South Atlantic by projecting her into the Southern Islands in order to weaken Argentina's position in the region, but was also trying to place Chile on the Southern flank of the Malvinas."[20]

Relationship to Geopolitical Thinking

The relationship is a simple and fundamental one: possession of the Malvinas Islands is the key to the geopolitical concept of a greater and tricontinental Argentina in which mainland Argentina is linked to Antarctic Argentina through Southern Insular Argentina. In the massive outpouring of passion, patriotism, excitement, triumphalism, and then defeat in Argentina in 1982, it was easy to overlook the fact that the recovery of the Malvinas, by force if necessary, has been a consistent theme among many Argentine geopolitical writers.

These currents of geopolitical thinking are linked to deeply felt emotions dealing with Argentine sovereignty and national unity in a country that has seen more than its share of fragmentation. Had the "Malvinas recovery" succeeded, the military regime might well have managed to hang on to power for an extended period of time, would have won its glorious place in Argentine history books, and would have perhaps also managed to wipe out the stain of the brutal excesses of the "dirty war." The basic geopolitical rationale for recovering the Malvinas in April 1982 met at a point in time with the impending collapse of the Argentine military government, the psychological need to do something about the islands before the one hundred fiftieth anniversary of their loss, and the growing realization of the implications of the Antarctic Treaty revision in 1991. Argentine geopolitical and strategic writers were stressing with increasing frequency in the early 1980s that "time was running out" for Argentina to assert itself in the South Atlantic and that, if it did not, then other countries would continue to make gains at its expense.[21] These considerations serve to illustrate the link between the retaking of the Malvinas and these profound currents of geopolitical thinking in Argentina.

Geopolitical thinking relevant to the Malvinas/Falklands conflict and Argentine unity also involves the frustrated search for a grand and unifying "National Project." Recovery of the Malvinas has frequently been described in Argentine geopolitical writings as an essential first step in this process in which the people and the armed forces would strive together to reach a goal that would integrate Argentina and liberate territory held by the British usurpers.[22]

The "recovery" of the Malvinas in April 1982 by military means was based on a widely held belief in Argentina that force was in fact justified. Even after decisive defeat in June 1982, these same geopoliticians argued for the need to "keep alive the possibility of a new, serious and objectively planned military attempt" to recover the islands. The same thought was echoed by a spokesman for the Argentine army's V Corps when he stated:

> Regardless of the setback we have experienced, we must look into the future by viewing the events which have occurred as the contemporary stage of the century-old battle that Argentina has been waging against Great Britain. . . . Great Britain is being prompted by a desire for hegemony in the South Atlantic and by the Antarctic region's economic potential. . . . Since the only concrete results will be those attained through our tenacity, the V Corps is getting ready for another war profiting from the situations already experienced. The V Corps has confidence in the justice of our cause and is strongly willing to defeat the British enemy, as happened on three occasions in the past.[23]

As indicated previously, the Malvinas issue for Argentine geopolitical thinkers has a transcendant importance related to the concept of tricontinental Argentina. These ideas go back to the maritime geopolitical thinking of Admiral Storni in the early twentieth century and have recently acquired new vigor with the related idea of "Atlantártida," which views the region as a single geopolitical entity under strong Argentine influence and control. Argentine geopolitical writers also have a keen awareness of the competing Chilean and British plans for influence and control in the area. For example, an article appearing in the Buenos Aires daily *La Nación* in late April 1982 spoke of the Malvinas as being a "British path to the Antarctic."[24] and developed the argument that Great Britain also had a broad geopolitical vision of the links between their Antarctic claim, the Southern Islands, and influence in the South Atlantic.

INFLUENCE IN THE SOUTH ATLANTIC

Introduction: Parties, Summary, and Geography

Even before the 1982 Anglo-Argentine conflict, there was enough competing strategic and geopolitical interest in the South Atlantic to make it necessary to analyze a potential conflict in that area. In contrast with prior South

American conflicts, this possible South Atlantic conflict would involve a wide variety of parties, including the two superpowers and South Africa, as well as the two largest nations of South America. The strategic importance of the South Atlantic (or at least the eastern portions of it) grew with the oil crisis of the early 1970s, the Cuban role in Angola from 1975 on, and the increasing Soviet and Cuban presence in the African continent. The South Atlantic also has an "Atlantic Narrows" of some 1,600 miles between northeast Brazil and the westernmost portions of Africa. Although this is hardly a classical choke point, it does have some features that bring it to the attention of geopolitical thinkers and strategic planners in South America and elsewhere. In a general sense the South Atlantic is a strategic vacuum involving large ocean areas with relatively low military presence by either superpowers or local littoral states. The value of the eastern portion of the South Atlantic has grown considerably with the increasing use of its sea lanes by tankers bringing Middle Eastern oil to European and U.S. markets. The Falklands/Malvinas war and the links to the Antarctic have served to focus additional attention on the southern portions of the South Atlantic. Proposals for filling this South Atlantic strategic vacuum have included: a broad South Atlantic Treaty Organization (SATO) involving some of the NATO and South American nations as well as South Africa; a limited alliance of the two Southern Cones of South America and South Africa; an exclusively South American alliance; and unilateral national projections of power into the area. For at least one country (Argentina), the southern South Atlantic acquires a vital importance as the integrating national link between the continent, the Southern Islands, and Antarctica.

As indicated, this conflict involves a large number of potential parties and serves as a useful transition from the basically bilateral conflicts analyzed previously to the highly multilateral potential conflict in the Antarctic. As a Brazilian geopolitican put it, the South Atlantic is an area where there is a "juxtaposition of the unknown of the Antarctic, the infantileness of Africa, and the adolescense of South America."[25] South American geopoliticians, especially those who are also naval officers with a budgetary axe to grind, tend to exaggerate the significance of the area and its potential value to the superpowers. Nevertheless, these individuals can point to the increased Soviet presence along the West African coastline, the undeniable importance of the oil sea lanes, and the corresponding reaction from the United States.[26] South American geopoliticians have responded to this superpower interest in the South Atlantic in a variety of ways. Some have argued for the broad SATO alliance, while others have appealed for what is essentially an isolationist South American solution as a counter to the entering wedge of superpower interest in the region.

The South Atlantic is also a primary theater in which the currents of Argentine-Brazilian competition and cooperation are being played out. To some Argentine geopoliticians who suspect Brazil's motives, Brazil is fulfilling its old traditional role as Argentina's nemesis with strong links to Great

Britain and the United States. Other South American geopoliticians of the integrationist school call for the creation of a new geopolitical doctrine built around joint Argentine-Brazilian efforts to fill the South Atlantic strategic vacuum before it is filled by outside powers.[27] A particularly intriguing party in the South Atlantic controversy is South Africa; there are indications that South Africa has seen the idea of a closer link to South American nations as a way of reducing the isolation it has been subjected to in recent years. In turn, some of the military regimes in South America have looked with favor on a closer relationship with South Africa for similar reasons.[28]

The geographic area under consideration in the South Atlantic must necessarily be the same broad region that South American geopolitical analysts use: it ranges from the southern limits of the NATO alliance south to Antarctica, and from the eastern coast of South America to the western coast of Africa.

Historical Background

The history of the contemporary struggle for influence in the South Atlantic can be traced back to the early years of World War II, when U.S. strategic planners expressed considerable interest in the northeast bulge of Brazil and the Atlantic Narrows. The interest was based on a real concern that, with France occupied, the Germans would have access to the old French colonies in West Africa and would thus control one-half of the Atlantic Narrows. Further, with bases in West African sites such as Dakkar, it would be relatively easy to cross the Atlantic Narrows and invade the Western Hemisphere using this route. This scenario was in fact the subject of a key speech by President Roosevelt in the dark days of mid-1940, and there are indications that German geopolitical thinkers had speculated on just this possibility.[29] Even after it became obvious that Germany had neither the capability nor the desire to pursue these ambitious plans, the Atlantic Narrows still played a key role. In this new capacity the Atlantic Narrows afforded a major alternate allied supply and aircraft-ferrying route to the North African and Mediterranean theaters of World War II. In the closing years of World War II, the United States, now linked in a close alliance with Brazil, built a series of air bases in northeastern Brazil to service this air logistical route. The South Atlantic also played a role in World War II naval actions, although on a lesser scale. There was close U.S.-Brazilian naval cooperation on convoy and antisubmarine operations in the Atlantic Narrows and South Atlantic. The area saw some limited naval engagements, most notably the tracking down of the German pocket battleship *Graf Spee*, which was sunk by its captain in Uruguayan waters rather than surrender it or face overwhelming odds. The British made use of their naval support installation on the Falkland Islands during that engagement, and this served to confirm the strategic importance of those islands to the Argentines.

For the Brazilians the strong U.S. interest in the northeast bulge and the sense of partnership with the United States were important foundations for the growing currents of geopolitical thinking that were emerging in that period. In particular, there was an increasing realization of the geopolitical and strategic significance of the northeast bulge, which was referred to by the Brazilian military during the war as "Brazil's stationary aircraft carrier," the "springboard to victory," and the "corridor of the Atlantic."[30] After the war it was logical for Brazil's fledgling school of geopolitics to focus these perceptions on a growing sense of Brazilian Manifest Destiny in the South Atlantic as well as on the South American mainland.

The recent history of the search for influence in the South Atlantic focuses on the events of the mid-1970s mentioned previously. These events include the oil crisis of 1973, the increasing significance of the Southeastern Atlantic oil sea lanes, the Cuban role in Angola, and the availability of West African ports to the Soviets. The actual Soviet naval presence in the South Atlantic has in fact remained rather modest, and many analysts concluded that if the Soviets wished to cut off the West's oil supply they could do it much more efficiently in places closer to the source, such as the Persian Gulf or the Strait of Hormuz. Nevertheless, these events of the mid-1970s gave rise to a renewed interest in South Atlantic security and spawned a series of geopolitical analyses and ideas, including the first serious proposals for a South Atlantic Treaty Organization.

The idea of a SATO was discussed at one of the periodic Inter-American Naval Conferences, which by coincidence was held in Brazil in 1976 shortly after the Cuban intervention in Angola. The discussions at the conference were never publicly released, but enough details leaked to permit considerable speculation (some of it rather wild) in the South American press. The basic SATO concept stemmed from the obvious fact that the NATO southern boundary was the tropic of Cancer and that therefore the Atlantic south of that line was not covered by any Western alliance or treaty structure. It should be pointed out that the Inter-American Treaty of Reciprocal Assistance, or Rio Treaty, does not extend significantly into the South Atlantic and in any case is not structured as an alliance like NATO. The political problem that emerged from any discussion of SATO was that it would have to include South Africa because of the proximity of the oil sea lanes to the Cape of Good Hope. However, any country (Brazil being the most obvious example) that valued its oil and trade links to African nations such as Nigeria could not afford to enter into alliances with the pariah state of South Africa. This dilemma led to heated internal discussions in the Brazilian government, with the navy taking a pro-SATO position, while the Foreign Ministry and important business and trade interests argued for the need to protect the access to oil. In the end prudence won out, and the idea of a SATO was quietly shelved, although it is revived from time to time by Southern Cone geopolitical analysts, particularly those who represent a naval line of thinking.[31]

Despite the failure of a SATO, the South Atlantic does have a subregional organization that permits some degree of coordination of strategic matters. This institution, the South Atlantic Maritime Regional Command (called CAMAS for its Spanish initials), is made up of Argentina, Brazil, Paraguay, and Uruguay. In practice it is a vehicle for Brazilian-Argentine naval and maritime shipping coordination and does not extend its influence much beyond the coastal sea lanes. There is also a Southwest Atlantic regional ecological and fishing commission involving these same countries.[32]

Recent Developments

The most significant recent development concerning the South Atlantic and its security has been the Falklands/Malvinas conflict and its aftermath, which includes linkages between the region and the Antarctic.

Several sources have focused attention on the fateful trip that General Leopoldo Galtieri made to Washington in late 1981 to attend the Fourteenth Conference of American Armies at Fort McNair. There is no indication that, during this meeting, any U.S. official encouraged him to believe that the United States would help Argentina recover the Malvinas, but this is apparently the impression he returned with.[33] Some Argentine sources view the Galtieri trip differently, seeing it as a sort of a trap set by the United States in collusion with Great Britain. Thus, an Argentine rear admiral, writing in a Buenos Aires journal a year after the invasion of the Malvinas/Falklands,[34] suggested that the United States tricked Argentina into invading the islands and then insured Argentina's defeat by helping the British. The U.S. motivation, argued the admiral, was to obtain the islands as a NATO base in order to insure the security of the South Atlantic.

The concept of a NATO base on the British-controlled Falklands has appeared in print and discussion many times since the Argentine defeat on the islands. Led by many geopolitical and strategic analysts, this line of thinking seems eminently plausible to a good many Argentines and other Latin Americans, since it provides a logical explanation why the British were so willing to fight and why the United States was so willing to back them up and guarantee Argentina's defeat. One of the first British construction projects after their victory in June 1982 was to extend the runway at Port Stanley to accommodate larger and more powerful fighter and transport aircraft. To the British this was an economic, logistical, and military necessity imposed by the requirement to defend and supply the islands directly from Ascencion Island, inasmuch as their old access to airfields on the South American mainland was now cut off. However, to many Argentine geopoliticians, the airfield had another explanation: it was to be a NATO base from which the British and their allies could project power into the South Atlantic, the other Southern Islands, and ultimately the Antarctic.[35]

One Argentine reaction to this prospect has been to revive the concept of collective regional security in the South Atlantic. Thus, while on a visit to Rio de Janeiro to express the Argentine navy's appreciation for Brazilian support during the conflict, Admiral (and junta member) Jorge Anaya suggested a pact between Argentina, Brazil, and Uruguay for the defense of the South Atlantic.[36]

Type of Conflict and Military Implications

The South Atlantic conflict includes both influence and resource issues. The influence element involves the projection of power into this large region, which does not fall under any treaty or security arrangements. For the superpowers this is a remote area of little intrinsic importance other than the oil sea lanes in the eastern portion and the access routes to the Antarctic and between the Atlantic and Pacific Oceans (Strait of Magellan and Drake Passage). To the regional states, especially Argentina and Brazil, the influence issue has an obviously much higher priority, and Argentina in particular considers it a "vital" national interest, since Argentina defines its own nationality in terms of sovereignty in the South Atlantic, the islands, and Antarctica.

The resource elements of the South Atlantic conflict are not so well defined. For the United States and Western Europe, the "resource" of greatest interest is the sea lane that carries Persian Gulf oil around the Cape of Good Hope and up the western coast of Africa. Fishing, seabed, and other maritime resources are of far less importance. For the South American littoral states (Brazil, Argentina, and Uruguay), the resource implications are greater, but still not significant.

The military implications of the South Atlantic can be seen from several perspectives. For the superpowers it is of secondary priority, although it could become an area of confrontation over sea lanes or Antarctic access. For the subregional littoral powers it is an important arena in which to project power in an attempt to secure expanded exclusive economic zones and improve their Antarctic claims. The navies, in particular, have a strong vested interest in focusing national attention into these areas since it gives them a justification for expanding their roles and their budget and equipment demands.

Relationship to Other Conflicts

The South Atlantic conflict situation has linkages to a number of other conflicts:

To the Malvinas/Falklands conflict by virtue of Argentine perceptions that the southwestern part of the Atlantic is an integral part of their national territory, and by British perceptions that they continue to hold sovereignty over the islands.

To the struggle for presence and influence in Antarctica because of the way the South Atlantic controls access to some of the more desirable and important sections of Antarctica, most notably the Antarctic Peninsula (Palmer Peninsula).

To the Argentine-Chilean Beagle Channel dispute due to the bi-oceanic principle under which Argentina will strongly resist any perceived Chilean penetration into the South Atlantic.

To superpower conflicts in terms of the oil sea lanes.

To law of the sea conflicts involving the extension of exclusive economic zones by littoral states of the South Atlantic region.

Relationship to Geopolitical Thinking

As suggested in Chapter 3, there is a strong link between South Atlantic strains and geopolitical thinking in the ABC countries of the Southern Cone, and most especially in Argentina. Geopoliticians in all three countries speak of their "mare nostrum," but it is in Argentine geopolitical writings that this concept is most strongly (and even vehemently) presented.

The Argentine geopolitical concern with the South Atlantic is, of course, related to its deeply held feelings about the Malvinas/Falklands and its conviction that it has sovereignty in the Antarctic sector. Argentine geopolitical thinkers, however, have gone beyond these land claims to develop a coherent and integrated vision of a Greater Argentina that controls the South Atlantic Basin. Figure 13 illustrates the scope of this "Argentine Sea" and shows how it serves to integrate mainland, insular, and Antarctic Argentina. The 1978 appearance of the book *La Atlantártida: Un Espacio Geopolítico* was a landmark in the process of presenting the concept of an integrated geopolitical region under strong Argentine influence. Its editor, Admiral Fernando Milia, refers to the "South Atlantic Basin" as an Argentine "mare nostrum" and as the "Argentine New Great Frontier." He closes the final chapter of the book with these words: "Therefore our future as a Nation is inequivocably linked to the knowledge, occupation and use we make of Atlantártida. Atlantártida is more than a neologism. It is a challenge to our capacity to fulfill the legacy given to us by our forefathers. It is the challenge to stop being merely a Country and to become a Nation."[37] Not surprisingly, Argentine naval officers enthusiastically embraced the concept and attempted to translate it into a vital national interest. They argued that, if Argentina did not take steps to project its national power into the South Atlantic effectively, then under the geopolitical "Law of Valuable Areas" other nations would get there first at Argentina's expense.[38] The Argentine concern with the South Atlantic also has a land component in terms of the empty spaces of Patagonia: Argentine

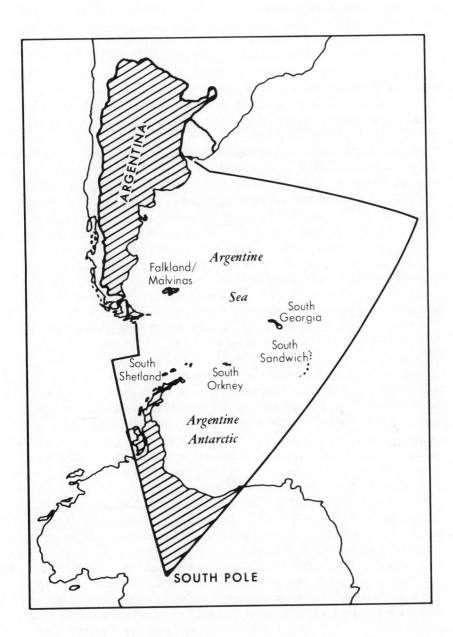

Figure 13. The "Argentine Sea."

geopoliticians are sensitive to the past history of Chilean occupation and incursions into Patagonia and argue that Argentina must occupy and develop this territory in order to make good its southern claims. For example, an editorial in *La Nación* during the Malvinas/Falklands conflict spoke of Patagonia as the "Argentine aircraft carrier in the South Atlantic" that is "fast becoming the place where our national strength is now at risk."[39]

Brazilian geopolitical thinking on the South Atlantic has two separate roots. The older one concerns itself with the Atlantic Narrows between the northeastern Brazilian "bulge" and the West African salient. This Atlantic Narrows was the subject of much analysis in the World War II period and shortly after, when its value to the Allied war effort was an important element in cementing the close Brazilian-U.S. relationship that lasted until the late 1970s. The newer and now more significant element of Brazilian geopolitical thinking concerns Brazil's emerging status as a subregional power that must inevitably project that power into the South American continent, the South Atlantic, and Antarctica. The declaration of a 200-mile territorial sea and the mounting of its first Antarctic expedition are taken as indications of this projection of power. These steps have been carefully noted by Argentine geopoliticians and have also appeared in the analyses of prominent Brazilian geopolitical writers such as General Meira Mattos and Terezinha de Castro. Professor de Castro has spoken of Antarctica, the 200-mile territorial sea and Brazil's Atlantic islands as "the forward lines of Brazilian defense in the South Atlantic."[40]

In the eyes of some Argentine geopoliticians, Chile too has South Atlantic pretensions. These would extend beyond the Beagle Channel Islands to what some Chilean geopoliticians call the "Arc of the Southern Antilles" (discussed in Chapter 5). This Chilean geopolitical concept would greatly strengthen Chile's position in the Antarctic and surrounding waters while practically demolishing Argentina's claims in the same area. Although there are few Chilean geopoliticians who seriously put forward this ambitious argument, in Argentine eyes this position is consistent with their perception of Chile as an expansionist nation that has moved against Argentina in the past. The overlapping Argentine and Chilean Antarctic claims further stimulate this sense of competition between these two countries in the extreme southern portion of the South Atlantic.

Uruguay is the last of the Southern Cone nations that has expressed geopolitical interest in the South Atlantic. Considering its size and resources, its geopolitical writers have been rather ambitious in suggesting a Uruguayan role in this region. Some of its geopoliticians have even argued that Uruguay should play a part in the South Atlantic down to, and including, the Antarctic, although the more common argument is that Uruguay should work closely with Brazil and Argentina to protect the South Atlantic from foreign incursions.[41]

THE CONTROL OF ANTARCTICA

Introduction: Summary, Geography, and Parties

The conflict over control of Antarctica[42] and its resources is potentially the most complex, wide-ranging, and dangerous of all the conflicts involving the South American nations. There are a number of reasons for this situation:

1. The legal status of Antarctica is in considerable doubt. Some nations have staked out traditional sovereignty claims; others have reserved the right to do so. Still others argue that the continent and its resources should be managed on a condominium or consortium basis among the nations that have been active in its exploration. Finally, a large group of nations with little activity in the Antarctic have pressed the argument that any benefits from the continent should be for the good of all nations.

2. Traditional international law is ambiguous and not particularly helpful in putting forth any single solution acceptable to the majority of the parties involved.

3. The Antarctic Treaty, which has provided the framework for the international regime prevailing in Antarctica since 1961, is open for revision for the first time in 1991. While it is not true that the treaty "expires" in 1991, it is fair to say that a number of the parties to the treaty (as well as some who are not) feel that they must improve their bargaining position before that year, especially on the sovereignty issue. There is a real danger that discussions over treaty revisions may break down and lead to an abandonment of the treaty regime.

4. Up until the 1970s, there was little prospect that Antarctica would yield any resources worth exploiting with foreseeable technology. However, that situation is now changing, and the real or perceived presence of economically viable mineral and biological assets has drawn new attention to the Antarctic and created the possibility of a conflict over resources.

5. Both superpowers are involved in Antarctica and have a considerable economic and strategic interest in the outcome. Although the United States and the Soviet Union agree on a number of key issues in Antarctica, including the position that there should be no national sovereign territories, there is also rivalry and the potential for a superpower confrontation. By the way of illustration, it should be noted that the Soviets have placed their installations in almost all the key geographic portions of Antarctica in order to establish their presence on the continent as a whole. In a similar fashion, one of the reasons why the United States has an installation at the South Pole itself is because "The pole is highly symbolic. By being here we maintain our status as first among equals of the treaty nations and prevent the Soviets from grabbing our base."[43]

6. The Falklands/Malvinas war has raised serious doubts about the ability of interested parties to settle their Antarctic disputes by peaceful means. There is a strong suspicion that one of the geopolitical motives for Argentina's invasion of the islands was to strengthen its Antarctic claim, and that one of the reasons for Britain's strong response was to protect its own claim. Further, the strategically and economically important Antarctic Peninsula is the site of overlapping sovereignty claims by the three states (Argentina, Chile, and Great Britain) that are most likely to reach armed confrontation over disputes in this area. Figure 14 shows the extent of these three claims and their geographic relation to the South American mainland and the Southern Islands.

7. Geopolitical writing and discussion in Argentina and Chile has been especially adamant about protecting these countries' Antarctic rights. In the last few years, Brazilian geopolitical analysts have joined the battle with a novel argument that would provide a piece of Antarctica for most of the Southern Cone nations, to the detriment of traditional Argentine and Chilean claims.

The physical, biological, and political geography of Antarctica is unique.[44] The continent has a surface area of approximately 13.5 million square kilometers (9 percent of the earth's surface and larger than the United States) and

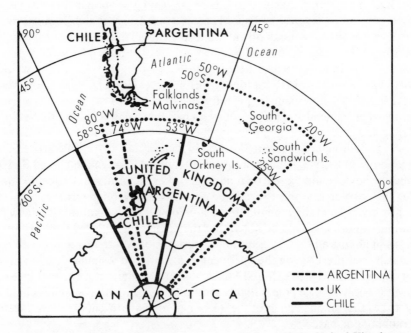

Figure 14. Antarctic claims of Argentina, Chile, and the United Kingdom.

yet has only about 2 percent of this surface area free from ice. Antarctica holds about 90 percent of all the world's ice, and were this to melt the oceans would rise approximately 60 meters. Since Antarctica consists of a circumpolar land mass, it is a mirror image of the Arctic, which is a circumpolar ocean surrounded by continents. Although there is no "Antarctic Ocean," some geographers refer to a "Southern Ocean," which consists of the portions of the South Atlantic, South Pacific, and Indian Ocean south of the Antarctic Convergence (about 60 degrees south latitude). The single most prominent topographical feature is the Antarctic Peninsula, which juts out toward South America and comes to within a few hundred miles of it across the strategically important Drake Passage. Physical conditions of temperature, darkness, and wind are extreme in Antarctica and make it the only continent with no indigenous human settlement. Human existence on Antarctica is possible only at considerable expense and isolation during the long polar winter. The biological chains that do exist are few, fragile, and closely tied to the sea.

The political regime in Antarctica is governed by the 1959 Antarctic Treaty, which came into effect in 1961. The treaty provides a useful way of categorizing the different parties involved in the control of Antarctica:[45]

1. Original consultative parties. These were the 12 nations that signed the Antarctic Treaty in the 1959–61 period. They were the countries that had the background of historical presence in Antarctica (i.e., discovery and early exploration) or subsequent activity in the 1957–58 Antarctic International Geophysical year. Although their status with regard to claims varies from country to country, they see themselves as the principal powers in any decision regarding the continent. These nations are Argentina, Chile, the United Kingdom, United States, Belgium, France, Norway, South Africa, the Soviet Union, Japan, Australia, and New Zealand.

2. Later consultative parties. These were the nations that signed the treaty after 1961 and were able to meet the treaty's requirement that they engage in substantial scientific research activity (at considerable cost and effort) and thus become consultative parties. Only Poland and the Federal Republic of Germany are in the category of later consultative parties. The total number of full consultative parties as of early 1984 thus stands at 14.

3. Acceding parties. These countries signed the treaty but have not met the requirements of scientific research activity to become consultative parties. These signatories include Rumania, Czechoslovakia, the Netherlands, Denmark, the German Democratic Republic, Brazil, Bulgaria, Uruguay, and India. These 9 acceding parties and the 14 consultative nations add up to 23 treaty signatories as of mid-1984.

4. Claimants. These are the nations that filed or declared Antarctic sovereignty claims prior to signing the treaty, which placed a 30-year moratorium on any new such claims. The seven claimant states are all original consultative

members: Argentina, Chile, the United Kingdom, Norway, France, Australia, and New Zealand. There are a number of anomalies and curious relationships between the claimant states. As indicated before, three claims overlap on the Antarctic Peninsula (those of Great Britain, Argentina, and Chile). The nations that formally recognize each other's claims are Australia, France, New Zealand, Norway, and the United Kingdom. Argentina and Chile recognize each other's right to claim but avoid acknowledging the limits of each others' claims by mutual understanding. The remaining consultative and acceding nations do not recognize these claims, although some (notably the United States and the Soviet Union) reserve the right to make claims in the future.

In the years since the signing of the Antarctic Treaty, there has been a growing feeling that the continent should not be the exclusive preserve of claimants or parties to the Antarctic Treaty alone. Rather, it should be the patrimony of all nations under some sort of international and all-inclusive regime, similar to that proposed for the oceans and outer space. The treaty members, and especially the claimant states, have been adamantly opposed to such proposals. This aspect of the conflict over Antarctica and its resources can potentially lead to some very strange international political bedfellows, such as the United States and the Soviet Union allied against the claimants, or Third World treaty signatories confronting the rest of the Third World over the patrimony issue. There are also possible ad hoc bilateral alliances such as Great Britain and Chile, or Argentina and the Soviet Union, or Chile and the People's Republic of China.

The individual Latin American positions[46] also show a considerable diversity that seems to contradict proclamations of Western Hemisphere solidarity and cooperation. Argentina and Chile as claimants and original consultative parties have the strongest positions in Antarctica, although there is tension between them generated by the overlapping claim and other differences. At the same time, they have cooperated in rejecting other claims and in opposing condominium or internationalization arrangements for the Antarctic. In both countries the issue of their Antarctic claims and rights are deeply grounded in the geopolitical writings and discussions prevalent there. The Latin American newcomer to the Antarctic scene is Brazil, whose geopolitical doctrines in this connection have now found operational reality in the expedition mounted in 1982. Two Brazilian geopoliticians (Therezinha de Castro and General Carlos de Meira Mattos) have developed and proposed the so-called frontage theory (*defrontação* in Portuguese). Under this theory each South American nation with unobstructed meridians to the South Pole would receive an Antarctic sector corresponding to those meridians, as illustrated in Figure 2. This would create a "South American Antarctic Sector" that would deny the rights of outside claimants, most notably Great Britain. The frontage theory has a certain appeal to countries such as Uruguay, Peru, and

Ecuador, which would get a piece of Antarctica under its distribution, but the theory is vehemently resisted in Chile and Argentina, which would have to give up large portions of their present claims.

Historical Background

The early history of Antarctica[47] is one of discovery, exploration, and adventure, with little concern for sovereignty, strategic significance, or exploitation of resources. In the nineteenth century the waters surrounding Antarctica saw considerable economic activity based on sealing and whaling, but there were no attempts to establish settlements or lay claims. There was an increase in Antarctic activity at the turn of the century, and during this period various Argentine governments proclaimed that Antarctica was part of Patagonia. However, the first formal claim was made by Great Britain in 1908 on the basis of early exploration; portions of this claim were later ceded to the Commonwealth nations of New Zealand and Australia. Hitler had dispatched a seaplane catapault ship to Antarctica in 1938, and to forestall a possible German claim Norway made its own claim in 1939, as did France. Argentina and Chile followed soon afterward in 1940 and 1943 respectively, basing their arguments on early exploration, the 1493 Papal Bull, and the Treaty of Tordesillas the following year.

With the advent of aviation and the tracked vehicle, it was possible to safely cover much greater areas of Antarctica than before. The technology of aviation, in particular, permitted U.S. expeditions in this period to explore most of the remaining parts of the continent. The possible military and geopolitical implications of Antarctica began to emerge after World War II, when the Soviets established their network of installations, and when the U.S. Navy mounted the largest expedition ever sent to Antarctica (4,000 men and 13 ships, including an aircraft carrier). In 1948 tensions rose as the British, Chileans, and Argentines sent military forces to the area where their claims overlapped, and there was at least one shooting incident involving British and Argentines on the Antarctic ice. In this period there was a growing appreciation of the strategic significance of the Antarctic Peninsula and the 700-mile wide Drake Passage separating it from the South American mainland.

The emphasis shifted to scientific experimentation and exploration with the International Geophysical Year of 1957–58. This proved to be a turning point in the history of Antarctica when the spirit of international scientific cooperation carried over into negotiations for the Antarctic Treaty. The treaty, which entered into force in 1961, provided for a moratorium on any new territorial claims (although it did not deny or recognize any prior claims); it also established that the Antarctic would be used solely for peaceful, scientific, and research purposes, banned any nuclear explosions or dumping of radioactive wastes, and provided for an inspection system, exchange of information, and periodic consultative meetings. Although the treaty itself has no expiration date, it does provide for a basic review at the end of the 30-year moratorium period, which comes due in 1991. Thus, those nations that have claims can be expected to take steps to reassert them toward the end of that period, and the nations that deny the possibility of claims can be expected to strengthen their arguments against them. Despite its many positive aspects, the treaty failed to make adequate provisions for the management and distribution of any mineral and biological resources, apparently because it was not foreseen in 1959 that this would be a contentious issue in the future. Thus, there is also considerable pressure building up among the treaty signatories to resolve this issue before the 1991 date is reached and before the nonsignatory countries can impose some sort of internationalization of Antarctic resources and territories.

Recent Developments

Recent developments in the Antarctic controversy have concentrated on the impact of the Falklands/Malvinas conflict and the early preparations for the 1991 review of the Antarctic Treaty. On the British side there has apparently been a reevaluation of its Antarctic policy, especially as it relates to the Falklands and the other Southern Islands. There is a special concern over the cost of a large permanent military garrison on the Falklands and the implications of confrontations with Argentina in the same area or farther south.[48] Despite the war and continued hostility between Argentina and Great Britain, both countries sent representatives to Antarctic Treaty consultative meetings in 1983-84 at Wellington, Bonn, and Washington. These meetings focused on the issue of mineral resources but made little progress.[49]

Government statements and press commentary in Argentina continued to relate the Malvinas/Falklands conflict to the Antarctic issue, casting aspersions on British motivations and suggesting in some cases that Argentina was the victim of a British-United States (or British-Chilean) conspiracy to deprive Argentina of its Antarctic rights along with the islands. An October 1983 commentary in *La Prensa* of Buenos Aires spoke of a report that "London and Santiago have harmonized their positions regarding future negotiations over the Antarctic which will have a negative impact on the Argentine territorial claim in the zone."[50] The Argentines also watched with interest the activities of the Brazilians in the Antarctic and far southern waters.

The Brazilians mounted their first independent Antarctic expedition using two naval vessels in the 1982-83 summer season, placing the Brazilian flag on Antarctic ice for the first time in January 1983 (the Brazilians had accompanied Chilean expeditions in the past). The broader significance of Brazil's Antarctic activities was not lost on its politicians or journalists, as indicated by a commentary in a São Paulo newspaper: "Brazil needs to go to the region before 1991. That is the expiration date of the period set by the Washington Treaty of 1961 to begin negotiations about who really has rights in the Antarctic. The countries that have not sent at least one expedition by 1991 will automatically be shut out of the negotiating table, and the Antarctic has a practically immeasurable economic and politico-military strategic potential."[51] The first Brazilian expedition was not without incident; it was intercepted by both Argentine warships and British fighter aircraft before it reached Antarctic waters.[52]

Other nations have also begun or continued their Antarctic activities in recent years. India sent its first expedition in early 1983, establishing a camp on what was called "the Southern Ganges" in honor of the geologic theory that holds that the Antarctic and India were once joined together in the continent of Gondwana. The Antarctic activity of India (and its signing of the treaty) raised some interesting questions as to whether India was operating in the Antarctic on its own or as a representative of the Third World nations that were not members of the "Antarctic Club."[53] Other countries that stepped up their interest in Antarctica included the People's Republic of China (which sent representatives with Chilean and New Zealand expeditions), the Federal Republic of Germany (which mounted a major expedition at a reported cost of $100 million, Cuba (whose representative joined a Soviet expedition), and Peru (whose Antarctic Studies Institute was attempting to arouse public and government interest in the area).

The growing interest of the Third World in Antarctica, and the resentment over exclusion from the "Antarctic Club," found an outlet in the 1983 General Assembly session of the United Nations, where the topic was discussed and aroused the opposition of several treaty signatories. In the end, the Third World initiative was relegated to a study group that would report back with its findings, thus practically assuring further controversy.[54]

Type of Conflict and Military Implications

The Antarctic conflict involves issues of influence, territory, and resources, but in ways that reflect the unique nature of the continent. To all the acceding states except the seven claimants, the basic conflict is for influence and the ability to project political and military power on the continent. The influence conflict extends beyond Antarctica itself to those international arenas where the fate of the continent is to be decided. The nonclaimant states also have a strong interest in preventing the claimants from making good their sovereignty or in staking viable claims themselves. This is especially true for the United States, which has very strong grounds for claims on the basis of extensive discovery, exploration, presence, and scientific work.

For the claimant states the issue is different. They must not only defend their claim from the nonclaimant treaty signatory states, but also from the rest of the world's nations that are not part of the treaty. The most aggressive of the seven claimant states are Argentina and Chile, which strongly feel that their claims have a variety of solid foundations and that their proximity makes it impossible in the long run to accept anything but sovereignty. The especially dangerous element in the Antarctic at present is the triple overlap of Chilean, Argentine, and British claims on the Antarctic Peninsula. If the poisoned state of Argentine-British relations continues, it is unlikely that a peaceful Antarctic compromise could be worked out, and this raises the possibility of a quick attempt to ensure sovereignty on the part of Argentina after the 1991 benchmark is reached. Of the other claimants, neither Norway nor France is likely to regard its claim as being vital to its national interest and could probably be persuaded to make concessions favoring either the status quo, condominium, or internationalization. The same would also probably hold true, although with a lesser degree of certainty, for New Zealand and Australia.

The resource dimension of the Antarctic controversy has been more prominent in recent years, but there is still much uncertainty about the value and exploitability of the resources.[55] One resource that is presently being exploited in limited quantities is krill, a variety of small shrimp with exceptional food value. The significance of Antarctic krill reserves can be seen from the fact that one single enormous school of these shrimp spotted in 1981 was estimated to represent about one-seventh of the total world catch of fish and shellfish in one year.[56] Although obviously abundant, there is some concern about excessive fishing of krill since it is at the base of a number of delicate Antarctic and sub-Antarctic food chains involving fish, whales, penguins, and seals. The geology of Antarctica suggests the presence of extensive hydrocarbon deposits, and some estimates have run as high as 45 billion barrels of recoverable oil and 3.3 trillion cubic meters of gas.[57] However, extracting these hydrocarbons would be exceedingly dangerous and expensive, especially if the nation doing it did not have a land support base close by. The morphology of Antarctic strata is similar to that of the Southern Cones of South America and South Africa (suggesting that the thesis of a single continent of Gondwana may be valid), and this in turn has led to speculation that Antarctica may contain minerals similar to those on nearby land masses. This could include copper, cobalt, chromium, iron, and uranium. One last mineral that is sometimes overlooked is the ice locked up in the massive Antarctic cap and surrounding bergs. Despite the perception, and in some cases the reality, of important resources in Antarctica, for the moment the exploitation of these resources is uneconomical and unlikely until basic political and sovereignty issues are resolved. However, the perception that valuable resources are present, even if they would be economically exploitable only in the distant future, fuels interest in the area and adds a resource dimension to the conflict possibilities.

The military implications of Antarctica, at least from the South American perspective, are primarily concerned with location and access from the Pacific to the Atlantic Ocean through the Drake Passage. This transoceanic passage would greatly increase in significance should the Panama Canal be closed. The possibility of trans-Antarctic air routes has been frequently suggested, especially by Argentine sources, but the traffic involved is not particularly significant, and there is not likely to be much change in this situation in the future. The Antarctic also lends itself to some specialized military applications, such as monitoring of communications and satellite traffic, and the installation of very low frequency antennas required for communications with submerged submarines.

Any military operations in Antarctica would be at the mercy of the incredibly severe weather conditions prevalent for most of the year. Except for a very brief period during the Antarctic summer, such operations would probably be mainly naval and at perhaps some distance from the Antarctic mainland. This would not, however, preclude incidents between the small contingents manning the permanent installations on the continent, such as occurred in 1952 when an Argentine detachment fired a machine gun at a British team unloading supplies at Hope Bay.[58]

Relationship to Other Conflicts

The conflict for control of Antarctica and its resources is linked to a number of other conflicts, including several involving extrahemispheric states. Among them:

1. The Southern Andean conflict between Chile and Argentina over the Beagle Channel Islands and influence in the South Atlantic.

2. The Falklands/Malvinas conflict. For Great Britain there is much value in having the Falklands (as well as South Georgia and the other Southern Islands) as a logistical base for Antarctic operations and to strengthen its overall claims to sovereignty in this area. Argentina does not require the Malvinas as an Antarctic base but realizes the need to deny them to its adversaries for this purpose, as well as to strengthen and protect its tricontinental unity.

3. The drive for influence in the South Atlantic. As the land mass between the southern portions of three major oceans (Atlantic, Pacific, and Indian), the Antarctic is linked to regional and superpower attempts to project power in these areas.

4. Argentine-Brazilian rivalry. With Brazil now establishing a presence in the Antarctic and proposing the frontage theory of Antarctic claims, the continent has become one more theater for Argentine-Brazilian competition.

This competition also involves several other states of South America, especially since the Brazilian theory proposes a much smaller sector for Argentina in order to provide portions of Antarctica to Uruguay, Peru, and Ecuador.

5. U.S.-Soviet rivalry in terms of competition for Antarctic resources or bases. It should be noted, however, that as superpowers the United States and the Soviet Union have generally been in agreement on Antarctic issues.

In addition to the above problems, the Antarctic Treaty regime itself tends to create two other conflicts. The first pits claimant states against nonclaimants. There is a possibility that claimant and nonclaimant signatories of the Antarctic Treaty may form ad hoc coalitions to defend their respective positions as the 1991 revision date for the treaty approaches. Argentina and Chile have already shown a tendency to coordinate their policies in this respect, despite the substantial overlap of their Antarctic Peninsula claims.

The second conflict aggravates North versus South relations. Because most of the treaty signatories are from the industrialized North, the treaty regime is frequently seen as a "rich nation's club" that deliberately excludes the rest of the world. Although there are some anomalies in this generalization (most notably Argentina, Chile, and India), there are signs of a North-South confrontation over the issue of Antarctic resources before 1991.

Relationship to Geopolitical Thinking

The subject of Antarctica and the concern over possible conflicts involving it are major themes in the geopolitical literature of the Southern Cone of South America. This is especially true for Argentina and Chile, the two nations closest to Antarctica and the only two Latin American claimant states. In Brazil, an acceding state, the themes are more recent and less significant but are still important elements in the contemporary geopolitical doctrine of that country. They were also key elements in raising Brazilian consciousness of Antarctica to the point of acceding to the treaty and mounting the first expedition in 1982. The Brazilian geopolitical frontage theory has also served to arouse the interest of geopolitical analysts in Uruguay, Peru, and Ecuador, who have written on how the theory would apply to their countries' share of Antarctica. Some common themes have emerged from these different national geopolitical approaches, including the need to protect an "American" or "Latin American" Antarctica from exploitation by outside powers.

For Argentine geopolitical writers, the subject of Antarctica is not only linked to tricontinental Argentina, but also to Atlantártida, national sovereignty, patriotism, and pride. This is a particularly touchy combination after the humiliating defeat of the Malvinas/Falklands conflict. The Argentine National Antarctic Directorate has professors of Antarctic geopolitics on its staff. Through the media, maps, and postage stamps (see Figure 15) and the

Figure 15. Argentine stamp showing its Antarctic sector. (Photo by the author.)

centralized educational system, Argentines are constantly taught and remind-
ed that there is an Argentine Antarctic just as much as there are Argentine
Malvinas. The need to assert Argentine rights in the Argentine Sea, islands,
and Antarctica is linked to dreams and national projects of Argentine greatness, as the following quotations suggest:

> A transcendant national objective is, without a doubt, the defense of our
> Antarctic rights. At the present international juncture it is essential to
> increase national power and strengthen our presence in the international
> community in order to confront with some success the tendency to in-
> ternationalize the Antarctic. . . . To consolidate our presence in the Ant-
> arctic and obtain the recognition of our rights will be the difficult task
> of the decade and constitutes a challenge to the Argentine vocation for
> greatness.[59]

I, and our youth, have a great responsibility. The Argentine (Antarctic) sector is in danger, we find ourselves alone, the Antarctic Treaty will be revised in 1991, and I have no doubt that on that date we will know how to fight to defend our legacy into which our predecessors poured life, sacrifices and struggles. . . . "[60]

In short, if Argentina had done nothing to occupy the Malvinas, they would soon have become the site for British, Russian, or U.S. military bases which, because they would have been immensely more powerful than the little British garrison sent home on the 2nd of April, would have prevented Argentina from exercising its dominion not only over the islands but also throughout the Argentine Sea and in Antarctica. As we have seen, this would represent the loss of a vast geopolitical and economic potential for Argentina.[61]

The Antarctic theme appears in Chilean geopolitical writings in a manner similar to that of Argentina, but with less emotion and less bombastic rhetorical linkages to "greatness." Chilean geopolitical writing has always had a strong naval and oceanic element, especially in terms of projecting power in the southwestern Pacific, the transoceanic passages (Magellan and Drake), and to the Antarctic. These themes were prevalent in the writings of General Cañas Montalva, who argued that Chile as the southernmost nation in the world had an unquestioned geographic continuity from the South American mainland to its claimed Antarctic territory.[62] The theme of Chilean rights in the Antarctic has been the subject of numerous geopolitical writings, especially in the 1940s and 1950s when Chile was pressing its Antarctic claim. Under the Pinochet regime the renaissance of Chilean geopolitical thinking has included a strong reassertion of the geopolitical basis for its Antarctic claims. Although there is much appeal to nationalism and history in the Antarctic claim, which is traced back to the writings of national independence hero Bernardo O'Higgins, there is also a shrewd assessment of important resources at stake for Chile, especially the possibility of finding the oil and gas that it so badly needs.[63]

Brazilian geopolitical interest in Antarctica is rather recent and is based on the ideas and writings of Therezinha de Castro. Her unique contribution was the adaptation of the sector principle that had been proposed by a Canadian geographer as a way of defining Arctic sovereignty. Her map of the frontage sector concept (see Figure 2) shows why this concept is so appealing to Brazilian geopoliticians: it gives Brazil the largest of the South American sectors, substantially reduces the Argentine sector, and provides sectors to all the other South American nations that have an unobstructed projection to the pole. This map was later included in an official atlas by the Brazilian Ministry of Education, although the Brazilian government has stopped short of any statement that this sector principle represents a Brazilian claim or formal position. Other Brazilian geopoliticians such as General Meira

Mattos and Professor Pericles Azambuja have echoed de Castro's ideas and expanded on them. De Castro herself in a later work linked the frontage theory to Brazil's strategic responsibilities as an emerging regional power with a mission to defend the South Atlantic area.[64]

As might be expected, Argentine geopolitical writers vehemently reject the frontage theory and ascribe the most cynical of motives to Brazil's Antarctic interest. The Argentines have suggested variously that Brazil is motivated by its drive for energy, by U.S. business or diplomatic interests, or as the ally of either Chile or Great Britain. In a sarcastic article in *Estrategia*, Carlos Mastrorilli argued that Brazil had an "evident anti-Argentine intention" as shown by its support of Chilean claims and its attempt to appeal to the dormant Antarctic aspirations of Uruguay, Peru, and Ecuador.[65] Geopolitical writers in these three countries did in fact pick up Brazil's frontage concept and used it to produce a series of articles supporting their own national sectors.[66]

NOTES

1. The Falklands/Malvinas conflict has generated a considerable volume of literature. Among the works that focus on the geopolitical and strategic factors of interest to this analysis are the following: Virginia Gamba, *Malvinas Confidencial* (Buenos Aires: Publinter, 1982); Jozef Goldblat, *The Falklands/Malvinas Conflict: A Spur to Arms Buildups* (Stockholm: SIPRI, 1983); Pablo J. Hernández, *Malvinas: Clave Geopolítica* (Buenos Aires: Castaneda, 1982); Gregorio Selser, *Reagan entre El Salvador y Las Malvinas* (Mexico: Editorial Mex-Sur, 1982); Jorge Alvarez Cardier, *La Guerra de las Malvinas: Enseñanzas para Venezuela* (Caracas: Editorial Enfoque, 1982).

2. The historical background can be found in Raphael Perl, *The Falklands Islands Dispute in International Law and Politics* (New York: Oceana, 1983).

3. Eduardo van der Kooy, "Malvinas," *Estrategia* no. 59 (July 1979): 37.

4. Juan E. Guglialmelli, "El Futuro de las Islas Malvinas," *Estrategia* nos. 43–44 (November 1976): 10.

5. Argentina, *Revista Militar* no. 704 (April–June 1981).

6. Ibid. See also *Revista Militar* no. 703 (January–March 1981).

7. Christopher Dobson, *The Falklands Conflict* (London: Coronet Books, 1982), p. 10.

8. *La Prensa*, January 24, 1982, p. 1, in *FBIS*, February 2, 1982, p. B-1.

9. *La Nación*, March 2, 1982, p. 1. See also Manfredo Schonfeld, *La Guerra Austral* (Buenos Aires: Desafío Editores, 1983), pp. 11–20.

10. *Buenos Aires Herald*, May 5, 1983, and June 16, 1983.

11. *La Prensa*, October 11, 1983 in *FBIS*, October 13, 1983.

12. *La Nación*, November 1 and 3, 1982; *Buenos Aires Herald*, June 30, 1983.

13. *EFE, Buenos Aires*, September 15, 1983 in *FBIS*, September 19, 1983; *La Nación*, November 5, 1982, and November 26, 1982; *Washington Post*, September 21, 1982; *Excelsior*, August 4, 1982.

14. *Washington Post*, November 10, 1982; *La Nación*, May 29, 1983, and December 23, 1982; *Excelsior*, January 13, 1983.

15. See, for example, Argentina, Air Force, special edition of *Aerospacio* no. 429 (September 1982); Her Majesty's Stationery Office, *The Falklands Campaign; The Lessons*, report to Parliament by the Secretary of State for Defence, December 1982; U.S. Navy, *Lessons of*

the Falklands (Washington, D.C.: Department of the Navy, February 1983); Goldblat, *Falklands/ Malvinas Conflict.*

16. *Christian Science Monitor,* January 12, 1983, p. 4; *La Nación,* November 24, 1982; *COHA-Washington Report on the Hemisphere,* April 19, 1983; Goldblat, *Falklands/Malvinas Conflict,* pp. 21-23.

17. *Philadelphia Inquirer,* May 10, 1983, p. 13; *Washington Post,* June 7, 1982, p. C-15. Goldblat, *Falklands/Malvinas Conflict,* pp. 16-18.

18. *Washington Post,* May 9, 1982, p. A-16. For a Guyanese reaction, see *CANA, Georgetown,* May 2, 1982, in *FBIS,* May 7, 1982, p. T-1.

19. Personal conversation with ex-President Julio Cesar Turbay Ayala, Washington, D.C., December 1983. *El Espectador* (Bogota), April 6, 1982 in *JPRS,* May 20, 1982.

20. Osiris Villegas, "Las Malvinas: Pleito Improrogable," *Geopolítica* no. 24 (1982): 53.

21. Juan E. Guglialmelli, "Islas Malvinas," *Estrategia* nos. 67-68 (November 1980–February 1981): 16-17; Armando Lambruschini, "Disertación del Comandante en Jefe de la Armada," *Estrategia* no. 69 (1981): 134-35.

22. Osiris Villegas, "No Ataco–Impugno," *Geopolítica* no. 23 (December 1981): 11.

23. Juan E. Guglialmelli quoted in *Clarín* (Buenos Aires), February 1, 1983, p. 10, in *FBIS,* February 8, 1983, p. B-2. *Bahía Blanca, DYN,* December 15, 1982, in *FBIS,* December 16, 1982, p. B-4.

24. "Las Islas Malvinas: Un Camino Inglés a la Antártida," *La Nación* (Buenos Aires), April 21, 1982.

25. Therezinha de Castro, "El Atlántico" in *Geopolítica y Relaciones Internacionales,* ed. Luis Dallanegra Pedraza (Buenos Aires: Pleamar, 1981), p. 57.

26. Vicente E. Palermo, "Latinoamérica Puede Más" in *La Atlantártida: Un Espacio Geopolítico,* ed. Fernando A. Milia (Buenos Aires: Pleamar, 1978), pp. 186-88. For a Soviet perspective, see L. Teplov, "Imperialist Plans for the South Atlantic," *International Affairs* (Moscow) no. 7 (July 1977): 92-100. For U. S. views, see Kenneth E. Roberts, *U.S. Defense and the South Atlantic,* Strategic Studies Institute, U.S. Army War College, Carlisle, Pa., December 1976.

27. For various perspectives, see Juan E. Guglialmelli, "Golbery do Couto e Silva: El Destino Manifiesto Brasileño y el Atlántico Sur," *Estrategia* no. 39 (March 1976): 5-24; Recaredo Lebrato Suarez, "Destino Geopolítico de la República Oriental del Uruguay," *Estrategia* nos. 49-50 (November 1977–February 1978): 61; "Estrategia del Brasil en el Atlántico," *La Nación,* May 19, 1982); Therezinha de Castro, *Atlas-Texto de Geopolítica do Brasil* (Rio: Capemi Editores, 1982); Bernardo Quagliotti de Bellis, *Geopolítica del Atlántico Sur* (Montevideo: Fundación de Cultura Universitaria, 1976).

28. Daniel Waksman Schinca, "Sudafrica, el Cono Sur, y la Mentalidad Bunkeriana," *Cuadernos de Marcha* (May–June 1979): 98, 103; Carlos J. Moneta, "Cono Sur de Africa y de América," *Geosur* fasciculo no. 9 (May 1980); Carlos J. Moneta, *Geopolítica y Política del Poder en el Atlántico Sur* (Buenos Aires: Pleamar, 1983), pp. 121-41.

29. Jack Child, *Unequal Alliance: The Inter-American Military System, 1938-1978* (Boulder, Colo.: Westview Press, 1980), p. 28.

30. Ibid., pp. 50-51, 54.

31. For a discussion of SATO, see ibid., p. 222. See also *Washington Post,* November 29, 1976; Daniel Waksman Schinca, "El Proyecto de la OTAS," *Nueva Politica* 2 (April–September 1977); da Costa in Dallanegra, op. cit., *Geopolítica* pp. 63-64.

32. Quagliotti de Bellis in Milia, *Atlantártida,* pp. 48-50.

33. Dobson, *The Falklands Conflict,* p. 10.

34. Horacio Zaratiegui, "Was the Malvinas a NATO Trap?" *Noticias Argentinas,* June 14, 1983, in *FBIS,* June 17, 1983.

35. See, for example, Virginia Gamba, "La NATO y el Atlántico Sur," *Nación,* June 1, 1982; *Diario las Américas,* January 23, 1983; *La Prensa,* July 25, 1983; *El País* (Madrid), May 26, 1982.

36. *Buenos Aires, DYN*, September 2, 1983, in *FBIS*, September 3, 1982.

37. Milia, *Atlantártida*, p. 250.

38. See, for example, the speech of Argentine Navy Commander Lambruschini, "Disertación del Comandante," p. 134.

39. *La Nación*, June 12, 1982, p. 8.

40. De Castro, *Atlas-Texto*; Carlos de Meira Mattos, "Atlantico Sul — Sua Importancia Estratégica," *A Defesa Nacional* (March 1980) no. 688, pp. 23–45.

41. Leslie Crawford, *Uruguay Atlanticense y los Derechos a la Antártida* (Montevideo: Ariel, 1974), pp. 5–9; Quagliotti de Bellis, *Geopolítica del Atlántico Sur*; see also his "Estrategia y Geopolítica en el Atlántico Sur," *Geopolítica* no. 5 (April 1978).

42. For additional information on the Antarctic, see Barbara Mitchell, "The Politics of Antarctica," *Environment* 22 (January 1980): 12–20; Barbara Mitchell, "Cracks in the Ice," *Wilson Quarterly* (Autumn 1981): 69–87; Joseph S. Roucek, "The Geopolitics of Antarctica and the Falkland Islands," *World Affairs Interpreter* 22 (April 1951): 44–56; U.S., Central Intelligence Agency, *Polar Regions Atlas* (Washington, D.C.: Government Printing Office, 1978); Edward Milenky, "Latin America and Antarctica," *Current History* 82, (February 1983); pp. 52–3, 89–90. Therezinha de Castro, *Rumo a Antartica* (Rio de Janeiro: Freitas, 1976; Deborah Shapley, "Antarctica: Up for Grabs," *Science* 82 (November 1982): 75–78; Carlos J. Moneta, "Antarctica, Latin America and the International System in the 1980s," *Journal of Inter-American Studies and World Affairs* 23 (February 1981): 29–68; F. M. Auburn, *Antarctic Law and Politics* (Bloomington: Indiana University Press, 1982); Oscar Pinochet de la Barra, *La Antártida Chilena* (Santiago: Editorial Andrés Bello, 1976); M. J. Peterson, "Antarctica: The Last Great Land Rush on Earth," *International Organization* 34 (Summer 1980): 377–403; James H. Zumberge, "Mineral Resources and Geopolitics in Antarctica," *American Scientist* 67 (January 1979): 68–77.

43. *Time*, February 22, 1982, p. 65.

44. This paragraph draws on Shapley, "Antarctica," Zumberge, "Resources and Geopolitics," and U.S., Central Intelligence Agency, *Polar Regions Atlas*.

45. For additional details see sources in note 42 above, especially Moneta, "International System"; Mitchell, "Politics of Antarctica" and "Cracks in the Ice"; and Auburn, *Antarctic Law*.

46. For the Latin American positions, see the general sources cited in note 42 above and the following national positions.

Argentina: Milia, *Atlantártida*; Eduardo de la Cruz, "Derechos Argentinos sobre la Antártida y Pretensiones Ajenas," *Estrategia* no. 3 (November 1976):60.

Chile: Pinochet de la Barra, *La Antártida Chilena*.

Brazil: de Castro, *Atlas-Texto*; Pericles Azumbuja, "Antártida: Derechos que Tiene Brasil, " *Geosur* no. 23 (July 1981).

Uruguay: Vicente Palermo, "Chile-China y algunas otras Cuestiones Antárticas," *Geopolítica* no. 13 (1979).

Peru: Arnoldo Zamora Lazo, "Proyección Peruana a la Antártida," *Geosur* no. 23 (July 1981).

Ecuador: Humbero Vera, "Derecho Territorial Ecuatoriano Sobre el Polo Sur," *Revista Geográfica Militar* (October 1981).

47. This historical account draws on Vera, "Territorial Ecuatoriano"; Mitchell, "Politics of Antarctica" and "Cracks in the Ice"; Milenky, "Latin America"; U.S., Central Intelligence Agency, *Polar Regions Atlas;* Shapley, "Antarctica"; and Auburn, Antarctic Law.

48. Peter J. Beck, "Britain's Antarctic Dimension," *International Affairs*, 59(3) (Summer 1983):429–444.

49. New Zealand, *Press Statement on Meeting on Antarctic Mineral Resources*, January 17–18, 1983; *Clarín* (Buenos Aires), July 23, 1983.

50. *La Prensa*, October 11, 1983, in *FBIS*, October 13, 1983, p. B-3.

51. *O Estado de São Paulo*, February 20, 1982, in *JPRS*, March 31, 1982.

52. *São Paulo Radio Bandeirante*, January 19, 1983, in *FBIS*, January 20, 1983, p. D-1; *Latin American Daily Post* (Rio de Janeiro) February 17, 1983, in *FBIS*, February 18, 1983, p. D-1.

53. *Washington Post*, February 1, 1983; *New York Times*, August 29, 1983; *World Press Review*, May 1982.

54. *Washington Post*, December 1, 1983, p. A-3; *El Mercurio* (Santiago), September 30, 1983, in *FBIS*, October 13, 1983; *Economist*, January 7, 1984, p. 33.

55. For a discussion of Antarctic resources, see Jorge A. Fraga, "El Futuro Incierto Político-Económico de la Antártica," *Estrategia*, no. 43 (November 1976): 36; Jose S. Campobani, "Atlántico Sudoccidental: Mar Argentino y uno de los Más Ricos e Importantes del Mundo," *La Nación*, April 2, 1982; Zumberge, "Resources and Geopolitics"; Beck, "Antarctic Dimension."

56. *Washington Post*, March 25, 1981.

57. *Washington Post*, December 1, 1983.

58. David W. Heron, "Antarctic Claims," *Foreign Affairs* 32(4) (1954): 661–667.

59. Cruz, "Derechos Argentinos," pp. 70–71.

60. José María Vaca Hernández, *Inquietudes y Realidades Antárticas: el Continente de Gondwana* (Buenos Aires: Ediciones Heraldo, 1977), p. 8. See also Jorge A. Fraga, *Introducción a la Geopolítica Antártica* (Buenos Aires: Dirección Nacional del Antártico, 1978); Vicente Palermo, "El Continente Antártico en el Contexto Internacional Contemporáneo," *Geopolítica* 5 (April 1978): 35–46.

61. Orlando Enrique Bolognani, "Por qué la Argentina ha Recuperado las Malvinas," *Revista de la Escuela de Guerra Naval* no. 642 (1982): 11.

62. Ramon Cañas Montalva, "Chile: El País más Austral de la Tierra," *Geosur* no. 23 (July 1981): 22–23.

63. Pinochet de la Barra, *La Antártida Chilena*; Emilio Meneses Ciuffardi, "Estructura Geopolítica de Chile," *Seguridad Nacional* (Chile) no. 21 (1981): esp. 142–45.

64. De Castro, *Atlas-Texto*; Carlos de Meira Mattos, *Brasil: Geopolítica e Destino*. Rio de Janeiro: Biblioteca do Exército, 1975), p. 68; Azambuja, "Antártida."

65. Carlos Mastrorilli, "Brasil y la Antartida: La tesis de Therezinha de Castro," *Estrategia* no. 43 (November 1976); Jorge Leal, "Algo mas Sobre el Petróleo y la Antártida," *Geosur* no. 22 (May 1981).

66. See, for example, Vera, *Territorial Ecuatoriano*, and Zamora Lazo, "Proyección Peruana."

7

THE SOUTH AMERICAN CARIBBEAN CONFLICTS

The conflicts involving the South American nations with a Caribbean coast have markedly different characteristics than those analyzed previously. For one, currents of geopolitical thinking are far less developed than in the Southern Cone nations, and the conflicts themselves have fewer features that can be ascribed to geopolitical thinking. Further, East-West and superpower concerns are much greater in the Caribbean area than in the Southern Cone, and Cuba plays an indirect role in several of these conflicts as a superpower surrogate. Lastly, some unusual new arms purchases and transfers in several of the countries involved in this area have given rise to concerns that, should fighting break out, it would be of a much more violent and destructive nature than in the past: the flow of Soviet bloc arms to Nicaragua and (before the October 1983 invasion) to Grenada and the Venezuelan purchase of advanced F-16 fighter aircraft clearly mark a departure from traditional levels of arms in this region.

NICARAGUA-COLOMBIA: SAN ANDRÉS AND PROVIDENCIA ISLANDS

Introduction: Parties, Summary, and Geography

The dispute between Colombia and Nicaragua over a series of Caribbean islands, cays, and banks is rooted in the past but has contemporary relevance in terms of ideological disputes in the Caribbean Basin. For many years this dispute was perceived as being dormant, with little probability of being revived. This complacency accounts for much of the shock felt in Colombia when the new Sandinista government in Managua in 1979 launched a diplomatic offensive to revive the issue, declare a past treaty null and void, and renew its claim to the islands and associated cays and banks. The United States was involved because of its close relationship with Colombia and the role it played in the signing of the original treaty in the 1920s. The reopening of the Nicaraguan claim also prompted Panama to state that it too had a colonial claim on the islands that should be considered. The geography of the dispute brings to mind the case of the Malvinas/Falkland Islands since the islands in question are controlled and administered by Colombia but lie much closer to Nicaraguan than Colombian coasts. The islands also have important strategic implications for Nicaragua, Colombia, Costa Rica, and Panama as well as Cuba. The dispute is further complicated by the possibility of oil in the area and the linkages to 200-mile maritime sovereignty issues.[1]

The territories under dispute (see Figure 16) include: San Andrés Island, located about 120 miles east of the Nicaraguan coast and 430 from the Colombian; Providencia Island, about 150 miles from Nicaragua and 460 from Colombia; Quitasueño Bank, due north of Providencia; Roncador Cay, due east of Providencia; and Serrana Bank, north of Roncador and East of Quitasueño. San Andrés is by far the most significant of these territories. It has recently undergone considerable development and is now an important Co-

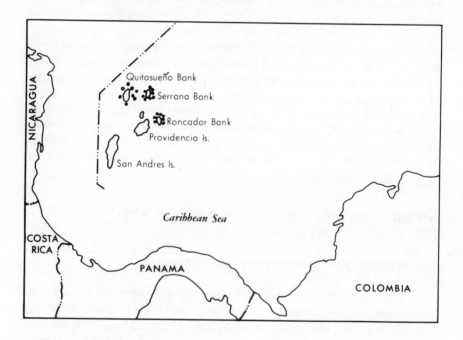

Figure 16. Islands and banks involved in the Nicaragua-Colombia dispute. (Not to scale.)

lombian resort area and free port; it is also the site of Colombian air and naval installations. The strategic significance of the islands stems from their location due east of Nicaragua, which suggests that they could be a "screen" between Nicaragua and the Caribbean. They also lie between Nicaragua and Cuba, and close to important Caribbean sea lanes leading to the Panama Canal. Should Nicaragua make good its claims, it would greatly expand its maritime boundaries and would make its maritime area one of the largest in the region.

Historical Background

A starting point for the conflicting claims of Colombian and Nicaraguan sovereignty is the colonial period when the islands were administered by the Spanish Crown through both the Viceroyalty of Nueva Granada (today Colombia) and the Capitancy-General of Guatemala (representing what is today Central America). The islands were subject to the attention of numerous pirates and travelers, and in the colonial centuries the original indigenous population was replaced by a population that was mainly black and English-speaking. In 1803 the Spanish Crown placed the islands under the administration of Bogota, and they remained under its jurisdiction until independence. Colombia bases its claim on this fact and on the reality that it has administered the islands ever since. The Nicaraguan argument, contained in their *Libro Blanco* of February 1980, rests on a later Royal Decree (of 1806) that seemingly restores control to the Capitancy-General of Guatemala.[2] The maritime boundaries of Colombia and Nicaragua were the subject of the controversial 1928 Barcenas-Esguerra Treaty, which awarded sovereignty to Colombia. However, the Sandinista government claims that the 1928 treaty was invalid because it was signed under pressure from the United States, at a time when the government in Managua had no legitimacy since it was under occupation by U.S. Marines. The Nicaraguans add that the United States was interested in giving the Colombians a "consolation prize" after losing Panama, and the simplest way to do it was to force Nicaragua to make concessions over San Andrés and Providencia. Colombia's maritime boundaries were also the subject of the 1972 Vasquez-Saccio Treaty between the United States and Colombia, which confirmed Colombia's claim over San Andrés and Providencia. This treaty languished unratified for many years in the U.S. Senate, and when it was finally ratified in July 1981 the Nicaraguan government interpreted the ratification as yet another attempt at intimidation by the United States.

Recent Developments

The immediate Colombian reaction to the Nicaraguan rejection of the 1928 treaty in late 1979 was one of disbelief and then shock. The Nicaraguan position was quickly rejected by both the Colombian government and overwhelming public and media opinion. As a precaution the Colombians moved a naval task force, a Mirage air squadron, and 500 marines to San Andrés Island. Colombians began to suspect the motives of the Nicaraguan government, and there were accusations that the Nicaraguan action was being pushed by Cuba, possibly in retaliation for Colombia's attempt to block Cuba's bid for a United Nations Security Council seat. During 1980 and 1981 relations were strained between Colombia and Nicaragua, and there were frequent clashes over the presence of Nicaraguan fishing boats near the islands.

Many Colombians saw some uncomfortable parallels between the Argentine invasion of the Malvinas/Falkland Islands in April 1982 and their strains with Nicaragua. This was one among several reasons for Colombia's very lukewarm support of Argentina and also accounts for some of Nicaragua's enthusiastic support for the Argentines. Bogota commentators spoke of the "bad example" that the use of force by Argentina set for other possible disputes in the Western Hemisphere, including their own;[3] the Colombian government responded by further reinforcing military units on San Andrés.

The Colombian position with regard to Argentina (and the United States) shifted noticeably when the new administration of Belisario Betancur took office in August 1982. There was a conscious move away from the previous close relationship with the United States and something of a repudiation of the position on the Falklands/Malvinas taken by the administration of President Julio César Turbay Ayala. A corollary to this was that relations with Nicaragua improved, and little has been heard regarding the San Andrés/Providencia issue from either Managua or Bogota since then.

Type of Conflict and Military Implications

The Nicaraguan-Colombian dispute is basically territorial (land and maritime) but also has important economic and strategic ramifications. The economic issue has to do with oil, which is badly needed by both countries. A U.S. petroleum company was licensed by the Colombians to prospect, but so far no results have been announced.

The strategic resource involved is basically the islands' location off the Nicaraguan coast. Because they are situated between Nicaragua and Cuba, the islands could provide an important military base from which to control air or maritime traffic into Nicaragua or the Panama Canal. The Colombian press has frequently speculated that U.S. interest in the islands is fueled by fears of Cuban expansion and by a desire for alternate bases from which to pressure Nicaragua. Further, there is a belief that the United States is interested in the islands out of a longer-range concern with Panama Canal security after the treaty with Panama expires in 1999.[4]

The military implications of the dispute stem from these considerations as well as the feeling in both countries that important national and superpower interests are at stake. Nicaragua has not challenged Colombia militarily and indeed has stated that it would press its claim only by peaceful means. For the moment this peaceful route is also a realistic one for the Nicaraguans, who have other pressing security concerns and have very little in the way of projectable military power with which to confront the Colombians. Colombia has a respectable military establishment by Caribbean standards. This includes a navy of 7,000, with 3,000 marines, four submarines, and numerous surface combatants; its air force relies on French Mirage fighters and U.S. AT-37s. In contrast, the Nicaraguans have only limited coastal craft and almost no combat aircraft. Although the arrival of advanced MiG aircraft in Nicaragua could quickly change the balance of forces, for the moment the Colombians have a clear military superiority despite the distances that tend to favor the Nicaraguans.

The Colombians have quite consciously linked their accelerated arms purchases to the need to defend the islands and are apparently using the purchase to send a message to the Nicaraguans that they would be serious about defending the islands with military force, if necessary. The Colombian government has also made it clear that it would not permit any foreign military bases on the islands (a thinly veiled reference to U.S. interest in such bases), but there would still exist the possibility of allowing the United States access and landing rights.

Relationship to Other Conflicts

As suggested previously, the Nicaraguan-Colombian conflict is linked to broader security concerns in the Caribbean-Central American area; that is, it includes politico-military interests of Cuba and the United States. During the period of fighting in the Falklands/Malvinas Islands, the Colombians felt somewhat isolated, and there were expressions of concern in Bogota that a Venezuelan-Nicaraguan understanding could be used to pressure Colombia because of the disputes it has with both of these countries. However, this isolation markedly diminished with the coming of the Betancur administration, and the Colombians no longer feel concern over such an unlikely understanding between Nicaragua and Venezuela.

Relationship to Geopolitical Thinking

Colombian geopolitical writings have not focused on this issue. The works of Londoño have been more concerned with Colombia's land borders and pay little attention to the islands. This is also a reflection of the general feeling in Colombia prior to 1979 that there was absolutely no question about its claim to the islands. Since 1979 there has been considerable commentary in the Colombian media, but not much of this has been in the strictly geopolitical category. Geopolitical writing in Nicaragua is not well developed, and most of the arguments made on the issue have been posed in historical and juridical terms.

COLOMBIA-VENEZUELA: THE GULF OF VENEZUELA DISPUTE

Introduction: Parties, Summary, and Geography

Relations between Colombia and Venezuela have generally shown some tension, which has tended to rise and fall depending on the specifics of the issue at hand and the relative compatibility of the governments in the two countries. Up to the late 1950s both countries had a political history of governments that were dictatorial and democratic. When both had the same type of government at a given time, relations tended to improve but tended to deteriorate if one had a democracy and the other a dictatorship. At present Colombia and Venezuela both have well-established elected regimes, and relations between the two countries have been reasonably good. A number of cooperative political and economic efforts have been taken by these two countries. These have been bilateral as well as multilateral in the context of organizations such as the Andean Pact, the Latin American Economic System (SELA), and the Contadora initiative. However, despite their political compatibility, there remains an undercurrent of some strain that is fueled at present by at least three sources of conflict: the dispute over the Gulf of Venezuela and the Los Monjes Islands; the flow of unemployed and undocumented Colombians into Venezuela; and the large-scale smuggling and drug trade that goes on along an essentially unguarded border. Of particular interest is the first of these three issues because of its links to other conflicts in the area (Nicaragua-Colombia and Venezuela-Guyana) and because of the way it draws upon geopolitical thinking for some of its arguments and foundations. The geopolitical foundation is especially influential in Venezuela.

The Gulf of Venezuela dispute is a good example of a territorial dispute that becomes far more serious when a valuable resource (in this case, oil) becomes involved. Figure 17 illustrates the area of the dispute and the maximum positions of Venezuela and Colombia regarding their maritime boundary and their claims on the Monjes Archipelago. The Gulf of Venezuela is the intermediate body of water between the oil-rich Lake Maracaibo and the open Caribbean Sea. Understandably, Venezuela is extremely sensitive concerning any territorial claim near this area, especially since there is a possibility that the Maracaibo oil formations might extend out into the Gulf of Venezuela.

Aggravating the dispute is the feeling among many Venezuelans that their country has suffered too many territorial losses in the past to its neighbors, especially during times when it was weakened by internal dissent and

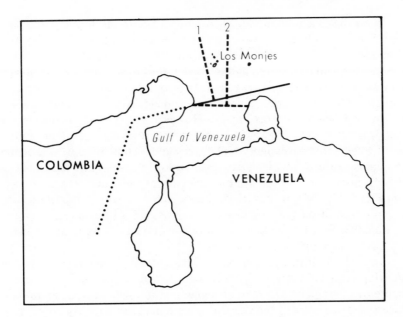

Figure 17. The Gulf of Venezuela dispute. Line 1 represents the limits recognized by Venezuela. Line 2 indicates Colombia's maximum claims.

political struggle. Venezuela today feels that it is recovering some of the greatness it had in the Bolivarian period shortly after independence in the early nineteenth century. Moreover, Venezuela believes that it now has the economic and military wherewithal to make itself respected in the region and effectively press its claims in border disputes with Colombia and Guyana.[5]

Historical Background

Strains between Venezuela and Colombia go back to colonial days and a sense of rivalry between Bogota and Caracas. Colombians tended to see (and to a certain extent still do) Venezuelans as a rather boorish, crude, undisciplined, and loud group who are more Caribbean than Andean. In recent years, with the advent of oil income, this image has also included a feeling that the Venezuelans are uncultured nouveau riche. In turn, the Venezuelans tend to see the Colombians as aloof, cold, austere, effete, and snobbish highlanders who put on airs about being more intellectual and literary than their neighbors. Commenting on the differences between these two peoples, Simón Bolívar is reputed to have said that Venezuela was a barracks and Colombia was a law court or a library.

As is the case in many South American territorial disputes, the basic problem stems from a very vague and imprecise definition of the frontiers under Spanish rule. The Guajira Peninsula area was not very attractive to the Spaniard, and population and interest in the area during the colonial period was low. The frontier between the two countries was supposedly settled in the 1941 Treaty on Border Demarcation and Navigation of Common Rivers (the Santos-López Contreras Treaty). However, many Venezuelans feel this treaty was overly generous to Colombia and represents a treasonous mutilation of Venezuelan sovereignty.[6] The areas under contention were the Guajira Peninsula (most of which was granted to Colombia) and the extension of the frontier from the Guajira into the Gulf of Venezuela. As can be seen from Figure 17, the Los Monjes Archipelago represents an important piece of territory in dispute; the nation that possesses the islands can extend its maritime frontier into the key mouth of the Maracaibo Basin and possible oil areas in the Gulf of Venezuela itself.

In the mid-1970s a long series of talks between negotiators for the two countries seemed to indicate that a final settlement of the Gulf of Venezuela dispute was imminent. However, a group of some 400 Venezuelan military officers publicly warned the Caracas government not to make concessions to the Colombians; given the past history of Venezuelan military politics, it is not surprising that this "warning" was taken seriously by the Venezuelan government, and the possible settlement was postponed.[7] Further attempts to reach a settlement in the late 1970s and early 1980s were compounded by a number of incidents when patrols from both nations strayed across the border or when Colombians residing in Venezuela complained of harassment and violence.

Compounding the territorial issue is the second source of friction: illegal immigration of Colombians into Venezuela. The border south of the Guajira Peninsula is one of the most populated frontier areas in Latin America. In contrast to typical Latin American border zones, it is not an "empty" area in which the frontier cuts through a region of low population density. This stretch of Colombian-Venezuelan border is populated by a rather homogeneous mestizo group that shares many ethnic traits and family ties with Colombians, making it relatively easy for Colombians to be assimilated when they cross. There is a significant differential in the standard of living and per capita income across the border, as well as a much higher rate of unemployment in Colombia. Further, the border area is relatively open and accessible. These elements all combine to produce a migration somewhat analogous to that along the Mexican-U.S. border, and an estimated 1.5 million undocumented Colombians live and work illegally in Venezuela.[8] Some Venezuelan employers in the border areas take advantage of the Colombians, and attempts by the Venezuelan authorities to control the flow of migrants have led to confrontations and violence on occasion.

The third element of tension has to do with historic and traditional smuggling activities along the rather porous border. In the contemporary context these have taken new life with an emphasis on drug and arms running, cattle smuggling, and kidnapping. Various guerrilla groups operating in the area profit from being able to cross national frontiers almost at will. Both Colombian and Venezuelan authorities recognize the problem and have in fact cooperated in trying to control it, but their efforts have not been up to the task, and the issue continues to irritate relations between the two countries.

Recent Developments

In October 1980 Venezuelan and Colombian negotiators managed to agree on a draft treaty that would have established a compromise position that would divide equally any oil found in the area. The draft treaty was leaked extensively to the press and was generally well received in Colombia. However, Venezuelan nationalists argued that it made too many concessions and managed to stir up enough negative public opinion to force President Herrera Campins to postpone any formal consideration of the treaty. An offer by the Latin American Bishops Council (CELAM) to mediate the issue was made in February 1981 but elicited no response. Shortly afterward the Venezuelan Supreme Court accepted a plea to nullify the 1941 Santos-López Contreras Treaty. This prospect was viewed with much concern by Colombians, who interpreted the action to mean that the Venezuelans were preparing to take a much tougher negotiating stance.[9]

Colombian concerns increased directly with the news of Venezuela's purchase of advanced fighter aircraft and indirectly with the events of April 1982 in the Malvinas/Falklands. Aggressive Venezuelan support for Argentina led many Colombians to believe that Venezuela might contemplate a similar military adventure. Further, the Colombians feared that a weakened Rio Treaty would not be an effective protection for them. In early 1983 Colombia showed signs of increasing impatience on the issue, and reports circulated that Colombia would soon place a deadline on negotiations; failure to sign a treaty in this time limit would presumably require the intervention of outside arbiters.[10] Border incidents involving troops from both countries increased concern in mid-1983.

Type of Conflict and Military Implications

The conflict is basically territorial (the maritime area in the Gulf of Venezuela) but is a resource one as well because of the possibility of oil in the area. It is also a border conflict because of the friction caused by Colombian immigration and the smuggling activities.

The military implications of the dispute stem from the fact that both countries have middle-size military establishments that are respectable in regional terms. Both countries also have other disputes that make their own military demands and create the possibility of linkages between otherwise unrelated conflicts. The Venezuelan drive to modernize their air force has resulted in a major purchase ($650 million for 24 F-16 fighter aircraft), which represents more than all the U.S. weapons sold to all of Latin America from 1970 to 1982.[11] Although the Reagan administration justified this sale on the grounds that it would serve to counter any Cuban threat to Venezuelan oil sea lanes, both Colombia and Guyana saw the purchase as an implied threat related to their disputes with Venezuela. Neither Colombia nor Guyana can possibly match this purchase, but there will probably be limited attempts to purchase defensive weapons against this perceived threat from Venezuela.

Colombia's defense problems are complicated by the endemic guerrilla warfare and banditry it has endured for many years. In fact, much of the military, especially the ground component, is tied down with security duty and counterinsurgency campaigns. Drug traffic and the corruption and economic distortions that accompany it in Colombia pose yet another major security problem.

Both nations are also involved in expanding their naval forces; in both cases this expansion is also a function of possible conflict situations with other nations (i.e., Nicaragua and Guyana). Interestingly, both nations have made a substantial investment in submarines, especially the miniature ones most suitable for coastal operations in the shallow waters prevalent around the Gulf of Venezuela.

Relationship to Other Conflicts

During their relative isolation at the time of the Malvinas/Falklands fighting, the Colombians were concerned over the way in which the Nicaraguans were establishing closer relationships with the other Latin American nations, and with Argentina and Venezuela in particular. This preoccupation decreased, however, with the Betancur administration. Many Venezuelans did not think it a coincidence that Colombia upgraded its relations with Guyana during the Malvinas/Falklands crisis, exchanging ambassadors for the first time in May 1982.[12]

Relationship to Geopolitical Thinking

The relationship between the Venezuelan-Colombian conflict and geopolitical thinking is different in these two countries. In Colombia there has been considerable attention devoted to the issue by geographers and politico-military analysts, but, as was noted in Chapter 3, this analysis is more in the field of political geography than in geopolitics. The principal Colombian author who has studied the problem is General Julio Londoño, who in works like *Nueva Geopolítica de Colombia* goes through a careful analysis of Colombia's border problems. But Londoño's analysis lacks the aggressiveness of the Southern Cone geopoliticians of the "living frontier" and *Lebensraum* schools.

In Venezuela, by contrast, there is a rapidly growing group of military and civilian geopolitical writers who have indeed focused on Venezuela's border problems with Colombia and Guyana. These authors stress that Venezuela has suffered unjust territorial mutilations in the past at the hands of these two neighbors; in the case of Guyana, the villain is Great Britain, with some help from the United States. As Ewell has noted, there is no unanimity among the views of Venezuela's geopolitical writers.[13] The "hardliners" take uncompromising positions on the territorial issues and are not above using demagoguery and inflaming public opinion to pursue their objectives. The more moderate analysts stress the pragmatic goals of seeking a secure and peaceful Caribbean in which Venezuela's sea lanes for shipping out its oil would be protected.

VENEZUELA-GUYANA: THE ESSEQUIBO DISPUTE

Introduction: Parties, Geography, and Summary

The Essequibo territory dispute between Venezuela and Guyana[14] involves not only these countries but also Great Britain as the prior colonial power and the United States because of its own participation in the nineteenth century arbitration process. According to some of the more alarmist Venezuelan analysts, Cuba is also involved because of a secret understanding that Cuba allegedly has with Guyana to come to its aid if the dispute ever reached the stage of military confrontation.

The area in contention (see Figure 18) is the so-called Essequibo territory of Guyana between the Essequibo River and the Cuyuni-Amakura Rivers, which is the present boundary between the two countries. This territory, comprising about 53,000 square miles, represents almost two-thirds of Guyana's total surface and is believed to contain important economic resources in the form of bauxite and possibly petroleum. It is also the site of the Maroni River hydroelectric project, which is seen by many Guyanese as vital to their country's development.

The dispute became more salient in 1981 and 1982 because of the convergence of three factors: Venezuela's strong support of Argentina's Malvinas/Falklands actions (which bear a historical similarity to the Essequibo situation); the expiration of a 12-year moratorium on the dispute; and Venezuela's acquisition of advanced fighter aircraft from the United States.

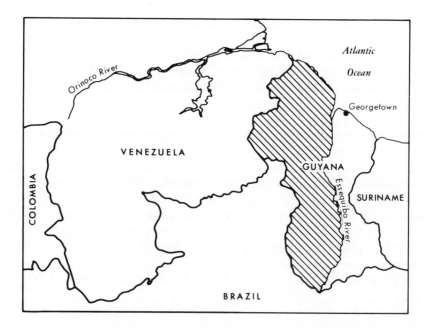

Figure 18.   The Venezuela-Guyana dispute. The shaded area between the Venezuelan border and the Essequibo River represents Venezuela's maximum claim (about two-thirds of Guyana).

Historical Background

The history of the dispute goes back to early rivalries between Spain and Great Britain (and, to a lesser extent, the Netherlands) over territories, resources, and influence on the South American mainland. In the early colonial period, when the Dutch controlled what is today Guyana, the border with Spanish territory was established at the Essequibo River, and it is this limit that the Venezuelans set as their maximum claim. In the early nineteenth century, shortly after Venezuelan independence, the British acquired Guyana from the Dutch and began to extend their influence west of the Essequibo River as British miners and explorers penetrated the area in search for gold and other reported riches. In this period a Prussian naturalist by the name of Schomburgk made a series of trips to the area and produced a number of maps. According to the Venezuelans, the first of these maps shows the border at the Essequibo River, but later ones indicate the border considerably further west. The Venezuelans argue that Schomburgk redrew his maps to show a more westerly border under British pressure and insistence. Venezuela was weak and disorganized during this mid-nineteenth century period and thus could not militarily protect its claim to distant and inhospitable territories against Great Britain.

Toward the end of the nineteenth century, Great Britain and Venezuela agreed to seek arbitration to settle the matter, and under the February 1897 Paneenfort-Andrade Treaty both nations accepted the establishment of an arbitration panel whose results would be taken by both countries as final. The arbitration tribunal included two British, one Russian, and two U.S. representatives (former President Benjamin Harrison and the chief justice of the U.S. Supreme Court). The Venezuelans were in fact not members of the tribunal, and their interests were represented by the Americans. The tribunal announced its decision on October 30, 1899, awarding the majority of the territory in contention to Great Britain and establishing the border as it is today (that is, essentially along the Cuyuni-Amakura Rivers to the triple point of Mount Roraima). The arbitral decision was not totally unfavorable to Venezuela, however, since it reconfirmed Venezuelan sovereignty at the mouth of the strategically important Orinoco River and granted Venezuela part of the territory it had been claiming. Although Venezuela was disappointed with the results of this arbitration and the resulting 1899 Treaty of Washington, it accepted the outcome and proceeded to mark the border with Great Britain in 1905. There the matter seemed to rest until Guyana began to move toward independence from Great Britain in the early 1960s.

In 1962 Venezuela unilaterally declared the 1899 arbitral award null and void because of alleged irregularities in the procedure. The Venezuelans based much of their case on the posthumous 1949 memoirs of Severo Mallet-Provost, a U.S. citizen who had been one of the junior lawyers in the case. According to the Venezuelans, the memoirs suggest that a secret deal was made between Moscow and London under which the Russian judge on the tribunal cast the decisive vote in favor of the British. Using colonial Spanish maps and documents, the Venezuelans subsequently argued that the border should be the original one shown on the first Schomburgk map, that is, the Essequibo River. In this strained climate Guyana became independent in 1966 over Venezuelan protests, which have prevented Guyana from entering the Organization of American States and have caused the nation economic and political problems ever since. In 1966 the three countries signed an agreement setting up a mixed border commission with the additional provision that if no settlement were reached by 1970 the parties would turn to the United Nations Secretary General or the World Court. No such settlement was reached by 1970, when a further agreement (The Protocol of Port of Spain) was signed. This 1970 protocol provided for a 12-year "cooling off period" that would be renewed automatically unless either Venezuela or Guyana objected. The protocol was considered to be in Guyana's favor, since it froze Venezuelan claims but permitted Guyana to proceed with the economic development and settlement of the Essequibo area.

In this interim period relations between Venezuela and Guyana have been strained by a series of border incidents involving alleged incursions of Venezuelans into disputed territory, the stirring up of rebellious movements among Guyanese indigenous people, and actual episodes of firing across the border.

In the late 1960s and early 1970s, a new factor entered the picture: Cuba. Faced with overwhelming Venezuelan economic, demographic, and military superiority, the Guyanese felt understandably vulnerable and turned to Cuba for support. This process was facilitated by the socialist ideology of Guyanese Prime Minister Forbes Burnham and was viewed with some alarm by Venezuela, the United States, and Brazil, among others. The Guyanese provided the Cubans with refueling and airport facilities during Cuba's Angolan and African incursions, and in 1976 there were strong rumors of large numbers of Cubans in Guyana. Guyana, in turn, accused the Venezuelans of stirring up these rumors to destabilize their government. Prime Minister Burnham has stated rather pointedly that if threatened Guyana would turn to any source that would offer help.[15]

Recent Developments

The Venezuelans strongly supported Argentina in the Falklands/Malvinas conflict and in the process revealed the depths of bitter anti-British feelings in Venezuela. A number of sources in Venezuela (including senior retired military officers) spoke of "the Argentine example" and the possibilities of taking military action against Guyana. However, the Venezuelan government never went this far, stressing that it continued to seek a peaceful solution of the dispute, but arguing that the Latin American solidarity demonstrated in the Argentine case should be focused next on the Guyana-Venezuela dispute. A series of border incursions by Venezuelan troops and aircraft further strained the situation in mid-1982. Guyana reacted strongly to what it perceived to be Venezuelan pressures and sought support from both Cuba and, with mixed results, from its English-speaking Caribbean Community and Common Market (CARICOM) allies in the Caribbean.[16]

Tensions further increased when the 12-year Protocol of Port of Spain expired in September 1982. Although the protocol could have continued indefinitely, Venezuela in effect did away with it by rejecting an extension and called instead for outside arbitration or other procedures to settle the issue. The Venezuelans proposed the secretary general of the United Nations, while the Guyanese indicated a preference for the International Court of Justice. The Guyanese finally acceded to the U.N. proposal in early 1983,[17] and this option appears to offer some hope for eventual resolution of the dispute.

The Burnham government has continued to respond to what it perceives as Venezuelan pressures by seeking political (and possibly military) support from a variety of sources. The March 1983 nonaligned summit provided Forbes Burnham with the opportunity to marshall Third World support against Venezuela to the extent that Venezuela was forced to withdraw its application for membership into the nonaligned movement. The Guyanese prime minister also remarked that he would seek help from anyone, "even the devil" if Guyana were to be invaded.[18] A further source of support for Guyana now appears to be Brazil, which is presumably not interested in seeing either Venezuela or Cuba extend its influence on its own borders. Forbes Burnham travelled to Brazil in late 1982 and was apparently successful in talks with his hosts regarding arms purchases. Although the Guyanese could not possibly afford enough weapons or a military establishment that could match the Venezuelan's, this action represented a significant step for both Guyana and Brazil.

Type of Conflict and Military Implications

The Essequibo dispute represents different things for the two major parties involved. For Venezuela the territorial aspects of the dispute are real, but somewhat marginal for a country that already has an abundance of natural resources and large expanses of empty territory. A major factor for Venezuela is the feeling of having been cheated in the past when it was weak and disorganized, and a sense that it must recover these lost territories to vindicate national honor and prestige. For Guyana the issue is much more one of resources and survival as a credible nation-state. Essequibo represents almost two-thirds of the surface area of the country, and its loss would result in a Guyana quite different from the one that achieved independence in 1966. Guyana is a poor nation with few energy resources, and the Essequibo region offers promise for national development in terms of bauxite, minerals, and hydroelectric potential. To this must be added the recent high-quality oil discoveries made in the Takutu Basin of the Essequibo area.[19] Thus, for Guyana the dispute goes beyond the territorial aspect to become one affecting its economic possibilities and its national identity.

The military implications of the conflict start with the obvious disparity between the Venezuelan and Guyanese forces. Venezuela is a respectable regional power, with an impressively modernizing force of some 41,000. In contrast, Guyana has only 7,000 soldiers, with very limited and rather obsolete equipment.[20] Guyanese links to Cuba and Brazil add an important and potentially dangerous dimension to any military confrontation. Because of the lack of roads in the area and the generally difficult terrain, any military operations would probably be coastal or by air.

Relationship to Other Conflicts

The relationship of the Venezuelan-Guyanan dispute to the problems that Venezuela has with Colombia has been noted previously in terms of a possible cooperation between Colombia and Guyana as a result of their common strains with Venezuela. Although there are indications of a greater degree of diplomatic involvement between these two nations, little of any concrete significance has emerged.

There has been speculation that a similar sort of commonality might emerge between Suriname and Venezuela over the fact that they both have border disputes with their common neighbor Guyana.[21] Surinamese leader Desi Bouterse visited Caracas in late 1982 and reportedly obtained support in his efforts to build an oil storage facility in Suriname and improve its military forces.

Brazil, the one country that shares a border with all of these nations (Colombia, Venezuela, Guyana, and Suriname) and yet has disputes with none of them, has watched these various conflictual strains with considerable interest. One theme in Brazil's geopolitical writing is that, as the United States begins its inevitable decline as a Caribbean power, Brazil must be prepared to fill part of the power vacuum that the United States will leave behind. With typical Brazilian discretion, Brazil's actions with regard to several of these states have begun to fill some of this perceived power vacuum. Thus, Brazil has offered military assistance and arms to both Guyana and Suriname, and has attempted to involve Colombia and Venezuela more deeply in the Amazon Pact under Brazilian leadership. Brazil's attitude toward Venezuela is tempered by a sense that they are to some degree competing for leadership in the area and that Venezuela's oil assets make it an economically powerful competitor. Brazilian military sources have also expressed concern that, if Venezuela does make any military move against Guyana, such a move could involve Venezuelan military incursions into Brazilian territory.[22] For all of these reasons, the creation of a Brazilian "rapid deployment force" and the strengthening of Brazilian garrisons along the northern borders have been interpreted as manifestations of increasing Brazilian concern.

As mentioned before, the strong Venezuelan support for the Argentine cause in the Malvinas/Falklands dispute has been consciously linked at all levels of official and unofficial Venezuelan circles with the somewhat parallel case of the dispute with Guyana. Argentine writers and geopolitical analysts have echoed the parallels, much to the consternation of many outside observers, who have difficulty understanding how so much bitterness can be generated over a seemingly anachronistic anticolonial struggle.[23]

Some Latin American analysts have taken note of the Venezuelan attempt to overthrow a long-established and confirmed arbitral award and have suggested applying this same approach to other conflict situations in the hemisphere. Thus, an Ecuadorean geopolitician writing in an Argentine geopolitical journal explored the Venezuelan attempt to declare the 1899 arbitration award null and void, and related it to the Argentine attempt to do the same with the Beagle Channel award.[24] He concluded his article emphasizing his own country's struggle to undo the 1942 Rio Protocol, which Ecuadoreans feel was so damaging to them and so favorable to Peru.

Lastly, the possible Cuban connection to the Venezuelan-Guyanese dispute has caused concern among geopolitical writers in both Venezuela and Brazil. The Cuban link motivated one Venezuelan geopolitician (in a pre–October 1983 reference to Grenada) to argue that there exists a threat to Venezuela from "a geopolitical arc in the Eastern Caribbean" that runs from Grenada to Guyana: "The day that this geopolitical grouping consolidates itself Venezuela will be subject to serious threats of political and economic destabilization. This danger is even more certain if one adds to the industrial development of (Venezuelan) Guyana the tremendous oil deposits in the Orinoco tar sand belt."[25]

Relationship to Geopolitical Thinking

As Ewell has noted, a considerable portion of the output of Venezuelan geopolitical writers has focused on issues of borders and national territory;[26] so it is not surprising that the Essequibo dispute has accounted for much of this. The parallel here to geopolitical writers in Argentina is strong. Both nations are geopolitically dissatisfied and believe that they have been wronged in the past by the same colonial power (Great Britain), working in conjunction with the regional neocolonialist power (the United States) to rob them of some of their national patrimony. This train of thought in Venezuela is echoed in the pronouncements of a small but highly vocal group of nationalists, many of them retired military officers.

In Guyana there is little conscious geopolitical writing or theorizing, which is perhaps the result of the small size of the military, their more British orientation, and the lack of anything like a "geopolitical school." Nevertheless, the Guyanese political leadership has shown a keen consciousness of the geopolitical need to fill its empty interior spaces and to fully occupy its empty territories.[27] The Guyanese are especially concerned about the low population densities in the Essequibo and generally in all the parts of the country away from the coast and major rivers. Attempts to persuade Guyanese to colonize and fill these areas have met with only limited success, and there have been a number of schemes designed to attract foreign settlers and colonizers into the Guyanese heartland. One of the more notorious and tragic of these schemes was that of the Reverend James Jones and his People's Temple settlement in Jonestown. According to Raymond Crist, one of the motivations of the Guyanese government in making the settlement attractive to the People's Temple was that the Venezuelans might be less likely to move against an area that contained significant numbers of U.S. colonists.[28]

GUYANA-SURINAME:
THE NEW RIVER TRIANGLE DISPUTE

Introduction: Parties, Geography, and Summary

Guyana and Suriname are the only two parties actively involved in the dispute, although at one time Great Britain and The Netherlands were the principals and to some degree still have an interest in the outcome.

The dispute is territorial in nature and involves about 9,000 square miles of land in the remote and uninhabited interior area of the "New River Triangle" formed by the Corentyne-Kutari Rivers and the New River. There is also a dispute over the maritime boundary of the continental shelf at the mouth of the Corentyne River.

Historical Background

The dispute stems from confusion and differences of opinion over which branch of the Corentyne River should form the boundary between the two nations. The agreed-upon boundary between British Guiana and Dutch Guiana in colonial days was the Corentyne River and its headwaters in the Kutari River; these rivers were mapped out by Robert Schomburgk in the 1840s. However, in 1871 another explorer, Barrington Brown, discovered that there was a second tributary to the west of the Corentyne, which he named the New River. Since the New River is larger than the Kutari, the Dutch argued that the border should follow the New River instead of the Kutari. Had it done so, the boundary would have been shifted westward at British Guiana's expense and would have given Dutch Guiana an additional 9,000 square miles of territory. The British rejected this claim, the matter was given little importance, and the Dutch had given up pressing this claim until after World War II. However, in the early 1950s both colonies began to gain a larger measure of self-government, and the issue was raised again.

After their independence in 1966, the Guyanese began to take a more aggressive stance on the border issue and in 1967 expelled a Surinamese surveying party in the disputed New River Triangle area. Suriname in turn threatened to expel all the Guyanese residing in its territory. Tensions reached the shooting stage briefly in 1969 when Guyanese troops landed on a border airfield and attacked a Surinamese police detachment.

The Guyana-Suriname dispute has been relatively dormant in recent years. Suriname gained independence in 1975 and since the "Sergeant's Coup" in 1980 has experienced much internal instability. The instability has been exacerbated by reports of activities of dissidents and mercenaries opposed to the government in Paramaribo. Some of these have operated from French Guiana, with which Suriname has a border dispute of lesser magnitude.

Recent Developments

Concern over the internal stability of Suriname and a possible Cuban role was intensified in late 1982 when 15 opponents of the regime of Lieutenant Colonel Desi Bouterse were killed "while trying to escape." Bouterse was identified with a pro-Cuban faction of the Surinamese armed forces, and there had been increased contacts with Cuba shortly before the killings.

These events in Suriname brought expressions of concern from Brazil, whose government warned that Brazil could not tolerate any threats to its security from that area, and specifically any "Cubanization" of the country. A few months later the Brazilians launched a campaign to counter the Cuban influence by offering the Bouterse regime a series of aid programs, including economic as well as military assistance.[29] Fears of Cuban penetration of Suriname have diminished considerably since the death of Maurice Bishop of Grenada; shortly after his assassination, Bouterse expelled a number of Cubans and reduced Suriname's ties to Cuba.

Type of Conflict and Military Implications

The conflict appears to be of a purely territorial nature, with some minor resource implications stemming from the fact that the area lies partly in the bauxite belt. However, the region is very remote, and transportation presents major problems.

The military potential of both Guyana and Suriname is low, and if only these two nations were involved the likelihood of any significant conflict would also be minimal. In mid-1983 Bouterse announced that he would soon be tripling the size of the armed forces by building up the Surinamese militia, but little seems to have come of this. Involvement by Cuba has diminished, and the Brazilians seem to be playing a stabilizing role.

Relationship to Other Conflicts

The only relationship to other conflicts appears to be a low-level one to the Guyana-Venezuela Essequibo conflict in terms of the advantages to Suriname if Guyana were distracted by a major problem with Venezuela. The Bouterse regime has signed a number of agreements, including military ones, with Venezuela.

Relationship to Geopolitical Thinking

No relationship to geopolitical thinking has been identified. Unlike the Essequibo area, there appears to be no push by either Guyana or Suriname to populate the New River Triangle as an important heartland. As long as it remains a low priority area of doubtful economic value, it is not likely to be the focus of geopolitical or military attention.

OTHER SOUTH AMERICAN CARIBBEAN CONFLICTS

There are at least three other potentially conflictual situations involving the South American and Caribbean nations, although these are at a much lower level of tension and appear to have little relationship to geopolitical modes of thought.

Suriname-French Guiana

In a situation roughly paralleling its dispute with Guyana, Suriname also has a contested border with its eastern neighbor, French Guiana. Here the problem lies in whether the Litani or Itary River should be the border in the most remote and uninhabited area of the frontier. Some 3,000 square miles of territory are involved, and its only economic significance is that there is rumored to be gold in the area.[30]

Venezuela-Trinidad and Tobago

The proximity of Trinidad and Tobago to the Venezuelan mainland (at one point as close as nine miles) has long caused problems stemming from fishing rights and maritime limits. Great Britain signed the Treaty of Paris with Venezuela in 1942 (and Trinidad and Tobago signed a subsequent treaty in 1977) in an attempt to settle the issue. Yet, there have been frequent disputes and arrests of fishermen allegedly outside of their own territorial areas. The situation was complicated in 1954 when Venezuela extended its territorial waters from 3 to 12 miles and again in May 1983 when Trinidad and Tobago declared a 200-mile exclusive economic zone.[31]

Venezuela-Netherlands Antilles

A somewhat similar situation exists between Venezuela and the Dutch island colonies of Aruba and Curacao, which lie just to the north of the Gulf of Venezuela and Venezuela's major oil producing area of Maracaibo. Here the issue is not fishing but oil, since wells have been drilled in the waters between Venezuela and the islands. Although Venezuela makes no claim on the islands proper, there was some nervousness on the islands during the time of the Falklands/Malvinas conflict, and there has been a move to obtain security guarantees for the islands from the Venezuelans and the Dutch.[32]

NOTES

1. Jorge Villacrés Moscoso, "El Caribe, Nueva Zona Conflictiva Marítima," *Geopolítica* no. 18 (June 1980); Gerhard Drekonja, *El Diferendo entre Colombia y Nicaragua* (Bogota: FESCOL y Departamento de Ciencia Política, Universidad de los Andes, 1982); Nicaragua, Ministerio de Relaciones Exteriores, "Declaración y Libro Blanco del Gobierno de Nicaragua," *Relaciones Internacionales* (Revista de la Universidad Nacional de Costa Rica) 1 (1980).

2. Nicaragua, Ministerio de Relaciones Exteriores, "Libro Blanco."

3. *Bogota, AFP*, April 13, 1982, in *FBIS*, April 14, 1982.

4. *El Espectador* (Bogota), March 9, 1982, in *JPRS*, May 6, 1982.

5. For additional information on the Colombian-Venezuelan dispute, see Hernando Holguín Peláez, *Proyecciones de un Límite Marítimo entre Colombia y Venezuela* (Bogota:

Editores y Distribuidores Asociados, 1971); Aquiles Monagas, *Testimonio de una Traición a Venezuela* (Caracas: Ediciones Garrido, 1975); Carlos Ramírez Faria, *La Clase Gobernante y la Frontera de Venezuela con Colombia* (Caracas: Talleres de Lithoformas, 1976); Hugo Trejo, *Basta de Concesiones a Colombia* (Caracas: Ediciones Venezuela Contemporanea, 1975); M. A. Padron, *¿Perderemos También el Golfo de Venezuela?* (Caracas: Aguilarte, 1978); Ruben Carpio Castillo, *Geopolítica de Venezuela* (Caracas: Seix Barral Venezolana, 1981); *El Tiempo* (Bogota), August 17, 1975, in *JPRS*, October 9, 1975; Hernando Holguín Peláez, *Los Monjes, Enjuiciamiento [sic] de una Traición* (Bogota: Editores Prosartes, 1975); Alfredo Vazquez Carrizosa, *Colombia y los Problemas del Mar* (Bogota: Imprenta Nacional, 1971); Germán Cavelier, *Memoria Histórico-Jurídico sobre el Asunto de los Monjes* (Caracas: Cavelier, 1977); Earle Herera, *¿Por qué se ha reducido el Territorio Venezolano?* (Caracas: Universidad Central de Venezuela, 1981).

6. See, for example, Trejo, *Concesiones a Colombia*, pp. 7–9.

7. *Times of the Americas*, January 8, 1975.

8. *Vision*, April 21, 1979, p. 21; *Washington Post*, January 9, 1981.

9. *Bogota, Cadena Radial Super*, October 8, 1980, in *FBIS*, October 10, 1980; *Bogota Radio Sutatenza*, March 6, 1981, in *FBIS*, March 10, 1981; *Bogota, AFP*, April 19, 1981, in *FBIS*, April 20, 1981; *Caracas, Ultimas Noticias*, January 2, 1981.

10. *Bogota, El Espectador*, May 14, 1982, in *JPRS*, June 17, 1982; *Bogota, Caracol*, January 13, 1983, in *FBIS*, January 14, 1983; *Bogota, Radio Super*, April 9, 1983, in *FBIS*, April 12, 1983.

11. *Baltimore Sun*, December 2, 1982.

12. *Georgetown, Guyana, CANA*, May 1, 1982, in *FBIS*, May 5, 1982.

13. Judith Ewell, "The Development of Venezuelan Geopolitical Analysis Since World War II," *Journal of Inter-American Studies and World Affairs*, 24 (August 1982): 302, 307–8; See also Carpio Castillo, *Geopolítica de Venezuela*.

14. For treatment of the dispute, see Leslie B. Rout, *Which Way Out? An Analysis of the Venezuela-Guyana Border Dispute* (East Lansing: Michigan State University, Latin American Studies Center, 1971); Venezuela, Ministerio de Relaciones Exteriores, *Summary of the Boundary Question with British Guiana, now Guyana* (Caracas: Editorial Arte, 1981); José Alberto Zambrano, *Speech to the National Congress*, June 17, 1982 (Caracas: Ministerio de Relaciones Exteriores, 1982); Guyana, Ministry of External Affairs, *A Search for Understanding* (Georgetown: Ministry of External Affairs, 1970); *New York Times*, June 21, 1982 and May 8, 1982; "Guyana Venezolana y Malvinas Argentinas: Reclamos Gemelos," *La Nación* (Buenos Aires), April 30, 1982; Jai Narine Singh, *Diplomacy or War* (Georgetown, Guyana: Cedar Press, 1982); Guyana, Ministry of Information, *The ABC's of Guyana's Essequibo Territory* (Georgetown, Guyana: Ministry of Information, 1981).

15. See note 14 above, as well as *Washington Post*, February 6, 1966, March 10, 1976, and October 11, 1981; *Christian Science Monitor*, March 11, 1976; *Business Week*, July 6, 1981.

16. *Times of the Americas*, July 7 and 21, 1982; *New York Times*, May 8, 1982; *CANA, Georgetown*, April 26, 1982, in *JPRS*, May 18, 1982; *AFP, Georgetown*, May 11, 1982 in *FBIS*, May 12, 1982; *EFE, Caracas*, September 3, 1982, in *FBIS*, September 8, 1982; *AFP, Caracas*, April 20, 1982, in *FBIS*, April 21, 1982.

17. *AFP, Caracas*, August 22, 1982, in *FBIS*, August 24, 1982, *Times of the Americas*, April 13, 1983; *DPA, Caracas*, March 28, 1983, in *FBIS*, March 29, 1983.

18. *CANA-Reuters, New Delhi*, March 8, 1983, in *JPRS*, April 1, 1983; *CANA, Georgetown*, February 16, 1983, in *FBIS*, February 18, 1983; *O Estado de São Paulo*, October 14, 1982, in *FBIS*, October 19, 1982.

19. *CANA, Georgetown*, April 26, 1982, in *JPRS*, May 18, 1982.

20. "Military Balance," *U.S. Air Force Magazine*, December 1982, pp. 134–40; People's Progressive Party, *Guyana Information Bulletin*, 19 (July 1982).

21. "Washington Report on the Hemisphere," *COHA*, September 7, 1982.

22. *O Estado de São Paulo*, April 17, 1983, in *FBIS*, April 18, 1983; Carpio Castillo, *Geopolítica de Venezuela*, pp. 219-20.

23. "Guyana Venezolana y Malvinas Argentinas: Reclamos Gemelos," *La Nación* (Buenos Aires), April 30, 1982.

24. Jorge Villacrés Moscoso, "Laudos Arbitrales Nulos," *Geopolítica* no. 21 (March 1981): 25-27.

25. Carpio Castillo, *Geopolítica de Venezuela*, pp. 215-16.

26. Ewell, "Venezuelan Geopolitical Analysis," pp. 298, 307-9; *Latin American Weekly Report*, October 29, 1982; Carlos A. Perez (president of Venezuela), "Geopolítica de Venezuela," speech to the Congress, *Geopolítica* nos. 5-6, (July-December 1976); statement by Foreign Minister Jose Alberto Zambrano, *LATIN-Reuters* (Caracas), October 15, 1982, in *FBIS*, October 19, 1982.

27. Peoples Progressive Party, *Guyana Information Bulletin*, 19 (October 1982); Guyana, Ministry of External Affairs, *Search for Understanding*; American University, *Area Handbook for Guyana*. Washington, D.C.: Government Printing Office, 1969, p. 202.

28. Raymond Crist, "Jungle Geopolitics in Guyana: How a Communist Utopia that Ended in Massacre Came to be Sited," *American Journal of Economics and Sociology* (April 1981).

29. *Folha de São Paulo*, December 24, 1982, in *FBIS*, December 28, 1982; *O Estado de São Paulo*, February 4, 1983, in *FBIS*, February 10, 1983; *O Estado de São Paulo*, April 20, 1983, in *FBIS*, April 25, 1983.

30. *Elseviers Magazine* (Amsterdam), January 15, 1983, in *JPRS*, February 17, 1983; John Keegan, *World Armies* (New York: Facts on File, 1979).

31. *Times of the Americas*, May 25, 1983.

32. *De Tijd* (Amsterdam), March 11, 1983, in *JPRS*, May 3, 1983; *NRC Handelsblad* (Rotterdam), March 14, 1983, in *JPRS*, May 3, 1983.

PART FOUR
CONCLUSIONS

8

GEOPOLITICS, BALANCE OF POWER, AND CONFLICT

GEOPOLITICAL THINKING IN SOUTH AMERICA

Geopolitical thinking in South America remains an obscure and little explored area for most outside scholars of the international relations of this region. Perhaps because of an inherent academic bias against the study of things strategic and military or perhaps because of the stigma still clinging to geopolitics since the World War II era, there is little serious analysis of this field of study. To compound the problem, not much of the prolific output of South American geopolitical writers makes its way into English translation or U.S. academic circles.

What is important, however, is not whether one approves of these geopolitical writings. Rather, the significance of geopolitical thinking in South America lies in the manner in which it has been put into practice by a number of governments in the last decade, the impact it has had on their international relations, and in the legacy that it is leaving. A study of geopolitical thinking in this area can provide an understanding of some of the mind-sets of South American leaders of this period, as well as suggest patterns of internal and international behavior in the future.

The geopolitician's basic vision of the state as an organism is instinctively rejected by many because of the way the individual is subordinated to the state. It is further repudiated because of the short step from this concept to a rationalization that individuals who oppose the regime in power are enemies who can, and must, be dealt with ruthlessly with little regard for their basic human rights.

As our analysis has shown, forms of geopolitical thinking have been most deeply rooted in those South American countries (Brazil, Argentina, and Chile) possessing large and sophisticated military establishments with a history of recent military rule and repression of political opposition. In the last decade the smaller states of the Southern Cone (Uruguay, Paraguay, and Bolivia) have tended to imitate both the geopolitical frames of mind and the politico-military systems of their larger neighbors. For a variety of reasons the nations of the northern Pacific and Caribbean coasts of South America (Peru, Ecuador, Colombia, Venezuela, and the Guianas) have not had geopolitical currents of similar depth in their military or government leadership. However, in the Spanish-speaking countries among them, one can identify many of the same elements of geopolitical thinking that are so prevalent in the Southern Cone.

The emergence of geopolitical thinking in the Southern Cone of South America must also be seen in the context of the declining U.S. ability to influence politico-military events in this part of South America in the 1970s and beyond. Congressional restrictions on military assistance and the linking of military assistance to human rights performance caused the Southern Cone military regimes to turn away from U.S. leadership in military matters. Not surprisingly, this has permitted the flourishing of local strategic doctrines, which tended to have a strongly geopolitical flavor. This lowering of a previous U.S. high profile in South America was in some respects inevitable given the greater capabilities, maturity, and independence of the larger nations of this area.

Geopolitical thinking in South America has gone through a number of cyclical changes. Before World War II it followed quite closely the seminal ideas of the Northern European and Germanic schools of geopolitics. In fact, in some countries (Argentina and Chile) these links were maintained even during the period when Germanic geopolitical thinking became associated with the Third Reich. After the war discussion of these ideas practically disappeared in Western Europe and the United States, but geopolitical thinking was kept alive by a handful of writers in the Southern Cone of South America. Although these writers were generally ignored by U.S. scholars and foreign affairs specialists, their ideas began to have a growing impact on key military and civilian decision makers through the military war colleges and specialized journals and books. In the late 1960s and 1970s there was a veritable renaissance of thinking, writing, and applying of geopolitics as the Southern Cone nations came under military rulers who paid a great deal of attention to these types of ideas. The accompanying decline in the U.S. ability to influence these same individuals gave further stimulus to geopolitical thinking. With the Malvinas/Falklands disaster, the loss of prestige of the Argentine military, and the severe economic and social problems facing the military regimes in the area, geopolitical thinking now seems on the decline in this region. If the moves toward democratization in the Southern Cone initiated in the early and mid-1980s continue, it would be reasonable to expect a decline in the military's political role and in the significance of geopolitical ideas in internal matters and foreign policy.

But it would be a mistake to dismiss geopolitical thinking as a short-lived phenomenon associated with a period of military governments in the Southern Cone in the 1960s and 1970s. The legacy of geopolitics will extend beyond these regimes because of the way geopolitical thinking became popularized in this period through the media and educational systems. Geopolitical thinking in the Southern Cone is also closely linked to nationalism, patriotism, and deeply felt beliefs about national sovereignty. These values, although strongly stimulated and manipulated by military regimes, also have an existence that is independent of military rule. To cite the Argentine example, the departure and discrediting of the 1976–83 military government have not diminished Argentine beliefs that the Malvinas should be theirs or that Argentina has a valid claim and a national patriotic mission in the South Atlantic, the islands, and Antarctica. While there is good reason to believe that an elected civilian regime in Argentina would not resort to irresponsible military steps to make good its claims, there is also little doubt that attempts to secure Argentine rights remain a high national priority and that geopolitical arguments supporting this goal will continue to have an impact.

The legacy of geopolitical thinking is a mixed one. The tendency to make negative value judgments on geopolitical thinking should be tempered by an appreciation of the different impact that geopolitical ideas and programs have on internal and external policies. The expansionary and aggressive tone of international geopolitics, with its emphasis on the living frontier, power politics, and revindication of lost territories, merits condemnation because of its hostile and bellicose tone. But there is an internal current of geopolitical thinking that argues for effective and rational employment of a nation's resources, cautious development, and planned systematic use of space, which should be seen as positive contributions made by the currents of geopolitical thought in South America. Further, the integrationalist current of geopolitical thinking offers some promising possibilities for cooperative international ventures in South America, particularly in the fields of trade, transportation, hydroelectric energy, and joint development of frontier areas.

Geopolitical thinking in South America has also served to draw attention to regions and resources that were previously ignored. The historical pattern of populating South America along the rim, and ignoring the hinterland and heartland, is now giving way to geopolitically inspired projects aimed at fully developing the interior empty spaces of the continent. Geopoliticians have also contributed to a reevaluation of the sea as a national asset and have influenced the Latin American and Third World movement toward declaring 200-mile exclusive economic zones and, in some cases, sovereignty. Geopolitics thus has contributed to a greater consciousness of the value of national space, be it land or sea, and of the relationship of that space to important resources. The emphasis on space, resources, and frontiers has also led to a deeper examination of national goals and interests.

Despite these positive elements, it is difficult to avoid arriving at a predominantly negative conclusion when assessing the contribution of geopolitical thinking in this period, especially under the military regimes of the Southern Cone. The close association between geopolitical thinking and the national security state, and to interstate conflict, overrides the positive contributions sketched out above. The negative vision of hostile nation-states struggling to survive in a highly competitive Darwinian struggle for diminishing resources and space is not a happy or optimistic scenario. The trend toward power politics, realpolitik, and militarization of important civilian sectors through geopolitical thinking has strongly negative connotations.

GEOPOLITICAL THINKING, THE NATIONAL SECURITY STATE, AND CONFLICT

The linkages between Southern Cone geopolitical thinking and the national security states in that region were developed in Chapter 4, where it was argued that the organic state concept is the starting point for most geopolitical analyses. It is also the basis for the corporatist and militaristic defense of the state that evolves from the national security doctrine. The link to conflict comes through the pessimistic and Darwinian vision of the organic state competing with others for scarce resources, space, and influence in a hostile environment.

South American geopolitical analysts (with the exception of the Brazilians) tend to harp on another theme that tends to justify their expansionist policies: the theme of geopolitical aggression committed against their country, usually by a neighbor. Thus, Argentina feels that it has lost territory to Great Britain and Chile; Chile to Argentina; Bolivia to all its neighbors, but especially Chile; Peru to Chile; Ecuador to Peru; Colombia to Venezuela and Panama; and Venezuela to Colombia and Guiana. In the case of countries which in colonial times contained the chief city of a viceroyalty, this feeling of loss carries over into dreams of restoring the greatness of the past, as in the case of Buenos Aires or Lima. This tendency to feel geopolitically victimized can be manipulated by nationalists and demagogues into a revanchist and jingoistic patriotism that can get out of hand and increase tensions with neighbors. Geopolitics feeds this process by providing a seemingly coherent and scientific foundation for these beliefs. The media, in turn, seek out and exploit those who are willing to present these arguments in public. The most dangerous combination occurs when a nation believes it has been victimized in the past by territorial losses, and is threatened once again by the same country, which has somehow managed to find allies with which to magnify its forces.

The aggressiveness of the national security states equipped with geopolitical doctrines is increased when the territory in contention is perceived to have important resources. This is especially true when the resources are energy ones and the nation competing for them is energy-poor. This has added a new and dangerous element to the old conflicts of South America, which generally dealt with relatively unimportant portions of territory in a continent that seemed still to have vast empty areas. The geopolitical "law of valuable areas" suggests that a nation had best move quickly to effectively control such an area before greed and the need for expanded space and resources persuade a neighbor to move first. Thus, the Argentine-Chilean, Peruvian-Ecuadorean, Colombian-Venezuelan, and Venezuelan-Guianese conflicts have a resource dimension that makes the issue far more important to both countries involved and thus much more difficult to resolve.

The close links between the military and the national security state, especially in the Southern Cone, make it more likely that government programs and policies will have a strong geopolitical cast. The role of the senior (or "superior") war college is a key factor in this process. Such institutions frequently play a major role as a source of ideas and doctrines for military regimes. As a matter of normal military academic activity, they play war games and generate "war hypotheses" against probable and possible enemies in a variety of situations. In general, these tend to be secret and are closely held in the hermetic inner circles of military institutions. However, at times they are published, and one can cite examples in Argentina of game hypotheses involving war with Brazil[1] or invasions of the Malvinas/Falklands well before 1982. If these war games and hypotheses are merely academic and stay within the senior war colleges, then they can be considered harmless training exercises in the same category as the U.S. Army's plans in the 1920s and 1930s to invade Canada and almost every country in Latin America.[2] However, one cannot assume such innocent implications when the government is in the hands of unelected military men whose intellectual formation is based on a strong dose of geopolitical theorizing and strategic war gaming.

TOWARD A GEOPOLITICAL BALANCE OF POWER IN SOUTH AMERICA?

Should geopolitical modes of thinking prevail in South America and should power politics dominate the relations between countries, then what might emerge is a geopolitical balance of power system involving a complex and inter-related set of antagonisms and alliances or understandings. Because of the geographic arrangement of the principal nations involved in such a system, it can be described as a network of diagonal alliances and perpendicular antagonisms. The danger inherent in such a system is that a conflict breaking out at any one point in the system tends to drag in the other linked antagonists or alliance partners unless the balance is quickly restored.

A South American balance of power system would not be unprecedented. Burr has studied nineteenth century balance of power arrangements in South America and concludes that shortly after independence two balance of power systems evolved in South America.[3] One was the system focusing on the River Plate estuary, in which Brazil and Argentina were the two principal actors and Uruguay and Paraguay the lesser ones. The second system was on the west coast, where a strong Chile was balanced by the combination of Bolivia and Peru. Toward the end of the nineteenth century and into the twentieth, these two systems began to merge as communications, trade, diplomacy, and other links began to draw them together. The end result was a single balance of power relationship dominated by four actors: Brazil, Argentina, Chile, and Peru. The three lesser states, Uruguay, Paraguay, and Bolivia, were relegated to the status of buffers between these more important actors. This balance of power system tended to regulate and dominate the international relations of the Southern Cone until first British and then U.S. influence began to play a predominant role. By the end of World War II, the ability of the United States to influence events in the Western Hemisphere was so great that it obliterated this balance of power system and ushered in the period of Pax Americana.

With the decline of Pax Americana in the 1960s and 1970s, and the concomitant increase in power politics in the Southern Cone based on geopolitical frames of thought, it can be hypothesized that the region may be moving back to something like the old nineteenth century balance of power system. However, the system now includes the added elements of geopolitics and the presence of a number of potentially explosive interstate conflict situations. The foundations for such a balance of power system lie in three geopolitical "laws" described previously: the laws of living frontiers, of valuable areas, and of discontinuous borders. As derived from geopolitical theorizing generally accepted by most of the Southern Cone practitioners, the laws mean the following:[4]

1. The law of the living frontier (sometimes also called the dynamic or flexible frontier) states that geopolitical frontiers are never static, despite what the map or the markers on the ground may show. Frontiers are the temporary resting point of two national forces in contact at a border; when one force gains strength, it pushes the border back into the neighbor's territory. The strength of the force involved is a function of national power in all its dimensions, be they economic, diplomatic, military, or psychosocial.

2. The law of valuable areas holds that, if there is a national area that is not being adequately populated or a resource that is not being fully exploited, there will be a tendency for other states to occupy or exploit it in their own interests, especially if it is near a common border area. This does not necessarily mean a physical or forceful invasion; under the "law of the living frontier," it may simply mean that settlers, investors, or firms cross the formal international border and thus push the "living frontier" at the expense of the weaker state.

3. The law of "discontinuous borders" argues that nations having contiguous borders have an inevitable tendency toward friction because of a range

of problems that might involve territorial claims, smuggling, political refugees, shooting incidents across a border, and so forth. On the other hand, the countries that are likely to get along best are those that are close enough to have high levels of economic, cultural, and human contact, but that are not actually contiguous.

If we apply these concepts to the geopolitical panorama of South America, we can structure a hypothesized balance of power system along the following lines. Venezuela, Colombia, and the Guianas are not really participants since in many respects they are Caribbean states. Uruguay, Paraguay, and Bolivia participate in the system as buffers between the larger powers and have relatively little independence within the power politics system. We are thus left with Brazil, Argentina, Chile, Peru, and Ecuador. The resulting system consists of four sets of perpendicular antagonisms and two sets of diagonal alliances (see Figure 19), as follows:

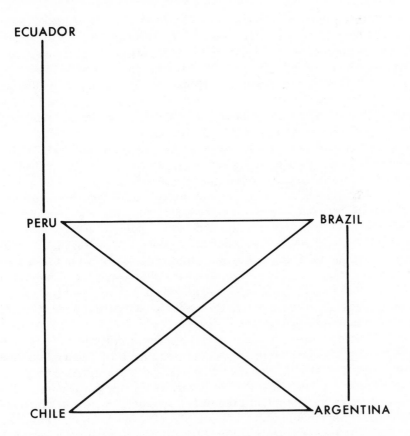

Figure 19. The pattern of perpendicular antagonisms and diagonal alliances.

The perpendicular antagonisms (i.e., East-West and North-South) correspond to those states that have contiguous borders and have had actual or potential conflicts over the years:

- Brazil-Argentina (the long-standing rivalry)
- Argentina-Chile (Beagle Channel and Antarctic conflict, exacerbated by Argentina's suspicions that Chile is collaborating with Great Britain)
- Chile-Peru (the War of the Pacific and Peru's lost territories)
- Peru-Ecuador (the Ecuadorean Amazon claim)
- Peru-Brazil (competing interest in occupying and developing the Western Amazon basin).

The diagonal alliances correspond to the states that obey the law of discontinuous borders (those that are close but do not touch):

- Chile-Brazil
- Argentina-Peru.

Some authors have suggested that other states could be added to this pattern. Thus, there is a certain tension between Venezuela and Brazil over Brazil's expansion into the Amazon Basin, and this could be balanced by a Brazilian-Guyanese understanding. Likewise, the tensions between Venezuela and its other two neighbors with which it has border problems (Colombia and Guyana) have led to speculation of a closer Colombian-Guyanese relation. Lastly, there are some indications of Ecuadorean interest in improving relations with Brazil as a counter to its difficulties with Peru.

This schema of a complex network of alliances and antagonisms held together by tensions and understandings is not entirely the product of the overactive imagination of geopolitical analysts. The history of past conflict and strains in the Southern Cone is consistent with this pattern. Whenever tensions rise between two nations in the system, there are usually indications that some of the other antagonisms and understandings come into play. For example, during the Malvinas/Falklands conflict, Chile's studied neutrality was seen as an unfriendly act by Argentina, and the Peruvian military responded by sending a flight of their border aircraft to Argentine airports close to the border with Chile. In this same period there were rumors of a secret pact between Argentina and Peru that would be activated if Chile took any sort of action against Argentina.[5]

The danger of a balance of power system such as the one described above is that should a conflict break out over one of the bilateral disputes it has the potential of spreading to others because of the interlinked nature of the Southern Cone conflicts. Thus, a worst-case scenario would have Chile moving against Argentina at a time when Argentina was confronting the British. Chilean mobilization to the south would offer a tempting target for the Peruvians (and Bolivians) who could justify moving against Chile because of their understanding to come to the aid of Argentina. Any Peruvian mobilization to penetrate Chilean territory would in turn provide an opportunity for Ecuador to recover its lost territories while Peru was distracted elsewhere.

There are, of course, a number of different scenarios and arrangements possible in the Southern Cone that compete with this pessimistic one. For example, the Argentine-Brazilian cooperation agreements of 1982 and 1983 suggest that there might evolve a sort of condominium arrangement between these two nations to stabilize any conflict situation in the Southern Cone. Or two sets of competing subregional systems might emerge, much like the early nineteenth century ones observed by Burr. In the contemporary context these might be Amazon Basin and Plata Basin, or the Atlantic States and Andean Pact States. A form of Pax Brasiliana might also evolve as Brazil moves ahead to its destiny and becomes the paramount subregional power. Lastly, there is always the possibility that democratization and the decline of military governments would be accompanied by a sharp decline in Southern Cone power politics and geopolitical mind-sets among the governing.

Even should such a decline occur and even if the geopolitical balance of power system sketched out above never comes to pass, the impact of geopolitical thinking in South America will continue to be a factor in any consideration of possible future conflicts. Most strongly in Argentina, Brazil, and Chile, but to a certain extent in all the Latin American countries of the area, modes of geopolitical thinking have left a durable legacy. While that legacy may find positive and productive output in schemes of national development and international integration, it seems more likely that geopolitical thinking will remain linked to narrow nationalism and jingoism. Major unsolved problems such as the Malvinas/Falklands and the Beagle Channel question will continue to be the focus of geopolitical analysis, distorted by patriotic filters and feelings of having been victimized in the past. The interlinked nature of many of South America's conflicts suggest that a crisis in any one of them will resonate in several of the others. And in a few of the possible conflicts with geopolitical implications, the interests of outside powers will add a further and more dangerous dimension to the conflict panorama of South America. Of particular concern are the interlinked Malvinas/Falklands, Beagle Channel, South Atlantic, and Antarctic conflicts because of the time pressure of the 1991 Antarctic Treaty revision.

NOTES

1. Pablo R. Sanz, *El Espacio Argentino* (Buenos Aires: Pleamar, 1976), pp. 335–51.

2. Jack Child, "From 'Color' to 'Rainbow': U.S. Strategic Planning for Latin America, 1919–1945," *Journal of Inter-American Studies and World Affairs* 21 (May 1979): 233–259.

3. Robert N. Burr, *By Reason or Force: Chile and the Balancing of Power in South America, 1830–1905* (Berkeley: University of California Press, 1965), pp. 3–4, 107, 136–37; Robert

N. Burr, "The Balance of Power in Nineteenth-century South America: An Exploratory Essay," *Hispanic American Historical Review* 35 (February 1955): 37–60.

4. See, for example, Armando Alsonso Pineiro, "El Equilibrio Geopolítico Sudamericano," *Estrategia* no. 30 (September 1974): 6. For a theoretical statement, see Howard E. Koch, "Some Theoretical Notes on Geography and International Conflict," *Journal of Conflict Resolution* 16 (March 1960): 4–14.

5. *Buenos Aires, TELAM*, July 7, 1982, in *FBIS*, July 9, 1982, p. V-2.

BIBLIOGRAPHY

Amaral Gurgel, José Alfredo. *Segurança e Democracia*. Rio de Janeiro: Livraria José Olympio, 1978.

Arbuet Vignali, Huber. *Antártida: Continente de los Más para los Menos*. Montevideo: Fundación de Cultura, 1979.

Argentina, Ministerio de Cultura y Educación. *Soberanía: Contribución Bibliográfica a la Afirmación de Derechos Argentinos Sobre las Malvinas, Islas y Sector Antártico*. Buenos Aires, 1975.

Arriagada Genaro. *Las Fuerzas Armadas en la Sociedad Civil*. Santiago: Talleres Gráficos Corporación, 1978.

_____., ed. *Seguridad Nacional y Bien Común*. Santiago: Talleres Gráficos Corporación, 1976.

Ascanio Jiménez, Austín. *El Golfo de Venezuela es Territorio Venezolano*. Caracas: Ediciones Garrido, 1974.

Atencio, Jorge E. *¿Qué es la Geopolítica?*. Buenos Aires: Pleamar, 1965.

Auburn, F. M. *Antarctic Law and Politics*. Bloomington: Indiana University Press, 1982.

Backheuser, Everardo. *A Geopolítica Geral e do Brasil*. Rio de Janeiro: Biblioteca do Exército, 1952.

Baptista María. *Antología Geopolítica de Bolivia*. La Paz: Ediciones Los Amigos del Libro, 1979.

Barra, F. de la. *El Conflicto Peruano-Ecuatoriano y la Vigorosa Campaña de 1941 en las Fronteras de Zarumilla*. Lima: Procer, 1969.

Basilico, Ernesto. *Sobre el Canal Beagle y las Islas Litigiosas*. Buenos Aires: Centro Naval, 1974.

Boscovich, Nicolás. *Geostrategia de la Cuenca del Plata*. Caracas: El Cid Editor, 1979.

Botelho Gosalvez, Raul. *Proceso del Subimperialismo Brasileño*. New York: Maity, 1977.

Briano, Jorge T. *Geopolítica y Geostrategia Americana*. Buenos Aires: Pleamar, 1966.

Burr, Robert N. *By Reason or Force: Chile and the Balancing of Power in South America, 1830-1905*. Berkeley: University of California Press, 1965.

Caillet-Bois, Ricardo. *Las Islas Malvinas*. Buenos Aires: Peuser, 1952.

Cardier, Jorge Alvarez. *La Guerra de las Malvinas: Enseñanzas para Venezuela*. Caracas: Editorial Enfoque, 1982.

Carlés, Fernando José. *Algunos Aspectos de la Geopolítica Boliviana*. Buenos Aires: Instituto de Derecho Público, 1950.

Carpio Castillo, Rubén. *Geopolítica de Venezuela*. Caracas: Seix Barral Venezolana, 1981.

Carrasco, German. *El Laudo Arbitral del Canal Beagle*. Santiago: Editorial Jurídica de Chile, 1979.

Carril, Bonifacio del. *El Dominio de las Islas Malvinas*. Buenos Aires: Emece Editores, 1964.

Cartaxo, Otacilio. *O Problema Geopolítico Brasileiro*. Rio: Ouvidor, 1965.

Ceresole, Norberto. *Geopolítica de Liberación*. Buenos Aires: Corregidor, 1972.

Chamero, Juan Angel. *Emergencia Geopolítica Argentina*. Buenos Aires: Libreria Hachette, 1977.

Chiavenato, Julio J. *Geopolítica, Arma do Fascismo*. São Paulo: Global Editora, 1981.

Child, Jack. "Geopolitical Thinking in Latin America." *Latin American Research Review* 14 (Summer 1979): 89-111.

Cirigliano, Gustavo. *La Argentina Triangular*. Buenos Aires: Humanitas, 1975.

Collins, John M. *Grand Strategy: Principles and Practices*. Annapolis: Naval Institute Press, 1973.

Comblin, Joseph. *A Ideologia de Segurança Nacional*. Rio de Janeiro: Editorial Civilizaçào Brasileira, 1978.

————. *The Church and National Security*. Maryknoll, N.Y.: Orbis Books, 1980.

Costas, Humberto. *Estudio y Difusión de la Geopolítica en las Fuerzas Armadas*. La Paz: Empresa Editora Universo, 1973.

Crawford, Leslie. *Uruguay Atlanticense y los Derechos a la Antártida*. Montevideo: Ariel, 1974.

Dallanegra Pedraza, Luis, ed. *Geopolítica y Relaciones Internacionales*. Buenos Aires: Pleamar, 1981.

de Castro, Therezinha. *Atlas-Texto de Geopolítica do Brasil*. Rio de Janeiro: Capemi Editores, 1982.

————. *Rumo a Antártica*. Rio de Janeiro: Freitas, 1976.

Drekonja, Gerhard. *El Diferendo entre Colombia y Nicaragua*. Bogota: FESCOL y Departamento de Ciencia Política, Universidad de los Andes, 1982.

Ewell, Judith. "The Development of Venezuelan Geopolitical Analysis Since World War II." *Journal of Inter-American Studies and World Affairs* 24 (August 1982): 295–316.

Fitte, Ernesto J. *La Disputa con Gran Bretaña por las Islas del Atlántico Sur*. Buenos Aires: Emece, 1968.

Foulkes, Heraldo. *Las Malvinas: Una Causa Nacional*. Buenos Aires: Ediciones Corregidor, 1978.

Fraga, Jorge Alberto. *Introducción a la Geopolítica Antártica*. Buenos Aires: Dirección Nacional del Antártico, 1979.

Gamba, Virginia. *Malvinas Confidencial*. Buenos Aires: Publinter, 1982.

Golbery, do Couto e Silva. *Geopolítica do Brasil*. Rio de Janeiro: Editorial José Olympio, 1967.

Golblat, Jozef. *The Falklands/Malvinas Conflict: A Spur to Arms Buildups*. Stockholm: Stockholm International Peace Research Institute, 1983.

Gómez Rueda, Hector O. *Teoría y Doctrina de la Geopolítica*. Buenos Aires: Editorial Astrea, 1977.

Grabendorff, Wolf. "Interstate Conflict Behavior and Regional Potential for Conflict in Latin America." *Journal of Inter-American Studies and World Affairs* 24 (August 1982): 267–294.

Gualco, Jorge Nelson. *Cono Sur: Elección de un Destino*. Buenos Aires: Fabril Editores, 1972.

Guglialmelli, Juan E. *El Conflicto del Beagle*. Buenos Aires: El Cid Editor, 1978.

_____. *Geopolítica del Cono Sur*. Buenos Aires: El Cid Editor, 1979.

Guyana, Ministry of Foreign Affairs. *A Search for Understanding: Patterns of Conflict Resolution*. Statements and Papers Relating to Recent Developments, Guyana/Venezuela and Guyana/Suriname Relations. Georgetown: Ministry of External Affairs, 1970.

Hernández, Pablo. *Malvinas: Clave Geopolítica*. Buenos Aires: Ediciones Castañeda, 1977.

Holguín Peláez, Hernando. *Los Monjes: Enjuciamiento [sic] de una Traición*. Bogota: Editores Prosartes, 1975.

_____. *Proyecciones de un Límite Marítimo entre Colombia y Venezuela*. Bogota: Editores y Distribuidores Asociados, 1971.

Ireland, Gordon. *Boundaries, Possessions and Conflicts in South America*. Cambridge, Mass.: Harvard University Press, 1938.

Kapur, Ashok. *International Nuclear Proliferation*. New York: Praeger, 1979.

Kasanzew, Nicolas. *Malvinas a Sangre y Fuego*. Buenos Aires: Abril, 1983.

Littuma, Alfonso. *Doctrina de Seguridad Nacional*. Caracas: Biblioteca del Ejército, 1976.

Londoño, Julio. *Nueva Geopolítica de Colombia*. Bogota: Imprenta de las Fuerzas Armadas, n.d., 1964?

López Herrman, F. Bolívar. *El Ecuador y su Problema Territorial con el Perú*. Quito: Industrias Gráficas CYMA, 1961.

Lucchini, Adalberto P. *Geopolítica del Cono Sur: La Cuenca del Plata*. Buenos Aires: Juárez Editora, 1971.

Luder, Italo A. *La Argentina y sus Claves Geopolíticas*. Buenos Aires: Editorial Universitaria de Buenos Aires, 1974.

Brasileña. Buenos Aires: Editorial Ciencia Nueva,

...aje del Beagle y la Actitud Argentina. Santiago:

...ina en el Océano Pacífico. Buenos Aires: Ediciones

...Geopolítica Marítima Chilena. Santiago: Univer-

...ation and the Near-Nuclear Countries. Cambridge,

...ítica e as Projeçóes do Poder. Rio de Janeiro: Jose

...Destino. Rio de Janeiro: Biblioteca do Exército,

...Amazonica. Rio de Janeiro: Biblioteca do Exercito, 1980.

Mercado Jarrín, Edgardo. *Seguridad, Política, Estrategia*. Lima: Ministerio de Guerra, 1974.

Methol Ferré, Alberto. *Geopolítica del Cuenca del Plata*. Buenos Aires: Pena Lillo, 1973.

Milia, Fernando. *Estrategia y Poder Militar*. Buenos Aires: Instituto de Publicaciones Navales, 1965.

_____. *La Atlantártida: Un Espacio Geopolítico*. Buenos Aires: Pleamar, 1978.

Molina, Franklin. *Doscientas Millas de Mar Territorial Ecuatoriano*. Quito: Imprenta ARPI, 1977.

Monagas, Aquiles. *Testimonio de una Traición a Venezuela: Demanda de Nulidad del Tratado de Limites de 1941 entre Venezuela y Colombia*. Caracas: Ediciones Garrido, 1975.

Moneta, Carlos J. *Geopolítica y Política del Poder en el Atlántico Sur*. Buenos Aires: Pleamar, 1983.

Moneta, Jose M. *¿Nos Devolverán las Malvinas?* Buenos Aires: Pleamar, 1970.

Monteza Tafur, Miguel. *El Conflicto Militar del Perú con el Ecuador*. Lima: Editorial Arica, 1976.

Mora Contreras, Oscar. *Defensa Integralista del Golfo de Venezuela*. Caracas: Imprenta Delforn, 1973.

Morzone, Luis Antonio. *Compendio de Soberanía Territorial Argentina*. Buenos Aires: Depalma, 1979.

———. *La Mediterraneidad Boliviana ante el Derecho Internacional: Posición Argentina*. Buenos Aires: Depalma, 1979.

Muller Rojas, Alberto. *Las Malvinas: Tragicomedia en Tres Actos*. Caracas: Editorial Ateneo, 1983.

Nicaragua, Ministerio de Relaciones Exteriores. *Declaración y Libro Blanco del Gobierno de Nicaragua*. Managua: Ministerio de Relaciones Exteriores, 1980.

Nolde, Kenneth. "Arms and Security in South America: Towards an Alternate View." Ph.D. dissertation, University of Miami, 1980.

Nunez, Carlos. *Brasil: Satélite y Gendarme*. Montevideo: Aportes, 1969.

Oblitas Fernández, Edgar. *La Geopolítica Chilena y la Guerra del Pacífico*. La Paz: Editorial Kullasuyo, 1959.

Ochoa, Octavio A. *Tragedia Ecuatoriana*, 1941. Quito: n.p., 1976.

Padron, G. M. *¿Perderemos También el Golfo de Venezuela?* Caracas: Avilarte, 1978.

Palacios Saenz, Carlos. *La Guerra del 41*. Guayaquil: Ediciones Ara, 1979.

Pereira, Osny Duarte. *La Seudo-rivalidad Argentina-Brasileña: Pro y Contra de Itaipú*. Buenos Aires: Corregidor, 1975.

Pereyra, E. F. *Las Islas Malvinas: Soberanía Argentina*. Buenos Aires: 1968.

Perez, Ulises. *Geopolítica del Uruguay*. Montevideo: La Oficina Nacional del Servicio Civil, 1975.

Perl, Raphael. *The Falkland Islands Dispute in International Law and Politics*. New York: Oceana, 1983.

Pinochet de la Barra, Oscar. *La Antártida Chilena*. 4th ed. Santiago: Editorial Andrés Bello, 1976.

Pinochet Ugarte, Augusto. *Geopolítica*. Santiago: Editorial Andres Bello, 1974.

Pittman, Howard T. "Geopolitics in the ABC Countries: A Comparison." Ph.D. dissertation, American University, 1981.

Ponce Caballero, Jaime. *Geopolítica Chilena y Mar Boliviano.* La Paz: Ponce Caballero, 1976.

Quagliotti de Bellis, Bernardo. *Constantes Geopolíticas en Iberoamérica.* Montevideo: GEOSUR, 1979.

_____. *Geopolítica del Atlántico Sur.* Montevideo: Fundación de Cultura Universitaria, 1976.

_____. *Uruguay en el Cono Sur.* Buenos Aires: Tierra Nueva, 1976.

_____. *Uruguay y su Espacio.* Montevideo: GEOSUR, 1979.

Ramírez Faria, Carlos. *La Clase Gobernante y la Frontera de Venezuela con Colombia.* Caracas: Talleres de Lithoformas, 1976.

Reyes, Salvador. *Fuego en la Frontera.* Santiago: Arancibia Hermanos, 1968.

Rodríguez, Gregorio. *La Geopolítica y sus Teorias.* Santiago: Academia de Guerra del Ejército, 1950.

Rodríguez Berrutti, Camilo Hugo. *Malvinas: Ultima Frontera del Colonialismo.* Buenos Aires: Editorial Universitaria de Buenos Aires, 1976.

Rodríguez Zia, Jorge. *De Mar a Mar: el Fallo del Beagle.* Buenos Aires: Editorial Moharra, 1978.

_____. *El Poder del Pan.* Buenos Aires: Editorial Moharra, 1977.

Rojas, Isaac. *Argentina en el Atlántico, Chile en el Pacífico.* Buenos Aires: Nemont Ediciones, 1978.

_____. *Intereses Argentinos en la Cuenca del Plata.* Buenos Aires: Ediciones Liberia, 1974.

Rout, Leslie B. *Which Way Out? An Analysis of the Venezuela-Guyana Border Dispute.* East Lansing: Michigan State University, Latin American Studies Center, 1971.

Sanz, Pablo R. *El Espacio Argentino.* Buenos Aires: Pleamar, 1976.

Schilling, Paulo R. *¿Irá Brasil a la Guerra?* Montevideo: Fundación de Cultura Universitaria, 1973.

_____., ed. *Una Situación Explosiva: La Cuenca del Plata.* Buenos Aires: Editorial Tierra Nueva, 1974.

Segundo Silioni, Rolando. *La Diplomacia Luso–Brasileña en la Cuenca del Plata.* Buenos Aires: Editorial Rioplatense, 1975.

Selser, Gregorio. *Reagan entre El Salvador y las Malvinas*. Mexico: Editorial Mex-Sur, 1982.

Taylor, William J., ed. *The Future of Conflict in the 1980's*. Washington, D.C.: Georgetown University, Center for Strategic and International Studies, 1982.

Terrera, Guillermo A. *Geopolítica Argentina: Población, Fronteras, Comunicaciones, Antropología*. Buenos Aires: Plus Ultra, 1979.

Tesler, Mario. *Malvinas: Como Estados Unidos Provocó la Usurpación Inglesa*. Buenos Aires: Editorial Galerna, 1979.

Travassos, Mario. *Projeção Continental do Brasil*. 2nd ed. São Paulo: Editorial Nacional, 1935.

Trejo, Hugo. *Basta de Concesiones a Colombia*. Caracas: Ediciones Venezuela Contemporánea, 1975.

Trias, Vivian. *Imperialismo y Geopolítica en América Latina*. Buenos Aires: Editorial Jorge Alvarez, 1969.

United States, Central Intelligence Agency. *Polar Regions Atlas*. Washington, D.C.: Government Printing Office, 1978.

Vaca Hernández, José María. *Inquietudes y Realidades Antárticas: El Continente de Gondwana*. Buenos Aires: Ediciones Heraldo, 1977.

Valencia Vega, Alipio. *Geopolítica del Litorial Boliviano*. La Paz: Librería Juventud, 1974.

_____. *Geopolítica en Bolivia*. La Paz: Librería Juventud, 1965.

Valois Arce, Daniel. *Reseña Histórica sobre los Límites de Colombia y Venezuela*. Bogota: Editorial Bedout, 1970.

Villacrés Moscoso, Jorge W. *Geopolítica del Mundo Tropical Sudamericano*. Guayaquil: Imprenta de la Universidad, 1963.

_____. *La Gran Vía Interoceánica Ecuatoriana a Través del Amazonas: Estudio Geopolítico*. Guayaquil: Imprenta de la Universidad, 1952.

Villalobos R., Sergio. *El Beagle: Historia de una Controversia*. Santiago: Editorial Andrés Bello, 1979.

Villegas, Osiris. *El Conflicto con Chile en la Region Austral*. Buenos Aires: Pleamar, 1978.

_____. *Tiempo Geopolítico Argentino*. Buenos Aires: Pleamar, 1975.

Wood, Bryce. *Aggression and History: The Case of Ecuador and Peru.* New York: Columbia University, Institute of Latin American Studies, 1978.

Ygobone, Aquiles D. *Cuestiones Fronterizas entre Argentina y Chile.* Buenos Aires: Plus Ultra, 1971.

Zorraguín Becu, Ricardo. *Inglaterra Prometió Abandonar las Islas: Estudio Histórico y Jurídico del Conflicto Anglo-Español.* Buenos Aires: Librería Editorial Platero, 1975.

Journals

A Defesa Nacional (Brazil)

Estrategia (Argentina)

Geopolítica (Argentina)

Geopolítica (Uruguay)

Geosur (Uruguay)

Revista Geográfica de Chile

Segurança e Desenvolvimento (Brazil)

Seguridad Nacional (Chile)

INDEX

ABOUT THE AUTHOR

Jack Child is Associate Professor of Spanish and Latin American Studies at The American University. He was born in Buenos Aires and lived in South America for 19 years. Dr. Child holds the B.E. degree from Yale University and the Ph.D. from The American University. He is a retired U.S. Regular Army officer (lieutenant colonel), and his military career has included teaching assignments at West Point and the Inter-American Defense College as well as a five-year tour with the Inter-American Defense Board and the Joint Brazil-U.S. Defense Commission.

His publications include *Unequal Alliance: the Inter-American Military System, 1938-1978* (Westview Press, 1980); *Latin America: International Relations — A Guide to Information Sources* (with John Finan; Gale, 1981); and *Maintenance of Peace and Security in the Caribbean and Central America* (International Peace Academy, 1984).